D0481786

NORTHERN WATERS

The Royal Institute of International Affairs is an unofficial body which promotes the scientific study of international questions and does not express opinions of its own. The opinions expressed in this publication are the responsibility of the authors.

NORTHERN WATERS

Security and Resource Issues

Edited by
CLIVE ARCHER and DAVID SCRIVENER

BARNES & NOBLE BOOKS
Totowa, New Jersey

© Royal Institute of International Affairs 1986

first published in the USA 1986 by
Barnes & Noble Books
81 Adams Drive
Totowa, New Jersey 07512
Printed in Great Britain

Northern Waters.

    Includes index.
    1. North Atlantic Ocean — Strategic aspects.
2. Barents Sea — Strategic aspects. 3. Natural resources
— North Atlantic Ocean. 4. Natural resources — Barents
Sea. I. Archer, Clive. II. Scrivener, David.
VA450.N67 1986   355'.03301631   86-14179
ISBN 0-389-20657-1

UNIVERSITY LIBRARY
180166 Lethbridge, Alberta

CONTENTS

Contributors

Abbreviations

Preface

1. Introduction
   Clive Archer and David Scrivener   1

2. The Law of the Sea and Northern Waters
   Patricia Birnie   11

3. Resource Endowment and Exploitation
   Tony Scanlan   42

4. Transportation of Resources from and
   through the Northern Waters
   Terence Armstrong   55

5. Strategy in the Far North
   Geoffrey Till   69

6. New Military Technologies and Northern Waters
   David Hobbs   85

7. The Control of Conflict in Northern Waters
   Elizabeth Young   97

8. The United States: Resource Interests
   Melvin Conant   109

9. The United States: Strategic Interests
   Steven Miller   115

10. Canadian Marine Resource Development in
    the Arctic
    David VanderZwaag   125

11. Canada's Security Considerations in the Arctic
    Nicholas Tracy   146

12. Norway in Northern Waters
    Willy Østreng   155

13. Greenland and the Faroes
    Jørgen Taagholt   174

14.   Iceland: Unarmed Ally
       Nigel de Lee   190

15.   The Soviet Union and Northern Waters
       David Scrivener   208

Index   234

Figures

1.1   The Northern Waters   xii
1.2   The Kola Peninsula   5
4.1   The Circumpolar Perspective   59
10.1   Tanker Routes in Northern Canada   128
10.2   Major Petroleum Areas in Northern Canada   129
10.3   Mineral Exploration and Mining: Northwest
       Territories — 1983   132
10.4   Delimitation between Canada and
       Greenland/Denmark   140
15.1   The Barents Sea and the Grey Zone   212
15.2   The Svalbard Archipelago   223

CONTRIBUTORS

Clive Archer, Centre for Defence Studies, University of Aberdeen

Terence Armstrong, Scott Polar Research Institute, University of Cambridge

Patricia Birnie, Department of International Law, London School of Economics

Melvin Conant, Conant and Associates Ltd, Great Falls, Virginia

Nigel de Lee, Department of War Studies and International Affairs, Royal Military Academy, Sandhurst

David Hobbs, Scientific and Technical Committee, North Atlantic Assembly

Steven Miller, Center for International Studies, Massachusetts Institute of Technology

Willy Østreng, Fridtjof Nansen Institute, Oslo

Tony Scanlan, Associated London Energy Consultants Ltd (ALEC)

David Scrivener, Department of Politics and International Relations, University of Aberdeen

Jørgen Taagholt, Commission for Scientific Research in Greenland

Geoffrey Till, Department of History, Royal Naval College, Greenwich

Nicholas Tracy, Department of History, University of New Brunswick

Elizabeth Young, writer, London

David VanderZwaag, Dalhousie Ocean Studies Programme, Nova Scotia

ABBREVIATIONS

ACE	Allied Command Europe
ALCM	Air-Launched Cruise Missile
API	American Petroleum Institute (refers to a measure of specific gravity)
ASW	Anti-Submarine Warfare
BMEWS	Ballistic Missile Early Warning System
BP	British Petroleum
CDE	Conference on Disarmament in Europe
CESAR	Canadian Expedition to Study the Alpha Ridge
CFP	Common Fisheries Policy
COLREG	Convention on Collision Regulations
CSCE	Conference on Security and Cooperation in Europe
DEW	Distant Early Warning
DOD	Department of Defense
dwt	deadweight
EC	European Community/Communities
ECE	Economic Commission for Europe
EEC	European Economic Community
EEZ	Exclusive Economic Zone
EFZ	Exclusive Fisheries Zone
ELINT	Electronic Intelligence
EORSAT	ELINT Ocean Reconnaissance Satellite
ESRO	European Space Research Organization
FAO	Food and Agriculture Organization
FPZ	Fisheries Protection Zone
FRG	Federal Republic of Germany
GDR	German Democratic Republic
GIUK	Greenland/Iceland/United Kingdom
GNP	Gross National Product
GPS	Global Positioning System
grt	gross registered tonnage
IAEA	International Atomic Energy Agency
ICBM	Inter-continental Ballistic Missile
ICC	Inuit Circumpolar Conference
ICES	International Council for the Exploration of the Sea
ICJ	International Court of Justice

ICNAF	International Convention for North Atlantic Fisheries
IDF	Icelandic Defence Force
ILO	International Labour Organization
IMO	International Maritime Organization
IOC	International Oceanographic Commission
IP	Independence Party
ISA	International Seabed Authority
ITLOS	International Tribunal for the Law of the Sea
IUCN	International Union for the Conservation of Nature
LNG	Liquefied Natural Gas
MARPOL	International Convention for the Prevention of Pollution from Ships (1973)
Milstar	Military Strategic-Tactical and Relay
MIRV	Multiple Independently Targetable Re-entry Vehicle
NAFO	Northwest Atlantic Fisheries Organization
NASCO	North Atlantic Salmon Conservation Organization
NATO	North Atlantic Treaty Organization
NEAF	North East Atlantic Fisheries (Commission)
NEAFC	North East Atlantic Fisheries Convention
NORAD	North American Air Defence System
NWT	Northwest Territories
OILPOL	Convention for Prevention of Oil Pollution from Ships (1954)
PA	People's Alliance
PIP	Petroleum Incentives Programme
PNE	Peaceful Nuclear Explosion
PP	Progressive Party
Prep. Com.	Preparatory Commission
RORSAT	Radar-equipped Ocean Reconnaissance Satellite
SACLANT	Supreme Allied Commander Atlantic
SDA	Social Democratic Alliance
SDI	Strategic Defence Initiative
SDS	Satellite Data System
shp	shaft horsepower
SLBM	Submarine-Launched Ballistic Missile
SLCM	Sea-Launched Cruise Missile
SLOCs	Sea Lines of Communication
SOLAS	Safety of Life at Sea
SSBN	Ballistic-Missile Nuclear Submarine(s)

SSN	Submarine(s), Nuclear
TAC	Total Allowable Catch
TFN	Tungavik Federation of Nunavut
UNCLOS III	Third United Nations Conference on the Law of the Sea
UNEP	United Nations Environment Programme
UNESCO	United Nations Educational, Scientific and Cultural Organization
WL	Women's List

PREFACE

In late 1979, the Scottish Branch of the Royal Institute of International Affairs established a study group to examine the inter-relationship of security, resources and jurisdictional issues in Northern Waters: that is, the sea area stretching from Canada's eastern seaboard to Norway's northern coast and the Barents Sea. The Northern Waters Study Group had as its original task the preparation of material for an International Colloquium on the subject, organized by the University of Aberdeen's Centre for Defence Studies in September 1980. The Study Group has continued its work by bringing together academics, businessmen, civil servants and serving officers interested in Northern Waters, and by arranging seminars and other international conferences.

This book reflects the Study Group's concerns, and a number of the contributions come from members of the Group. Other authors are overseas contacts made by the Group.

Any publication such as this is by its nature a collective effort. As editors we are grateful to the members of the Northern Waters Study Group for their attention to the subject and for their comments on chapter drafts. We are indebted to the staff of the Publications Department of the Royal Institute of International Affairs in London for their help. We particularly appreciate the work of Margaret McRobb and Fiona Docherty, who typed successive drafts of most of the chapters. Support from the Binks Trust and Britoil is also gratefully acknowledged.

Aberdeen
March 1986

Clive Archer
David Scrivener

Figure 1.1: The Northern Waters

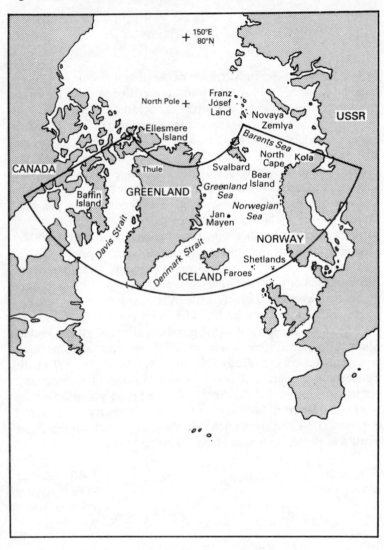

1 INTRODUCTION

Clive Archer and David Scrivener

Until the mid-1970s the literature on the economic and strategic significance of the Northern Waters was scarce and either focused on highly technical questions or dealt exclusively with the interests of particular countries in relative isolation. However, the general European and North American extension of fisheries and economic zones in 1977, hydrocarbon exploration and intensifying military activities have brought the importance of this maritime region into much sharper relief in the minds of policy-makers, academics and the public at large.

What are the Northern Waters? In geographical terms they comprise the maritime areas within the latitudes of 80°N and 60°N and from longitude 90°W to 40°E. These include the islands of Arctic Canada, Greenland, Iceland, the Faroes, Shetlands, Jan Mayen and Svalbard, and reach as far as the Kola Peninsula in the Soviet Union (see Figure 1.1). The area thus contains three important approaches: the Fram Straits between Greenland and Svalbard, which run from the Polar Sea out to the Atlantic Ocean; the waters of Baffin Bay/Davis Strait, which join the northern coasts of Alaska and Canada, and in particular the east coast of Canada and the USA, to the Atlantic Ocean; and finally, the Barents Sea and Norwegian Sea, which provide access to the Atlantic from the Arctic Ocean and to the northern coasts of Norway and the Soviet Union. In addition to their political and economic significance, these passages are of considerable environmental interest and concern, especially in relation to the movement of fresh water out of the Arctic Ocean and its high degree of vulnerability to pollutants.[1]

Northern Waters are of importance because of *the areas they join*: they are the northern rim of the sea lines of communication (SLOCs) between North America and Western Europe, and they are the approaches to the Arctic Ocean which itself has been said to typify both a 'sea between' (the North Atlantic and the North Pacific) and a mediterranean sea (an 'ocean in the middle' of the shores of North America and the northern stretches of Eurasia).[2] The interests of the two superpowers in the adjoining areas are clear; the extent of the riches of Siberia, Alaska and Northern Canada has only recently been appreciated. Likewise, while the security importance of the European continent has long been established, the strategic significance to Russia, America and the West generally of the Arctic lands has emerged over the past 35 years. Furthermore, this significance has waxed and waned as the 'bomber threat' was first supplemented by concern with intercontinental ballistic missiles (ICBMs), then reinforced by submarine-launched ballistic missiles (SLBMs) lurking in Northern Waters, and finally overlaid by the prospective deployment of long-range air-launched cruise missiles (ALCMs) and sea-launched cruise missiles (SLCMs).

As well as being an area of transit, Northern Waters have *their own intrinsic value.* Until recently the economic resources of the region consisted of the minerals extracted from land areas — coal from Svalbard, cryolite from Greenland, for example — and the seemingly ample fisheries stocks in the high seas that made up most of the Northern Waters. During the past ten years, the increase in the price of oil and natural gas and the advances in the technology needed to extract these products from deep waters has prompted the extension of the search for offshore energy into the Northern Waters. The lack of any detailed international agreement on the division of the seabed between neighbouring countries only began to present problems in this area with the realization that the underground resources there could be economically accessible.

The major traditional economic activity in the waters — fishing — was quite seriously affected by more powerful catching techniques by the mid-1970s, when the littoral states extended their national authority over previously high seas in the form of exclusive fishery or economic zones. The exercise of these new controls was justified on the grounds of fisheries conservation and of increasing the coastal states' share of the fish catch taken off their coasts. However, the uncertainty often surrounding the demarcation of these zones in Northern Waters, and their establishment before the United Nations Convention on the Law of the Sea had been drafted (let alone ratified) are now sources of tension in the management of Northern Waters resources.

Indeed, the division of resources has not been without conflict. Iceland's extension of its fishing limits out to 12, 50 and then 200 miles and the subsequent disputes, or 'Cod Wars', with the United Kingdom could have set the pattern for the whole region: 'The

1973 Cod War between Iceland and the United Kingdom was an example of the kind of conflict that could arise over national resources and the possible consequences for stability and security in the North Atlantic.'[3]

The 'fencing off', four years later, of maritime zones in which one nation had exclusive access to resources could have led to new versions of the Cod War. Very much in response to the fishing problems resulting from the Cod War, the European Community (EC) countries decided to extend their fisheries zones out to 200 miles from 1 January 1977, and they were joined by a number of other Western countries that independently chose to create exclusive maritime zones of varying descriptions. That conflict was largely avoided was partly due to the tacit agreement to follow the continental shelf delimitation — where this already existed — for the division of maritime zones. However, agreement on the seabed boundaries had not been reached in much of the Northern Waters, and the creation of fisheries and economic zones produced a need for delineation. The countries involved accepted that solutions should be reached by mutual agreement but, in the absence of detailed guidance from the Third United Nations Conference on the Law of the Sea (UNCLOS III), they could not always concur on the basis for delimitation. This was an inconvenient point when lines were being drawn on a map representing wide stretches of sea with a number of littoral states. Country could be pitted against neighbouring country; indeed some have been. For a brief moment in 1981 it seemed probable that Denmark and Norway would engage in a 'Capelin War' around Jan Mayen. Greenland's maritime borders with its eastern neighbours — Iceland and Jan Mayen — have been the subject of delicate negotiations, claims and counter-claims; and the Soviet Union and Norway are in dispute over a vast area of continental shelf in the Barents Sea. On the other hand, diplomacy has triumphed in many cases: the delimitation between Canada and Greenland in the Davis Strait; the seabed agreement between Iceland and Norway over Jan Mayen's southern zone; and even the annual Soviet-Norwegian accords over fishing in the 'Grey Zone' off their northern frontier reflect a preference for agreement over conflict.

Resource distribution and utilization in Northern Waters have proved to be the cause of tension or conflict between members of NATO (Britain and Iceland, for example) as well as between NATO states and those from the Warsaw Pact (as witnessed in the

Soviet-Norwegian relationship in the Barents Sea). More clearly, related security concerns have illustrated elements of East-West military rivalry in, around and above these waters. What remains to be seen is the outcome of the interaction between old and new elements of military competition, on the one hand, and, on the other, the need for mutual restraint in the form of explicit or tacit arms control measures affecting the area.

The most outstanding aspect of the Northern Waters' *strategic importance* lies in their value as an avenue of commercial and military transit. The submarine threat to the West's transatlantic SLOCs, so painfully experienced in World War II, has acquired a new and much expanded dimension in the form of the Soviet submarine force. The area has also seen an increasingly obvious projection of naval surface and air power by the Soviet Union, primarily drawn from the vast reserves of the Northern Fleet, based so precariously in the Kola Peninsula (see Figure 1.2). This development has been paralleled by NATO's concentration on the creation of a surveillance and anti-submarine-warfare barrier around the Greenland/Iceland/United Kingdom (GIUK) gap. The airspace in part provides a flight-path for ICBMs travelling to and from the heartlands of the USA and USSR, and strategic bombers would employ similar routes. The West, in particular, has erected a network of surveillance and early-warning systems, currently being updated, which are designed to track and thereby deter any hostile use of the airspace.

Much of the military activity undertaken in Northern Waters relates to movement through them and precautionary measures to check it, but the area also contains a number of territories with vital military bases, those on the Kola Peninsula being the most obviously crucial. The island territories are of military value in their own right, albeit mainly in their contribution to the effort to assist or frustrate transit through these waters. Indeed, military forces are thin on the ground in Greenland, Jan Mayen, Iceland, the Faroes and Shetlands. Nor do these islands contain air bases that shelter nuclear weapons in peacetime.

It is in the panoply of military activities and requirements centred around the deployment and containment of submarines that the Northern Waters have acquired their own peculiar strategic value. Rearward deployment of the latest generation of Soviet SSBNs — *Delta III* and *Typhoon* — in the Barents/Kola Seas and under the Arctic ice-cap itself will exploit the enhanced range of

Figure 1.2: The Kola Peninsular

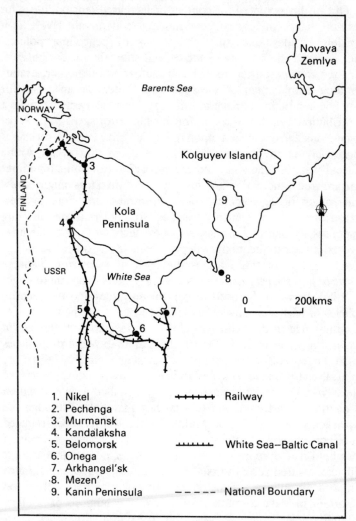

1. Nikel
2. Pechenga
3. Murmansk
4. Kandalaksha
5. Belomorsk
6. Onega
7. Arkhangel'sk
8. Mezen'
9. Kanin Peninsula

+++++++ Railway

┅┅┅┅ White Sea–Baltic Canal

– – – – – National Boundary

new SLBMs and SLCMs and profit from the advantages of reduced reliance on transit through the potentially hostile North Norwegian and Greenland Seas. In time of crisis or war, Western naval forces would be tempted to penetrate into the Barents Sea in order to conduct forward anti-submarine-warfare (ASW) operations, rather than ostensibly concentrate — as at present — on containment of Soviet submarine forces at the GIUK gap.

Sanctuarization of Soviet Arctic waters would not be conceded.

Out of this potential for conflict or increased tension, ideas for *restraint* have emerged at governmental and private levels. Is it possible or desirable, in the interests of peacetime political relations and the stability of the central strategic nuclear balance, for the two superpowers to arrive at mutual or unilateral restraints on their employment of the Northern Waters as an arena for strategic competition? Several existing general agreements make a contribution but leave room for further efforts. A number of discussions have touched upon possible arms control measures specifically in the Northern Waters: the creation of an Arctic nuclear-weapon-free zone and the recognition of anti-submarine-warfare-free sanctuaries are just two. Future ideas might stress non-armament agreements, or concentrate on more modest measures of arms control designed to constrain destabilizing responses by one or both sides to new technological capabilities incorporated into the military deployments of the other.[4]

A leitmotiv of this book is the level of *interaction between resource and security issues* in Northern Waters. That there might be a link between the need to control resources and the security policies of particular governments is by no means a new idea. Yet its resurgence in the West was closely connected with the rise in petroleum prices after 1973 and the fear that Western countries might be cut off from supplies of strategic material either by political chaos in the Third World or by Soviet action. Since the late 1970s, US declared doctrines have signalled a determination to maintain Western access to vital raw materials. Although the dependence of the USA on Middle Eastern oil has been reduced quite considerably, Professor Bruce Russett's recent observation does hold true in more general terms: 'major powers increasingly will seek assured access to vital raw materials, with that assurance achieved by political means. Access to raw materials will be too important to leave to market forces under conditions of political instability.'[5] He concludes that the 'risks of international great power confrontation stemming from economic causes will be critical in coming years'.[6] This is not to say that the USA and USSR will lock horns over the raw materials that may be found in Northern Waters, but the overlap between resource issues and security problems *does* exist there in three ways.

First, since the Northern Waters protect areas of transit, they are important for the *transportation of economic resources.* The crucial role here is that of guarding the trade routes to Northwest Europe from outside the European continent, especially from North America. It is clear from the experience of the last World War that plans have to be made to safeguard these supplies should West European countries wish to display a credible intention of surviving a period of crisis or blockade in the early stages of conflict. The military dispositions needed to demonstrate such resolve are much the same as those required to protect the SLOCs between North America and Europe for the purpose of reinforcement.

Second, there are *resources within the region* of Northern Waters which are of great strategic value. Prominent among these are the oil and gas reserves off the west coast of Norway, northern Norway and the Shetland Islands. They represent areas of industrial activity in the Norwegian and British maritime zones which could be targets for attack. They also constitute a large proportion of Western Europe's petroleum reserves, and could permit a less crucial dependence on Soviet and Middle Eastern sources. In the future, Greenland's uranium reserves may be another of the Northern Waters' intrinsically valuable resources in strategic terms.

Third, political actors in the area are able to make a deliberate *connection between resource and security* issues. This may be done by various parties to strengthen their bargaining position or to maximize their gains in resource negotiations by using their strength or value in the security dimension (or vice versa). This intermix has occurred in relations between Norway and the Soviet Union in Svalbard and the Barents Sea, and in the past was noticeable in Icelandic disputes with Britain over fisheries limits. There is, too, a potential in the Faroes and Greenland for security issues — the US and NATO presence — to be brought into discussions about resource issues.[7]

As well as being a region in which resource and security questions may, and sometimes do, overlap, Northern Waters also demonstrate the difficulty of divorcing legal and political issues. The international consequences of the extension of state control to much of the area have already been noted. The Law of the Sea, with its disputed, sometimes permissive and often unenforceable nature, has provided the cloak for conflict as well as the framework for cooperation. The creation of new economic and fisheries zones has led to demarcation disputes, some of which — such as that between Greenland and Canada — were rapidly solved by a mixture of political will and the use of the principles of international law. Others — such as that between Iceland and Norway over the Jan Mayen zone — have taken longer to conclude and produced a complicated settlement of a *sui generis* nature. There is a further group of jurisdictional disputes that have not yet been settled, either because of the complicated legal issue involved (the status of Svalbard's fisheries zone would come under this heading) or due to the lack of political will (the Soviet-Norwegian continental shelf delineation in the Barents). It is also noticeable that the political factors which sometimes interfere with the solution of demarcation disputes are not always manifestations of underlying security concerns or linked to security-related issues. Domestic fisheries interests in both Greenland and Norway have made the drawing of the line between Greenland's fisheries zone and that of Jan Mayen particularly sensitive.

The emerging law, as represented in the United Nations Convention on the Law of the Sea of December 1982, also has a bearing on the *preservation of the environment* in Northern Waters. The inclusion of much of this part of the world in the economic zones of the coastal states provides an opportunity — however guarded — for the control of marine pollution by coastal states as well as by flag and port states.[8] Furthermore, the Convention contains a section (Section 8, Article 234) on ice-covered areas which allows coastal states, under certain circumstances, to prescribe and enforce regulations for the control of marine pollution in ice-covered areas in their exclusive economic zones.

Transportation of resources through the territorial sea, straits and exclusive economic zones of the Northern Waters could be affected by the new Law of the Sea, especially in Articles 19, 39.2b and 211.5 of UNCLOS III. Plans for shipping-lanes into the Arctic areas of Canada (through the Davis Strait) and into the northern shoreline of the Soviet Union (across the Arctic coast of Siberia) offer both exciting and worrying prospects. The challenge is to produce the technology that can economically use the traditional Northwest and Northeast Passages. The danger is that this process may either run foul of the extreme climate or may pollute what is a fragile environment. Furthermore, neighbouring states have not always agreed about the conditions for such Arctic transport: the Greenlandic complaints to Canada about the proposed Arctic Pilot Project (which would involve carrying natural gas southwards through the Davis Strait) can be cited as an example.

New technology is making itself felt in another way in Northern Waters, by affecting military developments. Although a number of these will primarily strengthen defensive postures — surveillance, anti-submarine warfare, for example — some of the most disturbing changes may occur in offensive weapons. The advent of long-range air-launched cruise missiles and of sea-launched cruise missiles adds a new dimension to the Northern Waters, making them an arena in which East–West military conflict could be played out. An arms race in this field makes the need for arms control and the reduction of superpower antagonism even more urgent. If a new detente were reflected in this area of the world, it could foster restraint in the apparent growth of maritime armed strength in Northern Waters and encourage greater emphasis on cooperation, for example in scientific research and pollution control.

Whether the new significance recently attached to Northern Waters leads on balance to increased conflict in the area or to cooperation will depend partly on the attitude of the countries involved. The governments of Canada, Denmark (and the home-rule authorities in Greenland and the Faroes), Iceland, Norway and the United Kingdom (representing the Shetlands) have all shown a determination to take strong action to safeguard their resources and to protect the economic and security interests of their citizens. They have also shown a predilection for peaceful settlement of disputes — even the 'Cod Wars' cost no lives — and for compromise. However, the main determinants of peace and cooperation in Northern Waters lie outside the area: the two superpowers. It is their attitude towards security and resource-related questions which will finally determine whether the region remains calm or becomes more turbulent.

This book deals with the major features of the offshore tapestry in Northern Waters and reflects some of the concerns mentioned above. The legal perspectives given in Chapter 2 deal mainly with the developing regime that has been the framework for state activity in maritime areas over the past ten years or so. This has been codified and developed in the Law of the Sea Convention, which could provide the touchstone for international law considerations for ocean areas. How certain parts of the Convention might affect the legal status of Northern Waters is outlined in this chapter.

Chapter 3 characterizes the overall resource wealth of the area and outlines the existing and proposed exploitation of these resources, thus giving a picture of the intrinsic economic value of Northern Waters. The following chapter explains how these resources are transported either from the region or through the waters from the Arctic coastline. Included in this description is the type of shipping required for the particular needs of the Arctic seas.

Chapters 5, 6 and 7 deal primarily with security. The naval strategies of the two superpowers, and their allies, will decide the potential for conflict in the region, and the impact of new military technology (Chapter 6) could well determine the nature of the threat offered by potential rivals and the rate at which conflict and hostility might develop. It could also offer the means to detect and counter hostile forces in Northern Waters. Chapter 7 shifts the emphasis to how potential conflict might be controlled by political means, and estimates the chances for peaceful coexistence in the region.

Chapters 8 to 15 provide country profiles outlining the resource interests, security postures and attitudes to maritime jurisdictional issues of the major states in Northern Waters. In particular they seek to identify the various levels at which issues of access to resources, delimitation and security are linked potentially and in reality.

Notes

1. See Louis Rey, 'The Arctic Regions in the Light of Industrial Development: Basic Facts and Environmental Issues', in L. Rey (ed.), *Arctic Energy Resources* (Amsterdam: Elsevier, 1983), pp. 13-14.

2. These terms are used by Finn Sollie in a paper entitled 'Arctic Development and its International Relevance', presented at the International Symposium on the Sea, Tokyo, 16-20 October 1978.

3. North Atlantic Assembly Papers, *Security in the Northern Region* (Brussels: North Atlantic Assembly, 1979), p. 49.

4. Clive Archer and David Scrivener, 'Nordic Security Issues', *ADIU Report*, Vol. 5 (1983), No. 4, pp. 4-6.

5. Bruce Russett, 'Security and the Resources Scramble: will 1984 be like 1914?', *International Affairs*, Vol. 58 (1981-2), No. 1, p. 42.

6. *Ibid.*, p. 57.

7. See, for example, Clive Archer, 'Greenland and the Atlantic Alliance', *Centrepiece 7* (Aberdeen: Centre for Defence Studies, 1985), pp. 22-39.

8. United Nations Convention on the Law of the Sea, Part XII, Section 5 and Section 6, especially Article 220.

2 THE LAW OF THE SEA AND NORTHERN WATERS

Patricia Birnie

The Northern Waters area raises virtually every issue of the Law of the Sea that is comprehended in the 1982 Law of the Sea Convention (LOSC).[1] The failure of the Third UN Conference on the Law of the Sea (UNCLOS III) to reach consensus on the adoption and signature of the Convention, and the fact that the Convention has not yet entered into force and may not do so for many years, introduces an element of uncertainty into the jurisdictional limits and rights of the states bordering or using the area which will have considerable implications for policy-making.

These waters are of the highest strategic, economic and political importance to the two major superpowers and to their neighbours in the Northern Waters. Furthermore, both the states bordering the area and those active within it bear a special responsibility to preserve and protect this environment and the living resources it sustains, to develop a legal order for the Arctic Ocean and adjoining seas to this end, and to reduce the risk of jurisdictional conflicts. This chapter outlines and examines the extent to which the existing legal order achieves the objectives of Northern Waters states. It also identifies the problems and gaps that remain, which might be the subject of further legal developments, in the context of the outcome of UNCLOS III and the 1982 LOSC. This process has been widely, though not universally, endorsed by the international community, and the divisions which exist on relevant Law of the Sea issues are reflected in the differing positions of the states concerned in Northern Waters.

Also of relevance to Northern Waters is the question whether the Arctic Ocean qualifies, as does the Mediterranean, as a 'semi-enclosed' sea within the definition laid down in the LOSC. Much depends on how its approaches to Northern Waters are classified. Its geographical situation does mean that the bordering states of the Arctic and Northern Waters can legitimately, under current international law, increase their jurisdiction over the area by extending the outer limits of their continental shelves, fisheries or economic zones, as well as by placing many of the baselines from

11

which these are drawn at greater distances than previously from their natural coastlines. They are also now able to broaden the extent of their sovereignty by means of enclosing greater areas as internal waters, behind these baselines, and declaring wider limits for their territorial seas, though the precise limits of all these national zones remain in dispute in the current status of the relevant law of the sea, as do the methods of determining the boundaries between the zones of adjacent states.

The position in Northern Waters is further complicated by the fact that though the Arctic Ocean is a well-defined geographical unit, there is no internationally laid down boundary of the area, since, unlike Antarctica, it is not subject, as such, to any global or regional treaty identifying it, other than the Polar Bear Agreement.[2] Moreover it is difficult to draw a precise southern frontier for the surrounding circumpolar territories, and it has been suggested that criteria other than geographical should be used for this purpose, such as climatology or ecology, though numerous exceptions would have to be made.

Finally, in surveying the application of the Law of the Sea to Northern Waters problems, it becomes clear that the extreme sensitivity of the strategic and political aspects is an important constraint upon the eventual solution of such delicate questions as the establishment of boundaries and rights of passage through the numerous extended zones. At UNCLOS III the need to preserve the freedom to deploy and to monitor nuclear submarines, antisubmarine submarines and anti-submarine warning devices led the USSR and the USA to agree on many aspects of the relevant issues. This was especially the case for innocent passage through the territorial sea, transit rights through international straits, and navigational rights in fisheries and economic zones and on the high seas. The problems of Northern Waters and the Arctic beyond were always in the minds of US and Soviet negotiators even though neither area is specifically mentioned in the LOSC.

Framework of applicable law after UNCLOS I and II

Four conventions — on the Territorial Sea, High Seas, Continental Shelf and on Fisheries and Conservation of Living Resources — were adopted at the First UNCLOS in 1958.[3] These conventions remain in force, but have been modified to a certain extent or supplemented by developments in customary law, such as those concerning the extension of jurisdictional limits. The new LOSC (Article 311) specifically states that it will supersede the earlier conventions, but only for states party to the LOSC, and only as it enters into force. Denmark, the USA and UK are party to all four conventions, Norway and Canada are party only to the Continental Shelf Convention, and the USSR is party to all except that on fisheries. Only Denmark and the UK accepted an optional protocol on dispute-settlement machinery.

After the First and Second UNCLOS (1958, 1960) the framework of maritime law which became widely accepted by states bordering these waters was as follows. Coastal states could draw the limits of their territorial seas (over which they had sovereignty, subject only to a right of innocent passage exercisable by foreign vessels) and contiguous zones (in which they exercised certain enforcement powers limited to the prevention of violations of customs, immigration, and fiscal and sanitary laws) either from baselines that were based on natural coastlines or, where the coastline was deeply indented or there were fringing islands, from straight baselines. Bays, other than so-called 'historic bays', which were not defined, could be closed by a line not exceeding 24 miles* across the relevant points. The outer limit of the territorial sea was unfixed, but most states limited themselves to a 3- or 4-mile limit, though 12 was arguably acceptable on the basis of the ambiguities of the 1958 Territorial Sea Convention's Limit of the Contiguous Zone. In the territorial sea, all states had a right of innocent passage, the innocence of which was determined by the absence of threat to the peace, good order and security of the coastal state. The same right applied to international straits which fell within the territorial sea, although this could be temporarily suspended, and submarines exercising the right were required to navigate on the surface.

No fishing zones or fishing limits were provided for under the 1958 Conventions. However, the UK, Denmark and the USA (but not the USSR) became parties to the 1958 Convention on the Conservation of Fisheries and the Living Resources of the Sea, which required the fishing states concerned to cooperate with the coastal state and each other in order to conserve fisheries beyond

---

*Miles refer to nautical miles throughout.

the territorial sea of adjacent coastal states whose interest in maintaining such fisheries was recognized by the Convention.

The Convention on the Continental Shelf acknowledged the sovereign rights of a coastal state to explore and exploit the submarine areas adjacent to its coasts beyond the territorial sea to a depth of at least 200 metres and, beyond that depth, only so far as the areas were exploitable (i.e., available technology enabled exploitation in waters beyond 200 metres); but it explicitly maintained the status of the waters above as high seas and limited coastal states' jurisdiction over installations in terms related to what was necessary for the purposes of exploration and exploitation so as to avoid unjustifiable interference with other uses of the sea. This Convention also provided a formula for delimitation of overlapping shelves between opposite and adjacent states in the absence of any agreement. This is of particular interest in Northern Waters, where several delimitation problems arise between parties to the Convention. However, all areas beyond the territorial seas, over the shelf, being high seas were, under the 1958 Convention on the High Seas, open to all states for the exercise of the four freedoms of the seas identified in that Convention — navigation, fishing, overflight, laying submarine cables and pipelines — as well as others, unspecified but 'recognized by international law' (Article 2, High Seas Convention), which were widely assumed to include scientific research, waste disposal, and conducting military exercises. International obligations concerning conservation and control or prevention of pollution were both minimal and general under the Geneva Convention regime, but these gaps were filled to a large extent in the 1960s and 1970s by the conclusion of global and regional conventions outlined below.

In Northern Waters the fisheries regime used to be that of regulation by means of a 12-mile zone established unilaterally in the early 1960s by each coastal state, following the participation of most of them in the 1964 European Fisheries Convention, which was based on the compromise limits formula which had failed to gain acceptance at UNCLOS I. Beyond this 12-mile limit measures were laid down for the eastern part of Northern Waters by the North East Atlantic Fisheries Convention (NEAFC),[4] and by the International Convention for North Atlantic Fisheries (ICNAF)[5] for the western part. The NEAFC regulated fisheries by gear restraint, quotas and other limitations, and was backed by a Joint Enforcement Agreement,[6] which allowed mutual inspection for and reporting of violations. This basis for regulation changed to 200-mile limits in 1976/7 with a revised Common Fisheries Policy (CFP)[7] for application within the 200-mile limits of EC members. But the Faroe Islands (from 1974) and Greenland (from February 1985) were not part of the EC, and so they were not subject to the CFP. The European Fisheries Convention has not been denounced, but the NEAFC has been renegotiated to take account of the fact that the area, in which its members previously fished under high seas freedom, is now almost completely within the 200-mile fisheries zones of its parties and that the EC is required by its treaty to become party to such economic conventions in its own right, replacing its individual members.

The International Whaling Convention[8] applies in Northern Waters. It has adopted a moratorium on all 'commercial whaling', that is, whaling other than that by aborigines or for scientific research. Norway has formally objected to this ban, which enters into force 1985/6. Japan and the Soviet Union also formally oppose the ban but, in July 1985, the latter announced it would stop whaling for a year for technical reasons. Iceland meanwhile intends to take up to 200 whales for scientific research. Other Northern Waters states and non-governmental organizations have opposed the continuation of whaling.

Following several spectacular oil tanker casualties, there has been, since 1958, a proliferation of conventions for the control of oil pollution from ships, negotiated through the International Maritime Organization (IMO). The High Seas Convention, which is still in force, merely required that states take 'the measures necessary to prevent pollution from ships and seabed operations'. To this end the IMO has improved upon the 1954 Convention for Prevention of Oil Pollution from Ships (OILPOL) by introducing, in a 1969 Protocol to it,[9] controls which permit the Load on Top system for discharging oil en route and require special reception facilities on land, and also by concluding the 1973 Convention for Prevention of Pollution from Ships (MARPOL, as amended by a 1978 Protocol).[10] MARPOL improves the oil pollution control and includes annexes controlling discharge of garbage, sewage and some noxious and harmful substances, including chemicals. However, a subsequent 1978 amending Protocol[11] enables states to ratify by accepting only Annex I on oil; so only this is in force at present. The IMO has also fostered a series of Safety of Life at Sea Conventions (SOLAS), which provide measures for the safer operation of ships;[12] a Convention on Collision Regulations (the 1972 COLREG);[13] and another on Intervention on the High Seas in the case of Maritime Casualties (the 1969 Intervention Convention covers oil pollution casualties; the 1973 Protocol, which is in force, extends it to casualties involving noxious and hazardous cargoes).[14] A 1978 Convention on Training, Certification and Watchkeeping, concluded by the IMO and the ILO (International Labour Organization), tackles the contribution to accidents of insufficiently trained crews and officers.[15] The ILO has a whole series of conventions impinging on crew standards which constitute its 'Seafarers' Code'.[16] Liability for Oil Pollution Damage is covered by the 1969 Civil Liability Convention,[17] which is now backed by the 1971 Fund Convention (providing compensation for aspects of damage not covered by the former).[18] The limits and scope of both were raised in 1984 by Protocol. These and other IMO and ILO Codes and Conventions are applicable to all seas, including Northern Waters.

A number of conventions relevant to the prevention of pollution in Northern Waters and the Arctic have been negotiated outside the IMO, following the impetus provided by the 1972 Stockholm Conference on the Human Environment. These include the global 1972 London Dumping Convention[19] and, at the regional level, the Oslo Convention for Prevention of Pollution from the Dumping of Wastes from ships, aircraft and offshore platforms;[20] the 1974 Helsinki Convention for Prevention of Marine Pollution in the Baltic;[21] the 1974 Paris Convention for the Prevention of Pollution from Land-based Sources;[22] and the ECE's (UN Economic Commission for Europe) 1979 Transboundary Atmospheric Pollution Convention, a framework convention encouraging, if not requiring, states to begin to take measures to control and reduce pollution from such sources as so-called 'acid rain', to the extent that they can be proved to be harmful.[23]

Pollution from radioactive substances, i.e., from nuclear sources — weapons, nuclear-powered ships and submarines, cargoes of nuclear materials and wastes — is the area least satisfactorily covered. High-level waste dumping is banned under the London and Oslo Dumping Conventions. Low-level waste dumping, permitted under these conventions subject to conformity with IAEA (International Atomic Energy Authority) recommendations, is presently suspended under the London Convention pending a review, as a result of strong opposition from certain states, such as Australia, and non-governmental organizations, especially Greenpeace. There is a 1981 IMO Code of Safety for Nuclear Merchant Ships, and the IMO's Dangerous Goods Code makes detailed recommendations for carriage of radioactive materials by sea. Ad hoc Conventions relating to Carriage of Nuclear Materials,[24] and on Liability for Damage caused by Nuclear Ships,[25] are poorly ratified. The 1974 Paris Convention on Land-based Sources of Pollution requires its parties to adopt measures to forestall and, as appropriate, eliminate pollution 'from radioactive substances', and covers the North Atlantic. Pollution in all relevant conventions is defined in terms of causing harm or the likelihood of doing so, or introducing deleterious effects, all of which are often difficult to establish, especially in the short term.

Of especial relevance to the security issues in Northern and Arctic Waters is the 1970 UN Convention on Non-Emplacement of Nuclear Weapons and Other Weapons of Mass Destruction on the Seabed.[26] This Convention bans the permanent placing of such weapons on the seabed beyond a 12-mile limit drawn from the territorial sea baselines, but its wording is carefully formulated so as not to prevent the emplacement of anti-submarine warning devices on the seabed, nor to ban the use of submarines or other mobile vehicles above or resting on the seabed.

It is apparent that, outside the current LOSC, there is already a considerable body of law applicable to Northern Waters, and that either the coastal and user states are parties to the relevant conventions, or the conventions, or parts of them, can now be regarded as having entered the corpus of customary international law. The new LOSC (Article 311.2) prescribes that such treaties will not be superseded by it as long as they are compatible with its purposes and objects.

The effects of the LOSC on the area can occur in three ways: when the Convention enters into force for the parties to it; as it, or parts thereof, are put into practice by some states and gradually become part of customary law; or if there are immediate effects in relation to parts that can be regarded as codifying existing customs.

The LOSC and Northern Waters

The most immediate and awkward of the effects of the LOSC

derives from the fact that its text was not adopted unanimously (seventeen states including the Eastern bloc and half the EC member states — Belgium, the Federal Republic of Germany (FRG), Italy, Luxembourg and the United Kingdom — abstained on this vote, and four — including the USA — voted against). Furthermore, at the time of writing, although 159 states or other entities have signed it, including the Eastern and Nordic blocs, three states interested in Northern Waters and the Arctic have not signed the Convention: the FRG, the UK and the USA. The last announced that it would never sign or adhere to it in its present form, since the fundamental premises of its seabed regime are antipathetic to current US policies. The other two have indicated that they might do so — indeed would prefer so to do — if certain changes to the seabed provisions could be effected through the Preparatory Commission (Prep. Com.), which is currently preparing for the establishment of the International Seabed Authority (ISA) and for the International Tribunal for the Law of the Sea (ITLOS).[27] This at present seems unlikely. According to the Group of 77 states — supported by the USSR, Iceland, Denmark and Norway — states cannot 'pick and choose' the parts of the Convention package they are prepared to put into practice. They cannot, for example, ignore the deep seabed mining regime provisions, and adapt those on economic zones and the continental shelf to suit their own policies, while regarding the provisions on innocent passage through the territorial sea and transit passage through international straits either as codifications of existing customary international law or in process of becoming so by adoption into state practice — in other words, the policies that the USA proposes to follow.

The LOSC does not seem to express clearly the intention that any of its benefits should be available to non-parties (apart from those codified because they are already part of customary law). It clearly rules out reservations and is intended to be a 'package deal'. The United States regards its 1983 Proclamation of an Exclusive Economic Zone (EEZ) and the accompanying explanatory statements as an expression of its willingness, in return for being accorded the corresponding rights under the LOSC, to accept certain specified obligations, including those related to transit passage and to coastal-state jurisdiction over fisheries and pollution.[28]

The statements accompanying this Proclamation[29] make equally clear the US intention to retain a 3-mile territorial sea and to refuse to recognize 12-mile territorial sea claims unless the US is accorded its 'full rights under international law' therein. The US decided not to exercise jurisdiction over scientific research in its EEZs, but will respect the claims of others provided they are 'consistent with international law reflected in the Convention' and provided the coastal states concerned respect 'US rights and freedoms in such areas under international law'. The US will 'seek to facilitate access' by US scientists to foreign EEZs under 'reasonable conditions'. The US policy of regarding the territorial sea limit as three miles, in the absence of its being accorded the rights 'reflected' in the LOSC, leaves a corridor of high seas passage through most international straits 24 or less miles wide. To maintain these positions the USA will have to be active in pursuing them, including in Arctic waters. It stressed in these statements that unimpeded commercial and military navigation and airflight are critical to US national interests and that the United States 'will exercise and assert its navigation and airflight rights and freedoms on a worldwide basis in a manner consistent with the balance of interests reflected in' the LOSC.

Finally, the use of nuclear-powered merchant ships in Soviet Northern Waters[30] represents an increasing threat of radioactive pollution of these areas, given the series of disasters experienced by earlier Soviet nuclear-powered ships and submarines.[31] Coupled with the inconclusive conclusion of UNCLOS III and the contentious legal status of the resultant convention, this could introduce political turbulence into Northern and Arctic Waters, thereby exacerbating the difficulties already presented by the area's hostile climate. The issues most relevant to this area that are covered by the LOSC and the relevant positions of bordering and user states will now be examined.

Relevant LOSC provisions

There are two outstanding features of Northern Waters which determine the major international law issues in the area. The first is the vast extent to which the area consists of the continental shelves of Denmark (Greenland), the USA (Alaska and the Bering Sea), the USSR, Canada (Beaufort Sea and Arctic Islands) and Norway. Especially notable is the overlap of Soviet coastline and adjacent shelf to the east of Northern Waters, in the Barents Sea, with that of Norway, which gives rise to major delimitation problems, further complicated for Norway by Svalbard's international regime and the rich but relatively unexplored resource potential of the area.

The second special feature is the existence of the two major passages — the Northwest (through Canadian waters off the Canadian mainland and Arctic Islands) and the Northeast (off the Russian mainland) — both of which emerge into Northern Waters off southwest Greenland and northern Norway respectively, and also the passage from the Kola Peninsula into the North Atlantic, through the Norwegian Sea between Iceland and Norway, the Greenland Sea between Greenland and West Spitsbergen or the Denmark Strait between Greenland and Iceland.

Because of its 'package deal' nature, almost all the provisions of the LOSC, which has 320 articles and 8 annexes and is accompanied by four important UNCLOS Resolutions, including two on the deep seabed mining regime, have some relevance to the situation in Northern Waters. The issues most important in this area are: (1) the baselines from which national zones are measured; (2) the status of islands and ice formations; (3) rights of passage; (4) resource rights in fisheries or economic zones; and (5) resource rights on the continental shelves.

(1) Baselines and bays

The LOSC (Part II, Section II) includes, with minor additions, the baseline system adopted in the 1958 Territorial Sea Convention, which incorporated with some qualifications the International Court of Justice's decision on the Anglo-Norwegian Fisheries Case.[32] The ICJ accepted that straight baselines can be drawn along deeply indented coastlines or across bays (at points no more than 24 miles apart) and gulfs; or outside fringing islands that are so close to the coast as to be in effect part of it, so that characterizing the waters inside these lines as internal waters subject to the sovereignty of the coastal state, without a right of innocent passage, is appropriate. Such lines must follow the general direction of the coast and not depart too far from it. The LOSC excepts from these limitations 'so-called historic bays' (Art. 10.b), which it does not define or identify. The concept derives from customary law, which has developed two criteria for such claims, relating to bays with mouths wider than 24 miles: first, the bay must traditionally have been claimed as part of internal waters and jurisdiction exercised accordingly; second, other states must have acquiesced in this claim before it can be asserted against them.

Some Soviet lawyers contend that the whole of the Soviet northern seas (bays, inlets, seas and straits), including the Chukchi, East Siberian, Laptev, Kara and Okhotsk Seas, are Soviet historic waters subject to the USSR's sovereignty, and that, therefore, the Northeast Passage is their historical national route. Some relate the claim to Soviet efforts to open up and keep open this route, others to Soviet sector claims, of which more will be said later. Such claims go beyond those acknowledged in the UNCLOS I and III Conventions. In its 1982 Soviet Law on the State Boundary, the USSR does not specifically assert a sector claim but relegates to internal waters (Article 6.4) 'the waters of bays, inlets, coves, estuaries, seas and straits, historically belonging to the USSR', without identifying them.[33] It thus incorporates intact the provisions of an earlier statute of 1960 and perpetuates the ambiguity raised by a 1926 Soviet decree which regarded Soviet territory as including 'all *lands and islands* already discovered, as well as those which are to be discovered in the future' (emphasis added) in a sector extending north of the boundaries of the Soviet mainland to the North Pole.[34] This decree did not pronounce on the status of the intervening iced waters. The Soviet sector claim is disputed by other states in the area.

It is noteworthy, however, that the 1982 decree changes the former Soviet description of straight baselines: whereas the 1960 decree limited such baselines to 'localities where the coastline is deeply indented' or there are fringing islands, the 1982 one, in Article 5, merely describes them as 'joining appropriate points', the geographic coordinates of which are to be confirmed by the USSR Council of Ministers. In 1967 the USA sent icebreakers on a scientific voyage into the Kara/Laptev Seas, and they endeavoured to pass through the 22-mile-wide Vil'kitsky Strait connecting the two.[35] The USSR stated that its permission was required for this passage through its territorial sea. The USSR claims a 12-mile territorial sea (drawn from its prescribed baselines), the USA a 3-mile one (and it has not acquiesced in the Soviet baseline system). The USA did not on this occasion, however, attempt to assert a right of free passage, but attempted an alternative route before recalling its vessels.[36] The difficulty of asserting rights in such distant and hostile areas leaves the legal status of the Northeast Passage and Soviet coastal waters unclear, though the extreme claims of some Soviet lawyers would certainly seem to exceed the 'historic bay' concept as recognized in the LOSC.

(2) Islands, ice-shelves, ice-floes and ice-islands

No conclusive definition or categorization of islands has ever been arrived at in international custom or treaty. The 1958 Territorial Sea Convention merely defines an island as an area of land above water at high tide, but allows only fringing islands to be brought within the baselines.[37] The Continental Shelf Convention accepts that islands can have their own continental shelves, and it is generally thought that offshore islands may represent one of the 'special circumstances' which Article 6 of that Convention, in the absence of agreement, allows to be taken into account in adjusting the median or equidistance line laid down for purposes of delimiting the continental shelf between opposite or adjacent states respectively. The decisions of various international courts and tribunals,[38] as well as state practice endorsed by delimitation agreements, confirm this. The 1985 Libya-Malta decision reinforces the view that the uninhabited nature of an island is especially relevant in this context.[39]

The LOSC, in Article 121.3, provides that rocks which are uninhabited or cannot sustain human behaviour or economic life on their own cannot have an EEZ or continental shelf, though they may have a territorial sea. 'Rocks' are undefined, as are the nature and extent of habitation, etc., required. Current state practice does not support this categorization: for example, the UK's annexation of Rockall, 180 miles off the west coast of the Scottish Western Isles, and its use as a basepoint for the UK 200-mile fisheries zone in 1976.[40] Spitsbergen (Svalbard), a sparsely populated Norwegian archipelago, would not fall within Article 121.3, though some of the outlying rocks in the Svalbard archipelago might. Jan Mayen, another Norwegian island, is inhabited only by scientists but on a regular basis, and the delimitation of both its EEZ and continental shelf, originally contentious, has now taken place.[41] Ambiguities concerning the zones off islands still complicate seabed delimitation between the UK and Ireland; more recently between Denmark and Iceland concerning Rockall; and between Norway and the Soviet Union in the Barents Sea and off Svalbard.

The LOSC does not address the problem of the legal status of the ice-shelves, ice-floes and ice-islands which infest Northern Waters. The predominant view among commentators seems to be that ice-shelves attached to the land on a quasi-permanent basis could be considered to be land and included as basepoints for delimitation lines, as for example off Ellesmere Island, Severnaya Zemlya and Svalbard.[42] Canada has used them in this way. The status of ice-floes and ice-islands, though they are often used for meteorological and research stations, by the USSR and USA among others, is more uncertain, although in the Escamilla Case in 1970 a US court asserted jurisdiction over one of its nationals who had committed murder on a floating ice-station, then in the Canadian sector, on the basis that the offence was committed by one of its nationals against another national on the high seas.[43] The same year a Canadian court asserted jurisdiction in *R. v. Tootalik* over a hunter who had killed a bear on an ice-floe (an act that was an offence if committed on land), apparently on the basis that the ice-floe was in the Canadian sector for such jurisdictional purposes.[44]

(3) Rights of passage

Innocent passage.   Article 4 sets the maritime limit of the territorial sea at 12 miles for the first time in a global convention. The Soviet Union has long claimed this limit; Canada and Iceland now do so as well. Norway claims 4 miles, but Denmark, the UK and USA retain a 3-mile limit. A major innovation in the LOSC is that in addition to codifying the right of innocent passage 'for ships of all states' (Article 27), which implies inclusion of warships, it also defines in detail 'non-innocent' activities (Article 19) which are to be regarded as prejudicial to the peace, good order and security of the coastal state, thereby permitting that state to take the 'necessary steps' to prevent such passage. Non-innocent activities include the threat or use of force; conducting weapons exercises; the gathering of information or broadcasting of propaganda which prejudices the coastal state's security; launching, landing or taking on board military or other aircraft; acts of wilful or serious pollution; interference with communications systems; engaging in fishing or research activities; or — ambiguously — any other activity not having a direct bearing on passage. Ships' passage does not require prior consent, though many coastal states — including the USSR and Scandinavian states — insist on it. The USSR's 1982 State Boundary Law makes clear for the first time a Soviet policy change in favour of allowing warships rights of innocent passage in the territorial sea, though prior authorization for entry into Soviet internal waters and ports is still required, and Article 36 explicitly permits Soviet border guards and anti-aircraft defence forces to use weapons and combat equipment against violators of Soviet water boundaries in specific instances.[45]

There is no restriction in the LOSC on passage of nuclear ships or ships carrying nuclear or other inherently dangerous substances, though they must carry documents and observe any special precautionary measures established by international agreement.[46] The new Soviet nuclear-powered barge carrier for use on Arctic routes adds an additional pollution threat and makes urgent the clarification and development of the law regulating the use of such vessels in seas which are ecologically fragile, and therefore require special protection measures under Article 94.5 of the LOSC. Nuclear and hazardous cargo ships can be required to confine their passage to designated sea-lanes.

It has to be remembered that the LOSC is not in force and customary law remains as codified in the 1958 Territorial Sea Convention, which is less specific concerning non-innocent acts and special responsibilities, though under both conventions submarines are required to navigate on the surface and, under the LOSC, so are 'other underwater vehicles'.[47]

Transit passage.   The approval in the LOSC of the growing practice of asserting 12-mile limits for the territorial sea necessitates special provisions to preserve free passage through international straits[48] which are 24 miles wide or less. These previously had a high seas corridor running through them, but will now be completely enclosed within the territorial sea of one or more bordering states. Free passage for merchant and warships both on and under the water surface remains of vital importance: in the former case, especially so for the Soviet fleet; in the latter, for the nuclear submarines of the USSR, USA and UK. Thus none of these states welcomed the reduction in high seas freedoms introduced by the LOSC. The USA and USSR in particular fought for the inclusion in Part V of a right of unimpedable transit (not merely 'innocent' as heretofore) passage for *all* ships and aircraft through international straits, unless there were some suitable alternative route.

It is generally concluded that references to 'normal modes' of transit imply that submarines can navigate below the surface. It can be further deduced that the regime thus applies to passage below as well as on the surface. Bordering states are restrained from either hampering or suspending transit passage (Article 44).

There are therefore major differences from the regime laid down in the 1958 High Seas Convention, which made no reference to aircraft (unlike Article 34 of the LOSC) and endorsed the right in terms of 'innocent' passage, which could not be suspended but required submarines to navigate on the surface. Although the LOSC clearly implies that transit passage exists as of right for warships and military aircraft, some states maintain that their passage still requires prior authorization and have made declarations to this effect on signing the 1982 Convention.[49] The Soviet Union is likely still to maintain its requirements in this respect, as it did in denying passage to the US Coast Guard's icebeakers through the Vil'kitsky Strait.

Finally, it should be remarked that passage through straits which do not meet the LOSC's definition of 'international', if there is no alternative passage and if they are not already governed by a specific convention, falls under the provisions concerning innocent passage.[50]

(4) Resource rights in the Exclusive Economic or Fisheries Zones

The 1958 Convention on the Continental Shelf, following emergent custom, allowed coastal states to exercise certain rights over the continental shelf. The LOSC provides for complex interlinked compromises, mini-packages within the larger package deal, for fisheries and other economic rights over the water column, and for continental shelf rights. It provides first, in Part V, that coastal states have sovereign rights over living and non-living resources of the seabed and water column of the 200-mile Exclusive Zone defined as 'an area beyond and adjacent to the territorial sea'. These rights are, however, subject to the specific and very detailed regime established in Part V, 'under which the rights and jurisdiction of the coastal state and the rights and freedoms of other states are governed by the relevant provisions of this Convention'.[51] Thus, for example, coastal states have resource rights only for the purposes of exploring and exploiting, conserving and managing them. They have undefined sovereign rights concerning other economic exploitative activities (e.g., producing energy from water, currents and winds), but jurisdiction only, as specifically limited in other parts of the Convention, over establishing and using artificial islands, installations and other structures, marine scientific research, and protection and preservation of the marine environment.

The rights over the seabed and subsoil of the EEZ are further subject to the provisions on the continental shelf (Part VI); those over scientific research to Part XIII; and over the marine environment to Part XII and various other related articles. Thus even the EEZ, itself one of the mini-packages, is broken down into yet smaller packages.[52]

Fisheries.   Under the LOSC, as far as fishing rights are concerned, the coastal state has the right to determine the total allowable catch (TAC) and must determine the amount of this which is within its own harvesting capacity. Only if it cannot harvest all the TAC must it allow foreign states, subject to somewhat general criteria, access to the surplus TAC.[53] In Northern Waters, factors relevant to this allocation would be the significance of the fisheries to the economy and other national interests of the states concerned, and the need to minimize economic dislocation in states whose nationals have habitually fished in the zone.

Although none of the states bordering Northern or Arctic Waters has, by mid-1985, ratified the LOSC, all, whether or not signatories, have declared either 200-mile Exclusive Fisheries Zones (EFZs) (the UK, Canada and Denmark), or EEZs (the USA, Iceland, Norway and the USSR). Not all, however, have fully implemented EEZs, pending their acceptance of, or the entry into force of, the LOSC. The EC has now replaced its member states in all international fisheries commissions in the area of a purely economic character, such as the NEAF (North East Atlantic Fisheries) Commission, to which Denmark (in respect of the Faroe Islands only) Iceland, Norway, Sweden and the USSR are party, and NAFO (Northwest Atlantic Fisheries Organization), to which most non-EC states in Northern Waters (Canada, Denmark (Faroes), Norway, USSR, Iceland) are party. The EC conducts all negotiations with third states, such as Norway, for access to their fisheries. Individual EC members have denounced their membership of the former NEAFC and ICNAF. The USSR has been excluded from access to EC fisheries following the failure to negotiate an acceptable reciprocal agreement for access to the Baltic and Barents Sea fisheries in 1977-8. The EC and Norway, however, have concluded a series of reciprocal access agreements — though not without difficulty. The effective international management role of both the NEAF and NAFO has been much diminished by the reduction of the area of the former to the EC members' 200-mile jurisdictional zones and of the latter to Canada's 200-mile fisheries zone.

For some time Norway did not assert its 200-mile fisheries jurisdiction off Jan Mayen because of unresolved delimitation problems concerning the overlap of such a zone with the Icelandic zone, which might have had repercussions affecting the NATO base at Keflavik. However, these have now been amicably resolved and both the EEZ and continental shelf in the areas concerned have been delimited in an unusual and interesting manner.[54]

Scientific Research. The LOSC also has serious implications in Northern Waters in that it requires coastal states' consent for both sea and seabed research and it extends the geographical scope of the continental shelf to include the whole of the continental margin, thus leaving, especially in the Arctic, a comparatively small area of high seas in which the assumed customary freedom of research continues. The LOSC does provide (Article 246) that 'coastal states shall in normal circumstances grant their consent for marine scientific research projects by other states or competent international organizations' in their EEZs or on their continental shelves, but limits this to research for undefined 'peaceful purposes'. These are generally assumed to cover military research for defensive purposes; 'normal circumstances' are not defined. Such ambiguities and the definition of the circumstances in which consent can be withheld suggest that there may in future be delay and difficulty in obtaining consent. The LOSC also requires that research should increase scientific knowledge of the marine environment for the benefit of all mankind. Secrecy of research activity in EEZs will, therefore, be impossible to maintain legally even if it continues in practice. One concession is that on the outer continental shelf, between the outer limits of the 200-mile EEZ and of the continental margin (where this situation exists), the consent requirement applies only to areas designated by the coastal state for realistic seabed operations. Even if consent is obtained, it is subject to numerous conditions involving the optional participation of the coastal state or the rendering of assistance to it at virtually every stage — on board, in sharing and evaluating data and samples, and in submitting reports.

Clearly such unprecedented restrictions in such vast new areas could have a most adverse effect on research in large parts of these unique climatic and oceanographic regions. They are of interest to mankind as a whole, and research on them has been established by the Comité Arctique to be vital to this interest.[55] States are required by international law to observe treaty obligations in good faith, but the ambiguities and discretionary powers inherent in these provisions provide scope for severe restriction if they are not liberally interpreted and applied. A solution may be for more research to be undertaken in future through competent international organizations, as encouraged by the LOSC, though it does not specify the organizations concerned. The long-established and reputable International Council for the Exploration of the Sea (ICES),[56] of which all Arctic and Northern Waters states are members, is the most appropriate for this area, but its geographical scope is limited and does not include all Arctic Waters. UNESCO's International Oceanographic Commission (IOC) could also play a role. Bilateral or regional cooperation between coastal states could be instituted, but this is not without its own difficulties since it may unduly and harmfully limit the scope of the research in so far as the ecosystems and oceanographic features of Northern Waters are all interlinked or otherwise interrelated. The Comité Arctique cannot be designated as an 'organization' for these purposes, but if it develops as ICES did and founds its activities on a convention it could be so recognized, though this would be of real benefit only if the USSR participated (as it does in ICES).

Marine pollution.   The 1958 High Seas Convention dealt with this only briefly and then in general terms that required states to adopt regulations 'or measures for certain forms of pollution'.[57] These include measures to prevent pollution of the airspace above the high seas. Although recommended measures might include those against the sulphur and other chemicals contributing to 'acid rain', this is far from clear, since their harmfulness remains to be conclusively established in the view of the UK and USA.[58]

The Continental Shelf Convention required only that coastal states in the exercise of their jurisdiction must not unjustifiably interfere with other legitimate uses of the sea, and that they must, in the 500-metre safety zones they are permitted to establish round installations, take the measures appropriate to protect living resources from unspecified 'harmful agents'.

Especially since the 1972 UN Conference on the Human Environment, international law for the protection of the marine environment has grown. There have been many new conventions applicable to Northern Waters.[59] Numerous relevant codes of practice have been developed by the UN, IMO, IAEA, the International Union for the Conservation of Nature (IUCN) and the UN Environment Programme (UNEP), etc., which are not binding but are widely followed in practice. These include the UN's World Charter for Nature, the UNEP's Principles for Shared Natural Resources, the IMO's Code on Carriage of Dangerous Goods by Sea, the IUCN's World Conservation Strategy and a variety of IAEA recommendations both on carriage of dangerous goods by sea and on discharge of dangerous substances and of nuclear materials. The fishery commissions already referred to, including the International Whaling Commission, have become progressively more concerned at the possible, if as yet unproved, effects that the increasing amounts of wastes discharged into the sea and the intensification of uses of the sea, especially by the offshore oil industry, might have on living marine species and their habitats. The ICES has expanded its tasks to investigate these problems, at the request of its members. States adjacent to the Northern Waters are mostly party to all the relevant conventions and follow the codes of practice.

The LOSC lays down for the first time in a comprehensive convention the duty of all states to protect and preserve the marine environment without transforming one kind of pollution into another, and without transferring pollution from one area to another. It requires states to take the measures necessary to prevent or control pollution from all the existing six sources which it identifies: from land; from continental shelf and deep seabed operations; from dumping; from the atmosphere and from vessels. It specifies the means of developing these measures and of establishing required global standards at national, international, regional or sub-regional levels, either through international organizations or through diplomatic conferences. It gives coastal states much wider enforcement powers against vessel-source pollution, allowing the detention of vessels in their territorial seas or even — if the violations of applicable international standards are sufficiently serious — in the Exclusive Economic Zone. It also endorses the concept of port–state jurisdiction, whereby the next port of call of an offending ship can detain and prosecute it in certain circumstances at the request of the state within whose EEZ it committed the offence.

Semi-enclosed seas.   Part IX of the LOSC provides for enclosed or semi-enclosed seas, which it defines as 'a gulf, basin, or sea surrounded by two or more states and connected to another sea or the ocean by a narrow outlet or consisting entirely or primarily of the territorial seas and exclusive economic zones of two or more coastal states'. Clearly there are several seas bordering Northern and Arctic Waters which meet these criteria. Ambiguities concerning the lack of specification of criteria for determining 'narrowness', or whether there can be more than one outlet, cast doubts on the status of the North Sea or the Arctic Ocean or Baffin Bay. The Kara, Laptev and East Siberian, Barents, Norwegian and Greenland Seas are clearly excluded by this definition. If the Arctic Ocean can be regarded as meeting the criteria, which is highly doubtful in view of the width and diversity of outlets and the extent of remaining high seas area (albeit much diminished), then Article 123 applies, despite the frequent comparisons with the Mediterranean. This article, however, imposes on bordering states merely the obligation 'to cooperate with each other in the exercise of their rights and the performance of their duties under this Convention'. To this end they are required only to 'endeavour', either directly or through an appropriate regional organization (which is lacking for the Arctic), to 'coordinate' the management, conservation, exploration and exploitation of living resources; the implementation of rights and duties to protect the marine environment; and scientific research policies, undertaking 'where appropriate' joint research programmes in the area. They are also required to invite, as appropriate, other interested states or international organizations to cooperate with them in furtherance of these obligations.

Special areas.   Part XII, Article 211.b of the LOSC allows coastal states in clearly defined areas within their EEZs to adopt special mandatory measures for the prevention of pollution from vessels if international measures are inadequate to protect these areas in the special circumstances prevailing there. These can include oceanographical and ecological conditions, utilization and protection of resources and the type of traffic. The relevant evidence must be submitted to the 'competent' international organization (assumed to be the IMO), which can determine whether the area meets the requirements and whether its international rules for special areas are applicable. This could have a considerable effect in Northern and Arctic Waters, where many areas may qualify.

Ice-covered areas.   In some far Northern and Arctic Waters even greater effect could ensue from Article 234, concerning ice-covered areas. These are defined as areas 'where particularly severe climatic conditions and the presence of ice covering such areas for most of the year create obstructions and exceptional hazards to navigation'. Coastal states alone, without references to any international organization, are given the right to adopt and enforce non-discriminatory laws and regulations to prevent or control vessel-source pollution. This article was strenuously sought by Canada to validate its 1970 Arctic Waters Pollution Prevention Act,[60] which was protested against by the USA. In the absence of an effective Law of the Sea treaty, and in view of the USA's stance, it is far from clear whether this article can yet be regarded as codifying customary international law. Few states other than Canada seem to have adopted appropriate legislation to implement it, although it could be argued that the article attracted consensus during UNCLOS III.

Rare and fragile ecosystems.   Although such systems surely abound in Northern and Arctic Waters, the LOSC does not lay down criteria for identifying them. Article 194.5 stipulates that the measures required to be taken by all states to prevent or control coastal pollution from all sources must include those necessary to protect and preserve rare or fragile ecosystems as well as the habitats of depleted, threatened or endangered species. Neither the measures nor species concerned are identified, but it is commonly accepted that many cetaceans, pinnipedia and polar bears would be included. The cetaceans in the area are largely protected, as already mentioned, by the International Whaling Commission, of which all states in the area except Canada (which withdrew in 1982) are members. Having adopted the moratorium on commercial whaling, the Commission is likely to intensify its interest in habitat preservation in order to restore all species. The bears are protected by the successful Agreement on the Conservation of

Polar Bears, concluded in 1973 by Canada, the USA, USSR, Norway and Denmark. The IUCN has identified numerous threatened species in its Red Data Book. Again, in the absence of a treaty in force, it is not clear that the obligation specified under Article 194.5 is applicable, but clearly it is a matter on which states in the area need to act and to coordinate their activities. This could be done through existing organizations or, more appropriately and effectively, by establishing a regional mechanism on the lines of the Council of Europe's 1979 Berne Convention on the Protection of European Wildlife and Habitats, which lists in annexes the species whose habitats require protection.[61]

(5) Resource rights on the continental shelf

There are three aspects to the problem of resource rights that have been created by the changes introduced in the law relating to the definition and delimitation of the continental shelf both by the LOSC and by developments in customary law following the 1958 Continental Shelf Convention. They are the definition of this area, which is related also to the fixing of its outer limits, the demarcation of boundaries between opposite and adjacent states, or both, whose shelves overlap, and the sharing of revenue derived from exploitation of shelf resources in the areas beyond 200 miles to the limits of the outer margin.

The Geneva Convention limited coastal states' shelf rights to adjacent submarine areas, defined for legal purposes as the continental shelf, though the reference to 'adjacency' arguably introduced a geological element into the definition. Its limit was defined in terms of location (beyond the territorial sea), depth (200 metres) and exploitability (to the extent that water depth permitted this). The ICJ, in the North Sea Continental Shelf Cases of 1969, in stating that shelf rights derived from the character of these shelves as a natural prolongation of land territory, appeared to emphasize the geological or geophysical continuity of these areas rather than their exploitability, thus possibly extending coastal states' rights beyond the plateaux of the shelves. This has profound importance in evaluating the extent of coastal states' jurisdiction and control over the seabeds of the Arctic Basin and in all Northern Waters, with shelf rights remaining problematic in the Rockall Bank, the Barents and Beaufort Seas, and the Jan Mayen Ridge areas.

The 1982 LOSC simultaneously manages to clarify and confuse

these issues. It accepts the ICJ's dictum and defines the coastal state's continental shelf in Article 96 as comprising 'the seabed and subsoil of the submarine areas that extend beyond the territorial sea throughout the natural prolongation of the land territory to the outer edge of the continental margin'; but it also includes within the definition, where the continental shelf as defined above does not extend so far, the seabed areas that are comprised within the EEZ, namely, the areas 'to a distance of 200 nautical miles of the baselines from which the territorial sea is measured', regardless of geological or other criteria, though it places an ultimate limit on the shelf at 350 miles, or at 100 miles from the 2,500-metre isobath. Although a recent decision of the ICJ, which accepts that coastal states are now entitled, as a minimum, to a 200-mile 'continental shelf' as laid down in the LOSC, binds only the states party to that case, it will undoubtedly have a profound effect on claims in Northern Waters.[62] Claims to at least 200 miles of seabed are now likely to be made whether or not the LOSC enters into force and whether or not states in the region become party to it.

The LOSC requires states to establish the outer limits of their shelves, if they project beyond 200 miles, according to a complex formula related to thickness of sedimentary rock, distance and gradients in the outer areas. On submarine ridges, however, the 350-mile distance limit prevails, unless the elevations concerned are natural components of the continental margin, namely, its plateaux, rises, caps, banks and spurs. This delimitation of the outer limit must be submitted to the Commission on the Limits of the Continental Shelf, established under the LOSC, which can make recommendations upon it. Once established on the basis of these recommendations the limit is final and binding, but it remains unclear to what extent the coastal state must follow the precise advice of the Commission. Until the LOSC enters into force, no such Commission exists, and it is left to states to determine their own limits, though negotiation is required where claims overlap. The potential for conflict concerning seabed demarcation in Northern Waters that derives from this open-ended situation is obvious, since none of the 'rim' states has ratified the LOSC and not all have ratified the 1958 Continental Shelf Convention. Opinions are, however, divided concerning whether recent decisions of the ICJ will help or hinder future delimitation agreements.[63]

Clearly there will be many situations, including in northern areas, where the 'natural shelf' extends beyond 200 miles. Thus the LOSC (Article 82) requires that coastal states make payments or contributions in kind, through the Authority established under it, in respect of the non-living resources exploited in such marginal areas, according to a formula it lays down, the payments being shared out by the Authority on the basis of equitable criteria. It remains to be seen, pending ratification by the signatory northern states, whether some will eventually be restricted by this requirement and some, which do not become parties, will not. Demarcation may thus also determine which areas fall within these revenue-sharing requirements.

Some delimitation problems in Northern Waters

Delimitation disputes in Northern Waters may be affected by the 1980 conciliation which successfully settled the Jan Mayen Island dispute without recourse to judicial settlement.[64]

Details of the Iceland–Norway settlement over *Jan Mayen Island*, and Norway's response to it, are dealt with below, and this settlement and the problems concerning the unsettled boundary with Greenland have been exhaustively analysed by Robin Churchill in a recent article.[65]

Iceland adopted a 200-mile EEZ in 1979 (replacing its 200-mile fisheries zone) without delimiting its geographical scope. Norway provided for future establishment of an EEZ in 1976, which was also intended to apply to Jan Mayen. An EEZ was concluded in 1977 but for the mainland only, not for Jan Mayen. Negotiation led to an agreement in 1980 which established a boundary between the EEZs of Jan Mayen and Iceland, made arrangements for the management of fish stocks in the area and set up a Conciliation Commission to recommend a continental shelf boundary. In 1981 this Commission unanimously recommended that the continental shelf boundary should be identical to that established by the 1980 EEZ agreement and that cooperative arrangements for the exploration and exploitation of petroleum resources in an area overlapping the two islands' continental shelves should be established.

The Danish and Norwegian EEZs also overlap west of Jan Mayen. Norway contends that the boundary should be the median line; Denmark argues that Greenland's EEZ should be given full effect as the boundary, presumably because it regards Jan Mayen as a special circumstance which should not impair the full breadth of Greenland's zone. The conflict heightened when Danish and Faroese vessels began fishing for capelin in the disputed area in 1981. So far Norway has not acted upon a Danish proposal that the dispute be referred to arbitration, but prefers further negotiation. Greenland's withdrawal from the EC and the consequent removal of EC fisheries interests should facilitate a solution. Churchill suggests that the fisheries boundary should be drawn between the median line and the 200-mile Greenland EEZ limit, and that a Greenland-Iceland-Norway Commission should be established to manage the capelin and other joint stocks (replacing the existing Norway-Iceland Commission). For the continental shelf boundary he suggests the same delineation as the fisheries zone boundary but without the cooperative arrangements agreed between Iceland and Norway in their Jan Mayen settlement.

The unusual legal situation concerning *Svalbard* (Spitsbergen) derives from a treaty concluded in 1920[66] which gave Norway sovereignty over the Spitsbergen archipelago — until then unappropriated by any state. The treaty requires that nationals of all states party to the treaty be allowed to engage in 'all maritime, industrial, mining and commercial exploration on a footing of absolute equality' on land and in the territorial sea. The islands are non-militarized; Norway must regulate any activities on them, subject to the conditions of the treaty; and Norway is also required to apply to Spitsbergen only any taxes levied on the archipelago. A problem of most concern to this study is created by the increased jurisdictional control accorded to the coastal states in an extended territorial sea and in new maritime zones by the LOSC and also as developed in customary international law. The Svalbard Convention was concluded when most of its parties limited their maritime jurisdiction to the territorial sea only. Disagreement has since arisen as to whether the treaty now applies to the new 200-mile fisheries or economic zones and if so whether the parties will be entitled to equal access to their resources.[67]

A British commentator (Churchill) has analysed the extent to which the unique restrictions formulated in the Spitsbergen treaty apply to the maritime zones beyond Spitsbergen's territorial sea.[68] He considers that Norway has competence in international law to claim zones around the archipelago that should be measured from the basepoints of each separate island and not from the archipelagic straight baselines approved by the LOSC, since these do not apply to offshore archipelagos. Other jurisdictional disputes in the Northern Waters area are:

— Canada's inclusion of its Arctic islands in internal waters.[69]
— The dispute between Canada and Greenland (Denmark) over Hans Island.
— The effects of the overlap of conflicting Icelandic and Faroese fisheries zones and seabed claims.
— The delineation of the boundary between Norway and the Soviet Union in the Barents Sea.[70]
— The dividing line between the Svalbard and Greenlandic fisheries zones and continental shelves.

The following agreements have also been reached:
— The Canada-Denmark (Greenland) Continental Shelf Boundary Agreement, 1973.
— The Norway-Faroes EEZ and Continental Shelf Boundary Agreement, 1979.
— The Norway-United Kingdom Agreement on the Continental Shelf Boundary north of 60°N.
— The Norway-USSR 'Grey Zone' Agreement.[71]
— The Canada-Denmark Agreement on Marine Pollution, 1983.[72]
— A number of agreements on joint fish-stocks' management (e.g., the EC and Canada), on seals (Norway-Canada, Norway-USSR) and on salmon (EC-Faroes, EC-Canada).

Conclusion

More stress could be laid on the wide range of existing international treaties that are already applicable to the area and to which most regional states are parties. Furthermore, the acknowledgement in the Polar Bear Treaty that 'states of the Arctic region' have 'special responsibilities and special interests ... in relation to the protection of the flora and fauna' of that region could be extended to embrace both a wider area and a wider number of species. By coordinating national measures and research to this end, as successfully done in the Polar Bear Treaty, habits of peaceful cooperation and communication could be encouraged. It is also possible that the Comité Arctique could extend its scope and membership, in collaboration with the highly respected ICES.[73]

Without such developments the danger is that, in the absence of global support for the checks and balances instituted in the LOSC, and its identification of both the rights and obligations of states, jurisdiction will continue to 'creep', 200-mile economic zones will become 200-mile territorial seas in which passage will be permitted only if innocent and, in time, even the 200-mile limit itself will be displaced by the coastal states' extension of full sovereignty to all the waters and resources covering the continental margin. The effects of this on Northern Waters would radically change the existing strategic relationship of the superpowers and relations between all states bordering or using these waters.

Notes

1. Law of the Sea Convention, A/CONF. 62/122, 7 October 1982; XX *International Legal Materials* (hereafter *ILM*), 1982; Cmnd 8941, Misc. No. 11, 1983. Not in force.

2. Agreement on the Conservation of Polar Bears: II *ILM*, 1972, p. 1358; IV *New Directions in the Law of the Sea: Documents* (hereafter *ND*), pp. 214-17; in force 26 May 1976; Canada, Denmark (including Greenland), Norway, the USA and USSR are parties.

3. For the four treaties adopted at UNCLOS I, see I. Brownlie, *Basic Documents in International Law*, 3rd edn (Oxford: Clarendon Press, 1983), pp. 85-121. He gives details of parties and entry into force.

4. North East Atlantic Fisheries Convention, 1951: 231 *United Nations Treaty Series*, (*UNTS*), p. 200; in force 27 June 1963; 12 of the 18 ratifying states have denounced this Convention.

5. International Convention for North West Atlantic Fisheries, 1949: 157 *UNTS*, p. 157.

6. Scheme of Joint Enforcement; text in I *ND*, p. 484. See also Convention on the Conduct of Fishing Operations in the North Atlantic, 1967; I *ND*, p. 468; in force 26 September 1976.

7. For a detailed outline of the EC negotiations of a Common Fisheries Policy, see R. Churchill, 'Revision of the EEC's Common Fisheries Policy', *European Law Reports*, Vol. 5 (1980), 3-37 and 95-111; for an analysis of the final policy, see M. Leigh, *European Integration and the Common Fisheries Policy* (London: Croom Helm, 1983).

8. International Convention for the Regulation of Whaling, published by the International Whaling Commission, 1964: 161 *UNTS*, p. 74; in force 10 November 1948.

9. International Convention for the Prevention of Pollution of the Sea by Oil, 1954 (as amended in 1962, 1969, 1971), II *ND*, pp. 557-66, 567-79, 580-8, 589-91 respectively; in force 12 June 1953.

10. International Convention for Prevention of Pollution from Ships, 1973: IV *ND*, p. 345; in force 2 October 1983.

11. Protocol to above Convention; 1 June 1978; X *ND*, p. 32.

12. The most recent is the International Convention for the Safety of Life at Sea, 1974: 1980 *UK Treaty Series (UKTS)*, p. 46; in force 20 May 1980. Protocol to the Convention, 1978: 1981 *UKTS*, p. 40; in force 1 May 1981.

13. International Convention for Preventing Collisions at Sea, 1972; IV *ND*, pp. 245-84.

14. International Convention Relating to Intervention on the High Seas in Cases of Oil Pollution Casualties, 1969: II *ND*, pp. 592-601; in force 7 April 1974. Protocol relating to this Convention, 1973: IV *ND*, p. 451; in force 30 March 1983.

15. International Convention on Standards of Training, Certification and Watchkeeping for Seafarers, 1978; Cmnd 7543; in force 1984.

16. The most recent relevant Convention is that on Minimum Standards in Merchant Ships, 1976, ILO (International Labour Organization), Convention No. 147: VI *ND*, p. 449; in force 28 November 1981. For a brief reference to others, see R. Churchill and V. Lowe, *The Law of the Sea* (Manchester University Press, 1983), pp. 188-9, 190-2.

17. International Convention on Civil Liability for Oil Pollution Damage, 1969: II *ND*, pp. 602-10; in force June 1979.

18. International Convention on the Establishment of an International Fund for Compensation for Oil Pollution Damage, 1971: *ND*, pp. 611-32; in force 16 October 1978.

19. Convention for the Prevention of Marine Pollution by Dumping Wastes and Other Matter, London, 1972: IV *ND*, pp. 331-45; in force 30 August 1975.

20. Convention for the Prevention of Marine Pollution by Dumping from Ships and Aircraft, Oslo 1972: II *ND*, pp. 670-6; in force 7 April 1974.

21. Convention on the Protection of the Marine Environment of the Baltic Sea, Helsinki, 1974: IV *ND*, pp. 455-98; in force 3 May 1980.

22. Convention for the Prevention of Marine Pollution from Land-Based Sources, Paris, 1974: IV *ND*, pp. 499-513; in force 6 May 1978.

23. Convention on Long-Range Transboundary Air Pollution, Geneva (ECE), 1979: XVIII *ILM*, 1979, pp. 1442-55; in force 16 March 1983.

24. Convention relating to Civil Liability in the Field of Maritime Carriage of Nuclear Material, 1971: II *ND*, pp. 664-9; in force 15 July 1975; eleven ratifications.

25. Convention on the Liability of Operators of Nuclear Ships, 1962. See *American Journal of International Law (AJIL)*, Vol. 57 (1963), p. 268; not in force; six ratifications.

26. Treaty on Prohibition of the Employment of Nuclear Weapons and Other Weapons of Mass Destruction on the Seabed and Ocean Floor and in the Subsoil Thereof, 1971: I *ND*, pp. 288-91; in force 18 May 1972.

27. For an explanation of the UK position, see statement made in the House of Commons by Mr Malcolm Rifkind, Minister of State, Foreign and Commonwealth Office, in reply to a question from Mr D. Douglas, *Hansard*, 13 December 1983, Cols. 977-84. The FRG position is similar. Both the UK and the FRG are participating in the Preparatory Commission (Prep. Com.) as observers, having signed the UNCLOS Final Act. The USA, which also signed this Act, has not taken up its option to send an observer. The EC, having signed the LOSC, participates as a full member.

28. US Proclamation No. 5030 of an Exclusive Economic Zone, 10 March 1983, and accompanying Fact Sheet and Statement by the President: XXII *ILM* 1983, pp. 461-5. For the legal arguments concerning its significance in customary law, see L.T. Lee, 'The Law of the Sea Convention and Third States', *AJIL*, Vol. 77 (1983), pp. 541-68.

29. Reagan Proclamation, as Note 28 above.

30. See Armstrong, Ch. 4.

31. *The Daily Telegraph*, 28 May 1985.

32. Anglo-Norwegian Fisheries Case 1951, ICJ Reports, Vol. 1 (1951).

33. For details of this law and a general discussion of the USSR position on these questions, see W. Butler, 'The USSR and UNCLOS III', *Oil and Gas Tax Review*, Vol. 5 (1985), pp. 98-102.

34. B. Johnson Theutenberg, *The Evolution of the Law of the Sea: A Study of Resources and Strategy with Special Regard to the Polar Areas* (Dublin: Tycooly, 1984), pp. 38-40 (Soviet Claims).

35. For a description of US voyages in this area, see D. Pharand, 'Innocent Passage in the Arctic', *Canadian Yearbook of International Law, 1968*, pp. 15-38. See also W.J. Dehner, 'Creeping Jurisdiction in the Arctic: Has the Soviet Union Joined Canada?', *Harvard International Law Journal*, Vol. 13 (1972), pp. 281-5.

36. As Note 35, and Theutenberg, as Note 34, p. 45.

37. Territorial Sea Convention, Article 10.

38. E.g., North Sea Continental Shelf Cases, ICJ Reports (1969); Anglo-French Continental Shelf Arbitration, 1977, Cmnd 7438; XVII *ILM*, 1979, p. 397; Case concerning the Continental Shelf: Tunisia/Libyan Arab Jamahiriya, ICJ Reports (1982); Case concerning the Delimitation of the Maritime Boundary in the Gulf of Maine, ICJ Reports (1984); Case concerning Continental Shelf Delimitation: Malta/Libyan Arab Jamahiriya, 1985, ICJ Communiqué, No. 85111, 3 June 1985.

39. As Note 38. For a discussion of the significance of the islands in delimitation cases, see D. O'Connell, *The International Law of the Sea, Vol. 2* (Oxford: Clarendon Press, 1984), pp. 714-23.

40. For a discussion of the problems generated by this, see C. Symmons, *The Maritime Zones of Islands in International Law* (Dordrecht: Martinus Nijhoff, 1979); see also C. Symmons, 'Outstanding Delimitation Problems in the Irish Sea', paper given at the 19th Annual Conference of the Law of the Sea Institute, Cardiff, 24-27 July 1985 (publication of proceedings forthcoming); E.D. Brown, 'Rockall and the Limits of National Jurisdiction of the United Kingdom', *Marine Policy*, Vol. 2 (1978), pp. 181-211, 275-393. Use of Rockall as a basepoint for the UK's 200-mile Fisheries Zone was protested by Denmark on behalf of the Faroes and also by Ireland. Objection has also been made by these states and Iceland to UK continental shelf designation orders.

41. Agreement on the Continental Shelf between Iceland and Jan Mayen, October 22, 1981: XXI *ILM*, 1982, p. 1222; see Østreng, Ch. 12.

42. For discussion of the varying views, see D. Pharand, *The Law of the Sea of the Arctic with Special Reference to Canada* (University of Ottawa Press, 1973), pp. 181-203; Theutenberg, as Note 34, pp. 35-6; F. Auburn, *Antarctic Law and Politics* (Bloomington: Indiana University Press, 1982), pp. 32-8.

43. *US v. Escamilla*, 467 F.2d 341 (1972); see Pharand, as Note 42, Pt. V (3) for a discussion of this case; also Auburn, as Note 42, pp. 186-92.

44. *Western Weekly Reports (WWR)*, Vol. 71 (1969), p. 435; reversed on other grounds, *WWR*, Vol. 74 (1970), p. 774. For a discussion of the ambiguities relating to this case, see Auburn, as Note 42, pp. 23, 37; and I.T. Gault, 'The International Legal Context of Petroleum Operations in Canadian Arctic Waters', Working Paper No. 4, Canadian Institute of Resources Law, Calgary, 1983, p. 37.

45. Butler, as Note 33, pp. 99, 102.

46. LOSC, Article 23.

47. LOSC, Article 20.

48. LOSC, Pt. III. For different interpretative views, see J.N. Moore, 'The Regime of Straits and the Third United Nations Conference on the Law of the Sea', *AJIL*, Vol. 74 (1980), pp. 77-121; W.M. Reisman, 'The Regime of Straits and National Security: An Appraisal of International Lawmaking,' *ibid.*, pp. 48-76; see also Luke Lee, as Note 28.

49. See declarations by Iran, p. 19, and Yemen, p. 20, in *Law of the Sea Bulletin*

(*LOSB*), No. 1 (September 1983); by Egypt, *LOSB*, No. 2 (March 1984), p. 14; and by Spain, *LOSB*, No. 3 (February 1985), p. 15.

50. LOSC, Pt. II, Sec. 3, Articles 17-32.

51. LOSC, Article 55.

52. It is thus difficult for states to make unilateral declarations of EEZs without interlinking such declarations to the regimes laid down in other parts of the Convention for navigation, scientific research, pollution, the continental shelf, etc. See the US Reagan Proclamation, as Note 28.

53. LOSC, Pt. V, Articles 61 and 62.

54. See Østreng, Ch. 12.

55. L. Rey, 'The Arctic Regions in the Light of Industrial Development: Basic Facts and Environmental Issues', in L. Rey (ed.), *Arctic Energy Issues: Energy Research 2* (Amsterdam, Elsevier, 1983), pp. 11-25; proceedings of a conference of the Comité Arctique, Monaco, 1979.

56. ICES was originally based on an informal gentleman's agreement between scientists in 1902 and was not put onto a formal treaty basis until 1964: VI *ILM*, 1968, p. 302.

57. High Seas Convention, Article 24.

58. For the UK and USA views on this problem and the action required, see reports on meetings of this Convention in *Environmental Policy and Law*, Vol. 9 (1982), pp. 73-94; Vol. II (1983), pp. 46-7; and Vol. 12 (1984), pp. 48-51, 58-61, 86-91.

59. See pp. 12-17 of this chapter. Several global and regional conventions protecting wildlife and its habitats in the Northern Waters area have also been concluded: e.g., the Convention on International Trade in Endangered Species of Wild Flora and Fauna, 1973; Convention on the Conservation of Migratory Species of Wild Animals, 1979; and Convention on the Conservation of European Wildlife and Natural Habitats, 1979. The texts of these, as well as of the 1973 Polar Bears Agreement, are given in S. Lyster, *International Wildlife Law* (Cambridge: Grotius, 1985), accompanied by detailed analysis, as, too, is the text of the Convention Concerning the Protection of the World Cultural and Natural Heritage, 1971, which could be made relevant to the area.

60. Arctic Waters Pollution Prevention Act, Revised Statute of Canada, 1970 (1st Supp.), C.2, S.11. For discussion, see Pharand, as Note 42; and J.A. Beasley, 'The Arctic Waters Pollution Prevention Act: Canada's Perspective', *Syracuse Journal of International Law and Commerce*, Vol. 1 (1973), p. 226.

61. See Lyster, as Note 59: text at pp. 428-41; analysis at Ch. 8, pp. 129-55.

62. Malta/Libya Case 1985, as Note 38.

63. Compare A. Chircop and I. Gault, 'The Making of an Offshore Boundary: The Gulf of Maine Case 1984', *Oil and Gas Law and Taxation Review*, Vol. 3 (1985), pp. 173-81, with T.L. McDorman *et al.*, 'The Gulf of Maine Boundary: Dropping Anchor or Setting Course?', *Marine Policy*, Vol. 9 (1985), pp. 90-107.

64. As Note 41.

65. R. Churchill, 'Maritime Delimitation in the Jan Mayen Area', *Marine Policy*, Vol. 9 (1985), pp. 16-38.

66. Treaty Concerning the Archipelago of Spitsbergen, 1920; II *League of Nations Treaty Series*, p. 8.

67. See Østreng, Ch. 12.

68. R. Churchill, 'The Maritime Zones of Spitsbergen', in *The Law of the Sea and International Shipping: Anglo-Soviet Post-UNCLOS Perspective* (Dobbs Ferry, NY, and London: Oceana, 1985).

69. See VanderZwaag, Ch. 10.

70. See Østreng, Ch. 12.

71. *Ibid.*

72. See VanderZwaag, Ch. 10.

73. U. Jenisch, 'The Arctic Ocean and the New Law of the Sea', *Aussen Politik*, Vol. 35 (1984), English edition, pp. 199-217. He considers that since the problems of the marine environment are generally less controversial, they could serve as a vehicle to start regional cooperation in this area. But, as illustrated in D. Johnston (ed.), *Arctic Ocean Issues* (Hawaii: LOS Institute, 1982), pp. 6, 36-50, esp. pp. 37-8, 46, some participants in a workshop on this topic doubted whether the region yet needed any special legal regime. This is even more the case when considered in the Northern Waters context.

3 RESOURCE ENDOWMENT AND EXPLOITATION

Tony Scanlan

Resource endowment

The distinction in the title of this chapter is frequently expressed in mineral appraisals in terms of 'resources' and 'reserves', not just in polar but in all parts of the world. 'Resources' involves the concept of whether a geological mineral deposit does or does not exist, plus an attempt to quantify the volumetric extent of deposits in one geographical location or the number of deposits in a region possessing broadly homogeneous geological conditions. 'Reserves' of any resource implies that specific discovery and analysis of a regional resource has been completed, and a realistic assessment of the producibility of a proportion of the deposit has been established. The accessibility of an established reserve depends on technical ability to extract, economic acceptance of development costs at a level of volume considered competitive with alternative sources, and the time needed for operational development on a commercial scale. This last factor is referred to as 'lead-time' and is as essential as the technical and economic considerations in converting resources into reserves. Unfortunately, the term 'reserves' is often popularly used when mineral deposits are still at the resources stage, when their existence is speculative or unquantified, and with no clear assessment of how much will become an available reserve or when. The distinction is often blurred even in well-established and accessible mining regions, but in such frontier areas as the Arctic offshore regions it is absolutely vital to attempt to maintain it in order to achieve a realistic perspective of the potential access to minerals.

Access to minerals is the key concept. Finn Sollie has noted that, in contrast to Antarctica, a continent surrounded by vast oceans, the Arctic is an ocean surrounded by land belonging to some of the most developed industrial powers in the world.[1] Right of access to minerals is therefore also inevitably subject to differences in offshore exploration rights among neighbouring Arctic states. This can have a major impact on lead-time.

The extractable proportion of most mineral deposits, such as metals and coal, is sensitive to economic factors. A small change in price can make the cost of hitherto uneconomic ores or seams acceptable. It is cheaper to intensify extraction at existing sites from slightly inferior quality or deeper deposits than to project a major new expedition to polar regions or consider offshore technology which may not even prove to be feasible. Oil and gas are the exception. Not being solids, they migrate through geological time and preconditions for their entrapment in suitable rock formations are not a function of economics but of geology. Consequently the percentage of additional recovery made possible by technical and economic factors is often small or negligible, whereas with coal and non-energy minerals the converse is usually the case. The rate of depletion of oil and gas and the economics of offshore extraction, where their liquid or gaseous state is markedly easier to extract with existing engineering techniques than solids, both make a worldwide search for these two energy sources a practical and urgent necessity. Continental shelf production in temperate zones and onshore permafrost successes such as those on the Alaska North Slope and the Ob delta have developed oil and gas production technology to an unprecedented extent in the past two decades, pushing the frontier farther north. Is offshore oil and gas development in the Arctic poised to evolve over the next twenty years at the same pace as in the North Sea?

Apart from strategic political considerations, which could act either as an incentive or deterrent, there is a great deal not yet established about oil and gas resources in Northern Waters, and much more basic stratigraphic work, including drilling, must be done before the comparison with the North Sea can be dealt with analytically. Before the first oil was found in the North Sea, the geological knowledge of its origins was much further advanced than the current state of knowledge regarding Arctic offshore regions. North of 80°N is permanent ice-cap and ocean. It is correct to describe 60°N to 80°N as the next frontier zone for oil and gas, beginning in the south at the Shetlands, Leningrad and northern Alberta and ending at Svalbard and North Greenland, where all significant land mass and continental shelf gives way to the true Arctic Ocean.

The description of the Arctic as a true ocean, as distinct from a large sea of mediterranean stature, was controversial until relatively recent times. The rapid progress made in earth sciences, especially in the understanding and analysis of plate tectonics and the formation of the continents and oceans, that has taken place since International Geophysical Year (1957-8) has led to the publication of authoritative charts and geological maps (by the USA, the Soviet Union and others) which are not only in broad agreement on this issue but are supported by considerable analytical detail made possible by modern survey techniques.

If the Arctic had indeed proved to be another mediterranean sea, then the recent trend to extend offshore continental shelf mineral rights might have resulted in a median line settlement right across the region between North America and the Eurasian land mass. Instead, the Arctic region, which possesses some of the largest continental shelf areas in the world, is now known at its polar centre — roughly the region north of latitude 80°N — to have the main characteristics of a true ocean. This area extends nearly 2,000 miles from the Alaskan continental shelf to Svalbard, and over 1,000 miles from Ellesmere Island and Greenland to the East Siberian Sea. Along this latter axis there is, as in the Pacific, Atlantic and Indian Oceans, a distinct mid-oceanic ridge, the Lomonosov Ridge, on either side of which lie the Barents and Canadian abyssal depths. These features are repeated between Greenland and Norway: Iceland is largely volcanic rock formed by active movement on the North Atlantic Ridge, a branch of which separates southern Greenland from the Canadian Islands but does not succeed in penetrating into the Arctic Ocean as the Icelandic ridge does. The North Atlantic, Norwegian Sea and Lomonosov Ridges may be said effectively to divide Eurasia and America, with Greenland belonging to the American land mass. Although the distance between Svalbard and the edge of the North Greenland continental shelf at 80°N is only 200 miles, they belong to separate continents, with water over 3,000 metres deep dividing them. Svalbard is some 500 miles north of Tromsø but is linked to the Norwegian coast by continental shelf in water depths never greater than 500 metres, and about half is less than 200 metres in depth. North of Svalbard — Franz Josef Land and Severnaya Zemlya — the continental shelf ends rapidly with water depths of 1,500 to 3,500 metres occurring within an average of 50 miles from the 200-metre depth contour. The same rapid increase in water depth occurs north of Greenland and the Canadian Sverdrup Islands.

The significance for oil and gas resource prospects of the ending of the continental shelf is that oceanic geological development is almost totally devoid of sedimentary deposits, which are an essential precondition for the development of hydrocarbons. Equally devoid of sediments are the Archaean shield rocks, the core of continental land masses which came into being before the middle (Mesozoic) period of geological history, when the main hydrocarbon sediments were laid down (about 150-300 million years ago). The younger rocks, which Europeans generally classify with the Alps as 'Alpine' in age, include the most recent results of mountain-building (or tectonics) as younger and therefore less resistant sediments are compressed and folded by the pressures caused at the interface of the oceanic and continental shield plates, which cover the surface of the earth. These younger rocks have not yet had time to generate the more significant hydrocarbon deposits that are commercially viable.

The Mesozoic period lasted for over 200 million years, the great majority of it in stable tectonic conditions favourable to the accumulation of massive thickness of sediment. The most recent tectonic or mountain-building period has lasted less than ten per cent of this time-span and in generally unstable conditions, making it difficult for large-scale sediments to accumulate. The core or shield origin of the European continent is contained in the Fenno-Scandia shield, which covers northern Norway, Sweden, Finland and the Kola Peninsula up to the White Sea. In North America the Laurentian shield of Labrador and the Canadian northeast, including a large part of the Arctic Islands, similarly precludes the existence of large hydrocarbon deposits. Baffin Island and western Greenland are both largely comprised of Proterozoic rocks laid down over 2,000 million years ago, and Victoria Island, west of Baffin Island, is from Ordovician and Silurian formation between 400 and 500 million years ago, twice the age of the Mesozoic era.

Not surprisingly oil and gas exploration in the *North American Arctic* has been confined to the regions between the pre-Mesozoic and the younger western cordillera represented by the Rockies. This has resulted in Canadian exploration interest focusing on the Labrador Sea, in the Sverdrup Islands and the Mackenzie delta region. In the USA, the North Slope onshore successes have led to offshore prospecting in the Beaufort Sea and to interest in the Chukchi and Bering Seas off the west coast of Alaska, where the delimitation of the continental shelf involves a median line negotiation with the Soviet Union. That is perhaps an understatement in view of comments on Soviet offshore prospects which come later.

Off the coasts of Greenland there are sizeable areas of less than 200 metres' water depth, in the Davis Strait and its southern approaches off the southwest coast. These extend an average of 50 miles offshore, and the geological strata are of a more promising age for hydrocarbon potential than the older onshore formations. Little is known as yet of the centre of the vast *Greenland* mainland with its ice mantle over 2,000 metres deep in places, but in the extreme north Peary Land is considered to have hydrocarbon potential. On the east coast the width of the 200-metre offshore shelf is generally much less than on the west coast, but is believed to have some potential at about 70°N.

Some 200 miles east of Greenland at this latitude is the single island of *Jan Mayen*, a Norwegian territory about 30 miles by 10 miles in extent with some 50 miles of 200-metre contour shelf, which is regarded as having possible hydrocarbon potential. The Norwegian 200-mile offshore limit effectively produces a triangle between Jan Mayen, Svalbard and the Lofoten Islands which almost covers the entire Norwegian Sea, but the water depths are 2,000 metres or more over the vast majority of this area.

About 200 miles south of Greenland and Jan Mayen, *Iceland* does have some sediments up to 4,000 metres in depth off the north coast, but it is not a main prospective area because it is largely of volcanic origin.

The Faroes, a Danish group 250 miles southeast of Iceland, have a 200-metre offshore contour area of about 50 miles' radius around the islands, but little has been reported about hydrocarbon prospects. The uninhabited islet of *Rockall*, 500 miles south of Iceland at about 55°N, 14°W, lies some 200 miles west of the main UK 200-metre offshore contour and has flown the UK flag in order to establish British offshore territorial rights. It has its own 200-metre contour area of about 80 by 50 miles. However, even a 200-mile zone around Rockall largely lies south of 60°N, the southern limit of this study.

The extreme northerly extent of *British* North Sea oil and gas activities extends just north of 60°N: east, west and north of the Shetland Isles. Together with parallel Norwegian developments up to 62°N, this area is the centre of the most intense offshore oil development anywhere in the world, although it is not, strictly, within the scope of this study except for the strip between 60°N and 62°N, until recently the upper limit for Norwegian licences for offshore hydrocarbon development. Both Norway and Britain,

however, have advanced world standards — with the active participation of leading international oil companies from other developed
countries, especially the USA and France — in all aspects of offshore exploration and the development of oil and gas. Recent UK
and Norwegian licensing rounds demonstrate growing interest in
the region, and its future contribution to further technical advances
in the vanguard of fixed production platforms and innovative new
techniques for the extractive offshore industry will for many years
remain crucial to developments farther north. As a resource area
in this present context, however, it belongs more realistically to the
development of the North Sea region outside the scope of this
study. The northern limit of the 200-metre depth contour for the
main Northwest European Continental Shelf lies along the 62°N
latitude, about 50 miles north of the Shetlands.

Norwegian developments south of 62°N have been closer to the
median line with Britain. This is because inshore the deeper waters
of the Norwegian trench (up to 1,000 feet) were beyond the technical scope of the industry during the development of offshore
technology in the past 20 years, which advanced the frontier for
platform water depth from less than 30 to over 200 metres. North
of 62°N, with a few exceptions off Ålesund, Trondheim, the
Lofoten Islands and west of Hammerfest, the 200-metre contour is
very close inshore. The licensing north of 62°N, at Haltenbanken
(65°N) and Tromsø (71°N), has tended to reflect these areas of
shallower depths. Norwegian and other companies are now
beginning to project operations in much greater depths, so that the
considerable potential of the Norwegian Sea may be exploited.
North of Tromsø, 200 miles off North Cape, shallower zones re-
appear with less than 200 metres of water depth in a large area of
the western Barents Sea, extending over thousands of square miles
south and east of Svalbard. These shallower parts of the Barents
Sea also extend east of 30°E to 40°E from latitudes 74°N to 82°N,
in the sector directly north of Vardø and Murmansk. The combination of North Sea, Norwegian Sea and Barents Sea gives
Norway the largest geographical area of continental shelf hydrocarbon potential in Europe, in contrast to onshore Norway, where
the ancient geology offers no potential.

The *USSR*, taking both European and Asiatic offshore regions
into account, probably contains the largest potential for oil and gas
exploration in the entire Arctic. The sheer size of its northern offshore regions must constitute the largest continental shelf in the

world. They fall into five areas, the first of which is within the definition of Northern Waters offered in this book. The other four are Arctic areas of substantial importance not only for the Soviet Union but also for Western oil and gas consumers.

The Barents Sea area is vast, extending 1,000 miles north from the White Sea to Franz Josef Land and 600 miles east of Murmansk to the island of Novaya Zemlya. Geologically Novaya Zemlya is a northerly extension of the Ural Mountains, which form the Eurasian border. Franz Josef Land is mainly composed of earlier Ordovician and Silurian deposits, but the Barents Sea shelf is largely of Mesozoic structure with fertile sediments over 300 metres in depth. The southern and eastern Barents, including the Pechora Sea, has extensive areas within the 200-metre depth contour, rivalling the North Sea. The entire region is within the 500-metre contour, making it one of the most geographically extensive basins with hydrocarbon potential in the world. The onshore part of this basin in the extreme northeast of Europe, the Pechora region, is currently producing oil at nearly 500,000 barrels per day, with some commercial gas production.

The Kara Sea is another highly promising offshore area. It extends an average of 300 miles east of Novaya Zemlya and 700 miles north from the Ob and Yenisey deltas to the islands of Severnaya Zemlya. These islands are of similar geological formation to Novaya Zemlya, but at least two-thirds of the Kara Sea is known to be an extension of the West Siberian basin, which contains the largest onshore gasfields in the world. Except for a trench along the eastern shore of Novaya Zemlya the Kara Sea is less than 200 metres in depth.

The Laptev Sea extends from Severnaya Zemlya eastwards some 400 miles to the New Siberian Islands, and from the delta of the Lena it stretches about 300 miles north before the 200-metre depth contour is exceeded. Onshore the final section of the eastward-tilting extension of the Urals geology ends at the western edge of the Lena delta. The remote onshore basin has not been developed, but the basic geology onshore does not preclude the possibility of hydrocarbon potential extending offshore.

The East Siberian Sea is a vast untapped region three times as extensive as the Laptev Sea. It extends 600 miles east of the New Siberian Islands to Wrangel Island and an average of 400 miles north of the coastline, all within the 200-metre offshore contour, up to an average of 76°N. The geology of both island groups conforms with that of the onshore plains, indicating possible geological conformity throughout large parts of the seabed. Again, however, the onshore basin is too remote for hydrocarbon potential to be assessed, except to say that if the offshore is a homogeneous basin, the geological period is favourable.

The Chukchi and Bering Seas, from Wrangel Island to northeast Alaska, cover 400 miles, and the 200-metre offshore contour extends 500 miles north of the Bering Strait. The region south of the Bering Strait is equally large, so that the USA and USSR are joined at the 200-metre depth contour by a vast continental shelf over 1,000 miles in width from north to south and encompassing all the island groups in the Bering Sea north of 60°N.

The reach of the continental shelf north of the Soviet Union is very much more extensive than it is off Alaska. The 200-metre contour is never more than 100 miles from the north coast of Alaska, except in the western approaches, whereas the average distance off the Soviet coast is 400 miles in the regions east of the New Siberian Islands and 250 miles westwards to the White Sea. The total area exceeds one million square miles, five times the extent of the North Sea.

There can be little doubt that the Arctic regions justify the oil and gas geologists' prediction over the past thirty years that they could prove to be the only area of the world to rival the hydrocarbon resource potential of the Middle East. However, the polar offshore environment and the enormous distances involved are formidable obstacles to transforming these resources into accessible reserves.

Resource exploitation

The polar ice-cap is the main determinant of regional offshore development. Most regions above 75°N are under the permanent ice-cap, including the northern coasts of Sverdrup and Greenland. Along the continental shelf from Svalbard to Franz Josef and Severnaya Zemlya, the minimum line of permanent ice recedes to the edge of the shelf at about 82°N. The maximum extent of seasonal drift-ice, however, extends as far south as the southern coasts of Greenland and Iceland and across the Norwegian and Barents Seas, leaving an ice-free passage about 100 miles wide to the Kola Peninsula. From there eastwards the Soviet Union has managed with nuclear-powered icebreakers to maintain a shipping route along the northern coast for most of the year. The route lies through waters in the East Siberian, Laptev and Kara Seas, where ice is intermittent seasonally, except in the far more difficult regions of Wrangel Island and Severnaya Zemlya.[2] Alaska has a similar north coastal zone south of the permanent ice-cap with access to the Bering Sea, and the same conditions exist in the Davis and Denmark Straits on either side of Greenland.

Considerable attention has been given to the 200-metre off-shore contour. Although offshore drilling can take place in up to 700 metres of water, production platforms have been limited to 200 metres because of the need to design for stresses from giant waves up to 100 feet high. In the North Sea the platform installed by BP in the Magnus field in 1983, in 200 metres of water, weighs 40,000 tons so as to be able to withstand such extreme weather conditions. In less severe waters, however, structures can concentrate on using this weight to achieve greater water depth. For example, the Cerveza platform of Union Oil in the Gulf of Mexico stands in 300 metres of water but weighs no more than Magnus. The discovery of the giant Troll gasfield off the Norwegian coast at 61°N prompted Norsk Shell to announce plans for a fixed platform to stand in almost 400 metres of water at an approximate cost of US $6 billion.

The deep water in the Norwegian Sea, compared with the North Sea, will probably see giant fields such as Troll justifying a new generation of permanent platforms to operate in twice the water depth of Magnus and yet still be strong enough to withstand the wind and wave pressures. Statoil is also studying these new concepts which, in addition to fixed platforms, include tension leg platforms, articulated and guyed towers and subsea manifold gathering centres. The new technology is aimed at developing fields in still greater depths up to 1,000 metres, using flexible tied structures with perhaps underwater production-gathering manifold systems on the seabed, thus reducing the need for fixed platform strengthening and thereby the costs.

The Norwegian offshore is ice-free. Techniques for deep water operation in drift- or pack-ice surface conditions are still at the drawing-board. Even in temperate climates, these new platforms and subsea manifolds are still at the first practical stages of installation, and it will be some years before the experience can be adapted to the Arctic. There is at present no technology for offshore extraction and production in polar conditions; economical recovery may take decades to develop.

The decision to develop Arctic energy discoveries will be greatly affected by the size and nature of the fields concerned (whether oil or gas). So far the tendency has been for offshore and island archipelago hydrocarbon discoveries to be gas. This is true of the Canadian Sverdrup Islands, northern Norway and the enormous Ob delta gasfields in the Soviet Arctic. Prudhoe Bay remains the only giant oilfield developed in the Arctic Circle. A second major oilfield, of the kind that had been hoped for at Mukluk in the Beaufort Sea, would be developed with much greater incentive than gas, which at Prudhoe Bay is being reinjected to improve oil recovery. Plans for a commercial gas pipeline development have been shelved. Norway will have to accommodate Troll gas in European markets before plans to develop the offshore gas found much further north at 71°N can be advanced. The Soviet Union, the world's leading gas producer, has already sufficient proven reserves to continue at current output for 80 years. There are 11,000 bcm (billion cubic metres) in the Ob delta region — twice the proven gas reserves of the United States. Furthermore, the Soviets have the great advantage of an existing gas trunkline network linking the Arctic littoral with markets to the south. No such system exists in the North American Arctic.

The significance of recent drilling activities lies mainly in the collection of basic stratigraphic data and the accumulation of operating experience in some Arctic regions. The second half of 1984 and the first few months of 1985 saw the following announcements:

In *Alaska* Shell announced a discovery of light crude oil (40° API gravity) on Seal Island only twelve miles west of Prudhoe Bay. The US government has also licensed Amoco, Arco, Shell and Union Oil to conduct seismic surveys in the Navarin Basin southwest of Saint Lawrence Island in the Bering Sea. In discussions in 1984 with the Soviet Union on the median line, the USSR described the licensing as a provocative act.

Canadian offshore oil reserves comprise 30 per cent of the national total, with the Beaufort Sea and Mackenzie delta in the West accounting for 10 per cent or 0.75 billion barrels (thousand million); 0.5 billion barrels in the Arctic Islands in the extreme north; and 1.5 billion barrels off the east coast. Gulf Oil claimed a

0.5 billion barrel oil find off Tuktoyaktuk Peninsula, where several previous oil and gas finds have been made near the Mackenzie delta.

In *Greenland* Arco are shortly to be allowed to carry out the first offshore drilling on the east coast at Scoresby Island, 70°N, but up to five years is allowed before the first well need be drilled. On the southwest coast concessions in 150 to 200 metres of water in the Davis Strait have been awarded to a number of companies, including Amoco, Arco, Chevron, Deminex, Hispanoil, Mobil, Pancanadian and Ultramar. Total's drillship *Pelican*, while conducting pioneer drilling on the polar ice-cap, discovered traces of natural gas.

BP began seismic studies on the *Svalbard* archipelago in 1985, following earlier moves by Caltex, the Soviet Union, Statoil and Norsk Polar. Swedish Polar Energy (50 per cent Norwegian) will shortly follow BP.

In *Norway* Statoil's Snow White find was the first potentially major oil discovery in Tromsøflaket.[3]

The *Soviets* were recently reported to have discovered substantial amounts of oil in the central areas of the Barents Sea, to be talking of production within ten years and studying joint pipelines for landing energy in Scandinavia. These reports are believed to be premature in view of the fact that drilling has barely begun.[4] The USSR has also indicated the existence of many giant structures in the Kara Sea with 2,000 feet of Mesozoic sediments.

Whatever the commercial significance of these reports, and some could be highly significant, the overriding message is that positions are being taken by companies and governments as soon as or even before some of the political issues are settled. The next ten years will probably witness a continuation and consolidation of existing trends rather than any further moves north. This is because the most promising search areas in the region are now at some stage of evaluation, and the prospect of Barents oil with its ocean access, and of major structures in the Kara Sea, will absorb Soviet attention for many years.

The development lead-times will probably be in the region of ten years from discovery, as the Soviet announcement on the Barents stated. Where open sea routes for oil do not exist further delay is certain. Gas is more expensive to deliver, either by LNG (liquefied natural gas) tankers or pipeline, and markets are sluggish in the current economic recession. If the five years of appraisal in frontier areas such as Greenland and Svalbard lead to commercial prospects, there will still inevitably be no production of any commercial hydrocarbon supplies before the year 2000. Even then, unless really giant oilfields of the size of Prudhoe Bay are discovered offshore, development may not occur by the end of the century. Tromsø gas, it is estimated, will take 20 years to reach peak development.

The unprecedented lead-times with their long delays before payback and the uncertainty over accurate and acceptable levels of extractive cost make any specific forecast of financial thresholds unreliable. To illustrate this, the US Geological Survey gave a statistical appraisal of the likely oil resources in the Beaufort Sea. This showed a 95 per cent certainty of about 2 billion barrels with a 5 per cent chance of as much as 17 billion barrels (rounded to the nearest billion) and a mean of 7 billion. The greatest commercial problem lies in whether that 7 billion is in one or two giant structures, in which case it is likely to be developed, or whether it is in small offshore pockets over a wide area, which would perhaps preclude development.[5] A resource does not become a reserve until it is accessible on a commercial scale.

The current level of activity, designed, as it were, to stake claims, arises partly because the outlook is so speculative and the development lead-times so long. Two-thirds of the oil reserves in the non-Communist world are in the troubled Middle East. Over three-quarters of known recoverable oil and gas reserves lie in an arc from the Ob delta to Oman. The rest of the world, including developed nations, has barely enough indigenous hydrocarbons to sustain its current level of use without imports during the rest of this century. If political and technical access to Arctic resources, taking into account environmental difficulties, is to be effected, the viability of such projects lies in their future opportunity costs and not in those of 1986. What can be, and is being, secured now, wherever possible, is access to evaluate resource endowment in the Arctic as a prerequisite for eventual commercial reserve exploitation.

Notes

1. Finn Sollie, 'Polar Politics', *International Journal*, Vol. 39 (1984), No. 4.

2. See T. Armstrong, 'The Northern Sea Route, 1982', *Polar Record*, No. 134 (May 1983), and Ch. 4 in this book.

3. *Noriform*, No. 1 (1985).

4. *Petroleum Economist*, No. 10 (1984), p. 427. Finland was scheduled to deliver in 1985 the first semi-submersible rig to the USSR, designed for work in the Barents Sea.

5. See *International Petroleum Encyclopaedia 1983* (London: PennWell, 1983), p. 10, Table 1.

4 TRANSPORTATION OF RESOURCES FROM AND THROUGH THE NORTHERN WATERS

Terence Armstrong

The present pattern of shipping traffic

Northern Waters are not traversed by any major merchant shipping-lane. The transatlantic route, in its most northerly variant, lies to the south. They contain, rather, a series of routes which have a low traffic density but are nonetheless well-established. A significant fraction of Northern Waters — perhaps 10 per cent — is never used by shipping at all, since the ice situation is severe and there is insufficient economic incentive to overcome it.

The use made of these waters can be assessed under four headings: freight traffic to and from localities in the area: freight traffic through the area, to and from localities beyond; fishing within the area; and naval activity (which is dealt with in Chapter 5). So let us begin with freight traffic directly related to the area.

Statistics of *freight movement to and from* Northern Waters ports are hard to come by. Partial information could be extracted from *Lloyds List*, but this would not include much of the Soviet traffic. The only relevant indicator publicly available is the number of ships registered at ports in the area (see Table 4.1). From that one may form a very general impression of the activity at a given port and some idea of its comparative value.

There is much inshore trade up the Norwegian coast, mostly from southern Scandinavia, bringing passengers and mixed cargo. Fish and minerals are exported to many destinations. An important extension of the Norwegian coastwise trade is that to Svalbard, 800 kilometres to the north of Nordkapp (North Cape). The traffic here supplies the Norwegian coal-mining settlements and carries the coal back to Norway, Svalbard being its only source of coal. There are also Soviet coal-mines in the archipelago, and a similar traffic exists between Svalbard and north Soviet ports, notably Murmansk.

Iceland has sea links with all parts of the world, but principally with Scandinavia, and the main export is fish. Likewise the Faroes, which are constitutionally part of Denmark and so have their

Table 4.1: Merchant shipping of over 100 grt (gross registered tonnage) registered at ports in and near Northern Waters, 1983

Area	No. of ships	% of national total	grt (in thousands)	% of national total
Ports within Northern Waters				
Norway[a]	853[b]	52	2,556	14
Iceland	53[b]	100	71	100
Greenland	60	100	24	100
Faroes	186	100	84	100
Canada	none	—	—	—
Ports where ships are likely to use Northern Waters				
USSR (1980-81)				
Murmansk	619	11	—	—
Arkhangel'sk	179	3	—	—

[a]Bergen northwards
[b]Excludes fishing boats and other specialized vessels, of which there may be several hundred in Norway and a significant number in Iceland.
Sources: *Statistik Årbok 1984*, Oslo, 1984, pp. 144, 225, 469, 470; *Grønland Årsberetning 1983*, Copenhagen, 1984, p. 194; *Danmarks Statistik*, Copenhagen; personal communication, 15 November 1984; and *Registrovaya kniga morskikh sudov SSSR, 1980-1*, Moscow 1981.

closest links with Danish ports. Greenland carries out almost all its trade with the mother country, Denmark. The settlements are mainly on the west coast, which therefore receives most ships. The east coast has only three settlements, and no proper harbour.

Finally, Arctic Canada has some sea links with mainland Canada and with the world beyond. The most used is the Hudson Bay route, which carries grain from the port of Churchill through Hudson Bay and Hudson Strait to the North Atlantic. This trade is carried in about 20 to 30 ships, lifting 20 to 30 million bushels of grain. On a smaller scale is the traffic to Baffin Island and points north and west. If the Northwest Passage ever achieves the status of a functioning waterway, it is here that ships will enter and leave it. Traffic at present is concerned with the resupply of a few tiny settlements, and with the export of lead-zinc ore from the Nanisivik mine in northern Baffin Island and the Arvik mine in

Little Cornwallis Island. The two mines required a total of 14 voyages a year in 1983.

Freight movement through the area is even more difficult to determine. It can be assumed, however, that traffic to and from Murmansk and Arkhangel'sk constitutes the largest single component. Murmansk is, after all, the Soviet Union's only major ice-free port, handling much civil as well as military traffic; Arkhangel'sk is a major timber-exporting centre. Some traffic bound for the Northern Sea Route is no doubt also involved, but perhaps not as much as might be expected. There is almost no transiting of that route — that is, use of it as a link between the Atlantic and Pacific — and there is also virtually no non-Soviet use. Thus, Northern Sea Route traffic crossing Northern Waters is largely restricted to Soviet shipping coming out of Baltic ports and rounding Scandinavia, and some Soviet freighters carrying timber from the Yenisey river to various export destinations beyond the Barents Sea. It is not possible to quantify the Soviet traffic, but an indication of its scale may be derived from the fact that 619 merchant ships are registered at the port of Murmansk and 179 at the port of Arkhangel'sk; together these represent 14 per cent of the Soviet merchant navy. The greater part of these ships will undoubtedly traverse Northern Waters on their routine business.

Northern Waters have long been an important *fishing* ground. In 1980 (the most recent year for which statistics are available) they accounted for about 5.4 million tonnes in live weight equivalent of fish landed, or about 8 per cent of the world catch of fish at sea (see Table 4.2). The countries most actively engaged are the Soviet Union, Iceland and Norway, which between them generally account for at least three-quarters of the total catch. The sea areas most intensively fished are the Norwegian Sea, Icelandic waters and the Barents Sea, but there is a growing fishery in Greenlandic waters, both east and west. The main species caught are capelin, cod and poutassou. Although there is considerable annual variation in the way the figures break down, both by fishing area and by country, the aggregate has tended to remain rather stable over the past decade or so.

Navigational problems

By far the most significant of these is the presence of floating ice.

Table 4.2: Commercial fisheries' nominal catch of vertebrates and invertebrates (live weight equivalent of fish landed) in a sea area approximating to Northern Waters, 1980)

Sea area	Catch (in thousands of tonnes)
Barents Sea (ICES sub-area I)	1,046
Norwegian Sea (ICES sub-area IIa)	1,655
Svalbard waters (ICES sub-area IIb)	701
Iceland (ICES sub-area Va)	1,425
Faroe Plateau and bank (ICES sub-areas Vb_1, Vb_2)	227
Northeast Greenland (ICES sub-area XIVa)	203
Southeast Greenland (ICES sub-area XIVb)	75
Baffin Island (ICNAF sub-areas OA, OB)	3
West Greenland (ICNAF sub-areas IA, IB, IC, ID, IE)	102
Total, Northern Waters	5,437
Total, World Ocean	64,576

Sources: *Bulletin Statistique des Pêches Maritimes*, ICES, Copenhagen, Vol. 65 (1982); *Statistical Bulletin*, NAFO, Dartmouth, Nova Scotia, Vol. 30 (1982); and *Yearbook of Fishery Statistics*, FAO, Rome, Vol. 50 (1981).

Permanent ice-cover is found in only a small part of Northern Waters, chiefly in the Canadian archipelago and off northeast Greenland; but seasonal ice-cover stretches over more than half the total area (see Figure 4.1). The shipping operations referred to earlier naturally tend to avoid that half. But the possibility of encountering ice is still significant in certain parts of the area, depending on wind and temperature, and of course this becomes a probability if voyages are planned to less accessible parts, such as East Greenland, Svalbard in winter, and many islands in the Canadian archipelago.

The fullest description of the ice-cover of the Greenland and Norwegian Seas is given by Peter Wadhams, who also provides a list of references.[1] He does not deal, however, with waters west of Greenland, and the best description of this area is to be found in sailing directions.[2]

The main hazard is sea ice — the frozen surface of the sea — which may be encountered in the form of floes of greatly varying size and thickness. Level floes are the exception rather than the rule, since most sea ice is in continuous movement, and consequently newly frozen level ice is broken up by the collision of floes

Figure 4.1: The Circumpolar Perspective

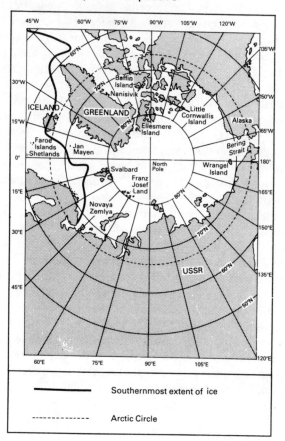

Source: *Atlas Okeanov: Severnii Ledovityi Okean* (Moscow: Ministerstvo Oboroni SSSR, 1980), p. 150.

and is soon given an uneven surface by the ridges and hummocks extending across it. Level ice is seldom more than 2 metres thick, though ridges may exceptionally reach 50 metres. In the horizontal dimension, individual floes may be several kilometres long.

Sea ice constitutes in area at least 99 per cent of floating ice, but the remaining one per cent or less may cause an almost similar degree of danger, for it is composed of icebergs, which are fragments of land ice (ice sheets, ice caps, glaciers) which have broken off and floated out to sea. Icebergs float much deeper in the water than sea ice (there are few recorded measurements, but they can draw several hundred metres), and the ice of which they are composed is stronger. Large icebergs can normally be seen and avoided, but they break down into 'bergy bits' and 'growlers' which, being less than 10 metres across and sometimes awash, are harder to see and identify, even with radar. However, such relatively small lumps of ice may weigh hundreds of tons and can easily hole a ship. It so happens, furthermore, that the major source of icebergs in the northern hemisphere is along the Greenland shore of the Davis Strait and Baffin Bay. These icebergs may circle the Bay before being borne by the Labrador current into the North Atlantic (where the *Titanic* and, more recently, the *Hans Hedtoft* struck one). Some are also found off the east coast of Greenland, carried southwards by the East Greenland current. Thus the western sector of Northern Waters — which provides the approach to Hudson Bay, to the waters of the Canadian archipelago and to the Northwest Passage — does present special problems in ice navigation, but these are by no means insuperable.

The other major factor in navigation is the availability or otherwise of electronic aids. Northern Waters east of Greenland are wholly covered by Loran C and Decca networks, but there is no such cover for Baffin Bay and the archipelago. Satellite navigation systems can be, and sometimes are, used throughout the area, but most ships do not yet have the rather expensive equipment required to benefit from them.

Ice-going equipment

If the challenge of floating ice is the major distinguishing feature of navigation in Northern Waters, then special importance attaches to the technology required for dealing with it. Merchant ships for use in ice fall into three categories: icebreakers, ice-strengthened freighters and submarines. *Icebreakers* may be either for use in and around ports (port icebreakers), in which case they are rather like strengthened tugs; or for use in sea areas remote from their base, in which case they are larger (up to 23,000 tonnes displacement) but are still not designed to carry any freight. The sea-going icebreakers may be for use in seas with seasonal ice only (the Baltic, the White Sea), or for use in Arctic seas, but the two roles are to some extent interchangeable. Of the countries with ports actually in Northern Waters, only Canada possesses sea-going icebreakers — eight of them. Norway and Denmark have none. However, the Soviet Union, whose ships are frequently obliged to traverse Northern Waters, has the most powerful flotilla of icebreakers anywhere in the world — 21 used regularly in Arctic Waters (see Table 4.3), not to mention at least as many again for peripheral waters and port work. The Soviet flotilla includes three nuclear-powered ships (the oldest of which, the *Lenin*, was the first surface vessel anywhere in the world to have nuclear power), and four more are currently planned. All of these ships are normally deployed on the Northern Sea Route, which is outside Northern Waters, but obviously any of them could at any time be sent to operate within this area. The United States, which might be expected to have a capability deployable in Northern Waters, has only five effective sea-going icebreakers, of which two are over 40 years old and two others have suffered from design defects. Sweden and Finland each own icebreakers, but these are primarily for Baltic use and seldom go farther afield.

Ice-strengthened freighters. It is obviously uneconomic to operate ships built to withstand Arctic ice in ice-free waters, so such ships tend to exist only in countries where ice conditions remain bad for much of the year. Again it is the Soviet Union which possesses far more of these ships than any other country. According to the Soviet merchant shipping register of 1980-1, the two top categories of ice-worthiness (ULA and UL), for which Arctic work is specifically permitted, contain 259 ships. Half of these, however, are tugs and salvage vessels, and almost none of them exceeds 20,000 tonnes deadweight. More than half of them, moreover, are registered at ports remote from Northern Waters (the Black Sea, the Caspian, and the Pacific).

Nevertheless, this situation contrasts strongly with that in the rest of the world, where in the equivalent categories (Ice Class 1* and 1A Super) there are altogether only 32 freighters of over 3,000 tonnes deadweight (dwt). In Canada, for instance, there is effectively only one freighter specifically built for Arctic work, the *Arctic*, of 28,000 tonnes dwt, and there are none in the USA. In 1984 Canada had 19 other vessels in these ice categories, but they were all tugs with a cargo capacity generally below 2,000 tonnes. In Scandinavia — Finland primarily, but also Sweden — there were 35 ships in these ice categories in 1984, and they included 11 dry

Table 4.3: Icebreakers of 10,000 shp or more operational in 1984 and which might be deployed in Northern Waters

Flag	Name	Where built	Power (shp)	Displacement in tonnes	Entered service
USSR	*Kapitan Belousov*	Finland	10,500	5,360	1954
USSR	*Kapitan Voronin*	Finland	10,500	5,360	1955[a]
USSR	*Kapitan Melekhov*	Finland	10,500	5,360	1956
USSR	*Lenin*	USSR	44,000	16,000	1959[b]
USSR	*Moskva*	Finland	22,000	13,290	1960
USSR	*Leningrad*	Finland	22,000	13,290	1961
USSR	*Kiyev*	Finland	22,000	13,290	1965
USSR	*Murmansk*	Finland	22,000	13,290	1968
USSR	*Vladivostok*	Finland	22,000	13,290	1969
USSR	*Yermak*	Finland	36,000	20,240	1974
USSR	*Admiral Makarov*	Finland	36,000	20,240	1975
USSR	*Artika*, later *Leonid Brezhnev*	USSR	75,000	23,400	1975[b]
USSR	*Krasin*	Finland	36,000	20,240	1976
USSR	*Sibir'*	USSR	75,000	23,400	1977[b]
USSR	*Kapitan Sorokin*	Finland	22,000	14,900	1977[c]
USSR	*Kapitan Nikolayev*	Finland	22,000	14,900	1978[c]
USSR	*Kapitan Dranitsyn*	Finland	22,000	14,900	1980[c]
USSR	*Kapitan Khlebnikov*	Finland	22,000	14,900	1981[c]
USSR	*Magadan*	Finland	12,400	—	1982
USSR	*Mud'yuga*	Finland	12,400	—	1982
USSR	*Dikson*	Finland	12,400	—	1983
Canada	*Labrador*	Canada	10,000	7,000	1954
Canada	*John A. MacDonald*	Canada	15,000	9,000	1961
Canada	*Louis S. St Laurent*	Canada	24,000	14,000	1969
Canada	*Pierre Radisson*	Canada	13,600	7,600	1978
Canada	*Sir John Franklin*	Canada	13,600	7,600	1979
Canada	*Canmar Kigoriak*	Canada	16,400	7,000	1979
Canada	*Robert Lemeur*	Canada	16,400	7,000	1982
Canada	*Des Groseilliers*	Canada	13,600	7,600	1982
USA	*Northwind*	USA	10,000	5,300	1944
USA	*Westwind*	USA	10,000	5,300	1944
USA	*Glacier*	USA	21,000	8,300	1954
USA	*Polar Star*	USA	18,000 60,000[d]	12,000	1976
USA	*Polar Sea*	USA	18,000 60,000[d]	12,000	1978

USSR	*Rossiya*[f]	USSR	75,000	25,000	1985[b]
USSR	Unnamed[f]	USSR	75,000	—	—[b]
USSR	*Taymyr*[g]	Finland/ USSR	52,000	—	1988[e]
USSR	Unnamed[g]	Finland/ USSR	52,000	—	1989[e]

[a] Probably withdrawn
[b] Nuclear
[c] Shallow-draught
[d] Gas turbines provide increase in power
[e] Nuclear, shallow-draught
[f] Under construction
[g] At design stage.

cargo ships and 10 roll on/roll off or passenger vessels.[3] There are also a number of freighters designed for Baltic trade which may be usable, though not highly effective, in the Arctic.

The most interesting new development is the introduction of the new SA-15 class. These are freighters of 19,500 tonnes dwt, built in Finland for the Soviet Union, and so powered and strengthened as to be capable of operating in ice one metre thick, unescorted by icebreakers. They entered service in late 1982, and early reports of their performance were all excellent. They seem to be a very successful compromise between icebreaking ability and freight-carrying capacity. There are now fourteen of these ships in operation, and more may well be ordered. Another new development is the construction of an Arctic-going lighter carrier of 33,500 tonnes dwt, which will have nuclear power. She will be called the *Sevmorput'*, and is due for launch in 1986.

The idea of a *submarine* freighter has often been put forward, and plans were even drawn up by an American shipbuilder several decades ago. The effectiveness of such ships in ice-filled waters would surely be great, but no one has been so keen to have one as to be willing to put up the necessary money. It is true that there would be difficulty in operating submarines in certain parts of the Arctic, because of the extensive areas of shallow water over the continental shelf; but while this drawback may be affecting Soviet consideration of their use (the continental shelf being most extensive off northeast Siberia), it would not be a major impediment in Northern Waters.

Other factors

Perhaps the most important factor, after the availability of suitable ships, is the provision of trained manpower. It is emphatically not sufficient to have seamen well trained in normal, ice-free navigation, since seamen are conditioned to keep well away from ice of any kind. Crews, and especially watch-keeping officers, of all ice-going ships need many years of training and experience. The only country which has such crews in abundance is the Soviet Union, for it has been operating at least 50 ships in Arctic waters every season since 1935.

Another factor is the availability of ice reporting and forecasting services. Much time can obviously be saved if ice is avoided rather than struggled through. An operational forecasting service requires frequent and regular input from reporting services, whether satellite, aircraft, or even ground stations. The Soviet Union has the most effective system in place, and it is able to reach the northeast regions of Northern Waters. Canada can manage some coverage west of Greenland, and this can be augmented if necessary by US support. The Russians alone, however, produce long-term forecasts, for periods of up to six months ahead, though these are not necessarily very reliable.

Further possibilities

The next decade or so could see considerable changes in sea transport in Northern Waters, which may be brought about by new exploitation of resources, new ship design, the opening up of new shipping-routes, changes in the ice situation or, of course, by any combination of these.

The most obvious development in resources might be the production of hydrocarbons close to, or in, the area. The Barents Sea, Svalbard and its waters and offshore Greenland, west and east, are all prospective locations (see Chapter 3). The first production would be Soviet — drilling ships are already active — and any oil or gas might, of course, be routed to home markets via Murmansk or some other Soviet northern port. But if used for export, the products would almost certainly have to traverse Northern Waters in tankers. The Svalbard area has been quite extensively explored, so far without positive result, but finds may yet be made. The oil or gas would be Norwegian, but the companies operating the wells might have any or no national allegiance. Svalbard is of course wholly within Northern Waters. So are the possible Greenland locations. West Greenland waters have been partially explored, without success, and the east coast is about to be investigated. Here again the shipping involved may come from any country. There is no Greenlandic, or Danish, monopoly.

Improvements in the power and design of icebreakers could be another factor in expanding the use of Northern Waters. What we have witnessed up to now has basically been increased power and strength applied to the traditional method of breaking ice by crushing it beneath the weight of the ship — more brute force in fact. Other techniques may be possible, and some have been the object of experiment: thermal, hydraulic, explosive, novel bow design. The only one to give positive results is the system of releasing air bubbles from below the waterline along the hull, in order to minimize ice formation. It is entirely possible that more impressive performance will result from other techniques, whether tried before or not. It has yet to be seen whether a surface vessel can make a way through floating ice anywhere at any time. A rough calculation, made for Antarctic use some years ago, indicated that 210,000 shaft horsepower (shp) would be required, using the traditional ice-crushing method. The most powerful icebreaker afloat today has 75,000 shp, but there has been discussion in the Soviet Union about building a ship of 150,000 shp. Such a ship would probably be able to overcome most of the ice found in the Arctic Ocean (icebergs apart) at most times of year, and its construction may be only a few years ahead. But it would still have to be handled with care, and there would still be obstacles it could not overcome.

Making extensive voyages in the central Arctic basin is indeed in sight. The Soviet Union has already mounted two spectacular voyages to this area. The first of these was that of the nuclear icebreaker *Arktika*, which reached the North Pole in August 1977, the first surface vessel to do so. She followed a triangular course, Murmansk — Laptev Sea — Pole — Murmansk, and covered the 3,852 nautical miles in 14 days, at the remarkable average speed of 11.5 knots. The following year *Arktika*'s sister ship *Sibir'* escorted the freighter *Kapitan Myshevskiy* on a course from Murmansk to the Bering Strait, passing north of the island groups. Though not in as high a latitude as the Pole voyage, this one was carried out in May/June, a much more difficult time than August. These two voyages were stated to be experimental, in a search to establish a direct route from Murmansk to the Bering Strait across the centre of the Arctic basin, which would cut 1,300 kilometres off the existing route along the Eurasian coast. But at present there is no call in the Soviet Union for direct freighting from Atlantic to Pacific (or the reverse): the usefulness of Arctic Waters is access they give to the Siberian rivers and coast, and for this purpose a route across the central Arctic basin would be a long way round, not a short cut.

The central route would, however, be useful in two contexts. One is if in future sea freighting *is* called for between the Atlantic and Pacific, and this might be either for Soviet use or for wider use by any of the world's shipping interests, perhaps with the Soviet Union acting in a kind of managerial capacity. The other is if there is a need to operate vessels of deeper draught than the 20,000 tonnes dwt freighters that are at present the norm and draw just under 10 metres, the limitation being essentially that of the shallow continental shelf along much of the Northern Sea Route. Neither context seems likely in the near future, but one may note that the first would lead to increased traffic through Northern Waters.

There has been no more action in the central Arctic since 1978, and the potentialities of the first voyages remain unexplored. The reason for this might be a lowering of priority due to the evident inability of the two new US icebreakers, *Polar Star* and *Polar Sea*, to present a serious challenge to Soviet pre-eminence in Arctic seafaring. Quite clearly, though, further probing of the possibilities of trans-Arctic basin navigation could be put in hand at any time, whenever the stimulus — rivalry with the United States or economic incentive — is sufficiently strong.

Another expansion of traffic traversing Northern Waters could come from increased use of the Northwest Passage. Of the possible variant routes, the one entering and leaving Northern Waters in Lancaster Sound is the likeliest to be employed. Such traffic as passes that way now is serving local ports in that general area. The Northwest Passage could become a significant shipping route if, for instance, major resources were to be exploited in the western islands of the archipelago or offshore in the Beaufort Sea — and both of these areas are promising. One such development is the Arctic Pilot Project, a scheme to carry liquefied natural gas from Melville Island to the Atlantic. It would have used the Lancaster Sound route, but was put into abeyance in 1983. The Northwest

Passage was also one of the options available for the transport of Prudhoe Bay oil from Alaska, and it was rejected only after experimental voyages had been made by the strengthened tanker *Manhattan* in 1969 and 1970. These proposals, or others like them, may well come up again. A research group at Dalhousie University under the direction of Professor Douglas Johnston is indeed now at work on identifying the arrangements that must be made by Canada if a Northwest Passage is to function smoothly. It was thought in 1980 that various hydrocarbon developments might require some hundreds of transit voyages a year by the early 1990s, but this projection is now seen to be much exaggerated.[4]

The most enigmatic, but perhaps the potentially most far-reaching, cause of change in the shipping pattern in ice-covered waters is the possibility of change in the ice situation itself. The seasonal and interannual variations in the extent of ice-cover are already large, but the secular change over periods of decades is of real concern. It is believed by many, particularly in the Soviet Union, that ice conditions for shipping on the Northern Sea Route have been deteriorating over the last 10 to 15 years: 1972, 1973, 1978, 1979, 1981 and 1983 were all significantly bad. In 1983, 51 ships were caught in the ice for a period of weeks, and one was sunk. Some forecasters predict continuing deterioration.[5] Technological improvements have by and large up to now offset past disadvantageous effects, but there may come a time when this will no longer be the case. However, the Soviet Union, which would be the country most affected by such changes, shows little sign of being dismayed at the prospect.

Conclusion

Northern Waters are not among the world's busiest, but significant traffic is found in their southern and eastern sectors. Much of this traffic is concerned with fishing, since the area is one of the world's major fishing grounds. The largest flow of other (non-fishing) traffic is probably Soviet shipping using Murmansk and White Sea ports.

The most obvious difficulty encountered is the presence of floating ice. This can be, and is, overcome, at least to some extent, by the use of specialized ships, trained personnel and ice prediction services. In all these the Soviet Union excels.

The future offers possibilities for expanding use of these waters. If new resources are found in the area, or new shipping-routes required across it, then the technology is certainly available to boost the current level of traffic. The least-known factor in any future expansion is the ice itself, which may cause problems so great as to inhibit very seriously the possibility of greater shipping activity.

Notes

1. P. Wadhams, 'The Ice Cover in the Greenland and Norwegian Seas', *Reviews of Geophysics and Space Physics*, Vol. 19 (1981), No. 3, pp. 345-93.

2. For instance, the British *Arctic Pilot*, Vol. 3; the Canadian *Pilot of Arctic Canada*, Vols. 2 and 3; or the American *Hydrographic Office Publications*, 15, 16, 76 and 77.

3. I am indebted to *Lloyd's Register of Shipping* for kindly supplying relevant extracts from their 1984 issue.

4. D. Pharand and L.H. Legault, *The Northwest Passage: Arctic Straits* (Dordrecht: Martinus Nijhoff,1984), pp. 82-3.

5. N.A. Volkov and V.F. Zakharov, 'Evolyutsiya ledyanogo pokrova v Arktike v svyazi s izemeneniyami klimata', *Meteorologiya i Gidrologiya*, No. 7 (1977), pp. 47-55. A. Arikaynen and G. Burkov, 'Ukhudshayutsya li ledovyye usloviya v Arktike?', *Morskoy Flot*, No. 6 (1985), pp. 36-7.

STRATEGY IN THE FAR NORTH

Geoffrey Till

In 1944, the Soviet Foreign Minister, Molotov, gave his Norwegian counterpart, Trygve Lie, a lesson in maritime geography. 'The Dardanelles,' he said, 'here we are locked in ... Oresund ... here we are locked in. Only in the north is there an opening, but this war has shown that the supply line to northern Russia can be cut or interfered with. This shall not be repeated in the future. We have invested much in this part of the Soviet Union, and it is therefore important for the entire Union's existence that we shall in the future ensure that northern Russia is permitted to live in security and peace.'[1]

The strategic importance of the North

Forty years later, the strategic importance of this area to the Soviet Union and its possible adversaries is at least as great as ever it was, and arguably much more so. Now, as then, Soviet naval aspirations are bedevilled by the fact that unkind circumstances oblige the country's admirals to divide their assets into four semi-autonomous fleets (not to mention a river flotilla or two) in a way which makes creating a concentration of naval force against a powerful adversary extremely difficult. Three of these fleets can only reach the open oceans by transiting narrow straits currently under the control of the Soviet Union's adversaries, and three (not the same three) have difficult climatic operating conditions to contend with. It is therefore not surprising that the Soviets continue to emphasize the strategic value of the waters to the northwest of the USSR as being the only place where reasonable access to the open oceans and manageable operating conditions coincide.

If Soviet leaders are to play their proper part on the world stage, then, as Admiral Gorshkov, currently Commander-in-Chief of the Soviet navy, has repeatedly said, they must use sea power to do it, and this means that Russia must continue its historic struggle for access to the open oceans. Northern Waters are, however, as useful to hostile naval forces coming in as they are to a Soviet fleet going out. Admiral Gorshkov has accordingly also often echoed Molotov's warning that throughout its history Russia's enemies have frequently used the sea as a means of projecting military power against it, and that this is a menace which must still be zealously countered.

More recently, the traditional strategic importance of Northern Waters to the Soviet Union has been reinforced by various technological developments. The area has become the front line between the United States and the Soviet Union for the transpolar exchange of ballistic missiles and intercontinental bombers. An increasing percentage of the submarine component of Soviet strategic nuclear forces operates in these waters. Because of this, and the extensive military and commercial investment in the territories bordering the Barents and White Seas, Northern Waters have become even more crucial to the Soviet Union now than they were in 1944.

The ancient and modern significance of the area has made the Northern Fleet one of the two main Soviet fleets, and the Soviet navy currently deploys rather more than 40 modern ballistic-missile-firing submarines (SSBNs) in the region. Normally this total includes over 20 *Delta* SSBNs, whose SS-N-18 missiles can reach the USA when launched from Soviet waters. The gigantic *Typhoon* submarine has made an appearance here too; its 20 SS-N-20 missiles have a similar range but between 6 and 9 individually targetable warheads each. The remaining SSBNs in the area are older *Yankee* submarines.

About 40 nuclear-powered and 50 diesel hunter-killer submarines spearhead the rest of the fleet. The surface ship component, which normally comprises about 30 major combatants and a host of minor ones, has been reduced in number over the years, but the individual quality of these ships and their increased effectiveness as a blue-water force is most convincingly demonstrated by the *Kiev*-class aircraft-carriers and the *Kirov* nuclear battle-cruisers. The fleet's capacity for local amphibious warfare is modest but becoming more significant.

The fleet is based at Severomorsk, to the north of Murmansk on the Kola Fiord: a long seaway studded on both sides with defence installations and industrial centres, particularly the city of Murmansk itself, which are linked by recently enhanced road and rail communications. Although there are a couple of small shipyards at Murmansk (at Sovmorput and Glavryba), such capacity is mainly to be found about 600 kilometres to the southeast across the White Sea in the vicinity of the city of Arkhangel'sk, particularly in the huge covered submarine construction yards at Severodvinsk. Nevertheless, the capacity of these yards would not be enough to sustain the Northern Fleet's repair and refit requirements in a prolonged conflict. To fight and prevail in a long war with a serious adversary, the Soviet Northern Fleet would need access to the shipyards of the Baltic.

Ashore, the Soviet Northern Fleet has a naval airforce which includes some 95 *Badger* and *Blinder* bombers, although some 40 formidable *Backfire* bombers are expected to be deployed north from the vicinity of Leningrad in order to operate from Olenogorsk, an airbase in the Kola Peninsula. Several hundred other various naval aircraft are deployed from over 20 major and minor airbases in the area.

It is difficult to be precise about the Kola-based ground forces garrison and air defence assets, because the peninsula is only a part of larger military areas, the Leningrad military district and the Arkhangel'sk air defence district respectively, but normally there are the equivalent of two motor rifle divisions and about 120 interceptors in the area. Substantial reinforcements could, however, be drafted in should the need arise.

Force comparisons with possible adversaries are more dependent here on critical assumptions about the length of warning-time and the influence of events elsewhere than is the case on the Central Front. Probably the main source of uncertainty would be about the presence and composition of NATO's Striking Fleet Atlantic,[2] a major variable in the equation about which it is difficult to be precise. It might be there early on in massive strength, or it might not. There are also very considerable differences between NATO's air and ground forces in the area in normal times and what might be available through reinforcement in periods of tension. Without cataloguing possible forces in various states of readiness and alert, it seems fair to conclude that in normal times NATO's forces in the Northern Waters area are very small: a few hundred Norwegian troops deployed in Finnmark and about 80 interceptor aircraft; a few naval vessels and maritime patrol aircraft; and that would usually be all.

Since the Soviet Union is clearly hypersensitive about its rights in Northern Waters, and because the Scandinavian countries adopt interestingly complex defence postures, the area is normally one of low tension and careful restraint. Peacetime deployments are intended to deter possible adversaries as well as reassure local allies, but they are judiciously modulated so as not to appear provocative. The North is not an area of major East-West confrontation, and both sides currently seem happy to keep things that way. By contrast, in the event of a major conflict, the area would be fiercely contested, because control of it would yield so many strategic advantages to the victor.

Predominance would allow either side to use the area for its strategic purposes and deny those uses to its adversary. Were the Soviet Union to achieve control of Northern Waters, it would be able to use them for the secure deployment of the submarine component of its strategic nuclear forces. It would also win access to the North Atlantic and the open oceans beyond, which would allow it to attack NATO's maritime lines of communication, thereby impeding the flow of reinforcement and resupply shipping and occupying the attention of forces otherwise free to threaten Soviet interests elsewhere. As NATO's SACLANT recently remarked, 'the battle of the Atlantic must be fought in the Norwegian Sea'.[3] Soviet predominance could also extend into waters to the south, which would result in the physical outflanking of NATO's position in Scandinavia. This in turn could lead to local feelings of insecurity in peacetime, and lay Norway open to amphibious assault in war. Territory seized in the north could be used as a base for subsequent air, naval and land attacks directed to the south or indeed across the North Sea against the UK itself. Finally, Soviet predominance would prevent NATO forces from using the area to launch attacks on Soviet territory.

Western interests in predominance in the North are the mirror image of all this. Furthermore, both sets of strategic interests incidentally demonstrate the particularly close relationship here between control of the sea and control of the land.

The struggle for sea control

The battle for sea control, or what Admiral Gorshkov calls 'favourable operating conditions', would probably consist of four elements. The first would be a struggle for control of inshore waters, which in the early stages of any conflict would be primarily the responsibility of the Norwegian navy and air force. The

Norwegians would make maximum use of the topographical features of their coastline — with its islands, skerries, inlets, long deep fjords and mountainous shores — to harass incoming naval forces with a host of fast patrol boats, inshore submarines, mine warfare vessels and heavily protected coastal defence forts. Their concept of total defence envisages continuous harassment of enemy forces even after the main body has gone past. Perhaps remembering the tenets of its own New School in the early 1930s and the initial losses suffered by the Germans in their invasion of 1940 (particularly the loss of the heavy cruiser *Blücher* in Oslofjord), the Soviet navy would take this threat seriously.

Further out to sea, the main variable in the sea control equation would be the carrier battle-groups of the US navy. The question here is how many would be available and when they would arrive. The local Europeans are well aware of the possible need to hold the fort until the carriers arrive. As West Germany's Vice-Admiral Bethge has recently remarked: 'In view of the global commitments of the United States Navy, the security of these waters would, especially at the beginning of any armed conflict, be pre-dominantly the responsibility of the maritime forces of the North-West European NATO countries.'[4] Their task would be to make sure the Soviet navy could not successfully launch a *fait accompli*. They would do this by maintaining effective surveillance and, afterwards, by engaging in a campaign of attrition (particularly by submarine) against Soviet forces in the Norwegian Sea. In some respects this would be like the campaign conducted by the German High Sea Fleet against the British in the first two years of World War I. As in that earlier struggle, the intention could well be to improve the odds for the contest between the two main naval forces that might be expected to follow later. Such a campaign would doubtless involve British, Dutch, French, Norwegian and, since their 1980 decision to abandon their self-imposed operational boundary of 61° North, West German naval, air and naval air forces. During World War I, this type of attack with limited means (especially mines and submarines) forced the British to behave with some circumspection lest they fritter away their superiority before the main opponent (Scheer's battle-fleet) arrived on the scene, and it is not inconceivable that it would have a similar effect on the Soviet Northern Fleet.

The balance to be struck between the two remaining elements in the contest for control in the North, namely barrier operations and forward operations, has caused public debate, especially in the United States. The notion that NATO's naval forces should blockade Soviet forces by creating a defensive zone across the Greenland/Iceland/UK gap is well established. This would probably be the baseline of a system that would in fact extend forward to the Bear Island/North Cape line and so offer defence-in-depth through the progressive attrition of exiting Soviet forces by means of submarines, deep water mines, aircraft and surface ships. The Soviet navy has a similar system, comparable in its intention, which even partially overlaps in geographical terms, but is of course oriented in the opposite direction.

The really controversial issue is the extent to which NATO's Striking Fleet Atlantic should seek to challenge that system by engaging in what have become known as 'forward operations' against the main seat of Soviet maritime power in the North, the Kola Peninsula and the Barents Sea. Ever since Elizabethan seamen attacked the Spanish navy in its own ports, this most direct and ambitious method of securing command of the sea has exercised a particular fascination for the strategists of the major maritime powers. In its modern guise it has been well summarized by a recent Chief of Naval Operations of the US navy:

We must fight on the terms which are most advantageous to us. This would require taking the war to the enemy's naval forces with the objective of achieving the earliest possible destruction of his capability to interfere with our use of the sea areas essential to the support of our overseas forces and allies. In this sense sea control is an offensive rather than a defensive function. The prompt destruction of opposing naval forces is the most economical and effective means to assure control of the sea areas required for successful prosecution of the war and support of the US and allied war economies. Our current offensive naval capabilities centred on the carrier battle forces and their supporting units are well-suited for the execution of this strategy.[5]

Such ideas are also associated with US Navy Secretary John Lehman, who has been accused by his critics of using such arguments mainly to justify the US navy's carrier construction programme. They believe the real target of this strategy is not the Soviet navy in the Kola, but economizers in Congress. They conclude that this is a political rather than a military strategy. Lehman and his defenders point, however, to the traditional advantages of seizing the initiative in this way. Tactically, it would make the most of what is believed to be the Soviet navy's weakness in responding quickly and efficiently to unexpected situations; strategically, it would prevent the Soviet Union from deciding the rules of the game and deploying its forces to its best advantage.

More specifically, forward operations would relieve immediate and long-term pressure on NATO's sea lines of communication. Lehman has argued: 'Forward operations are especially valuable in drawing down enemy forces, keeping pressure on the enemy's interior lines of communication and buying time for the capabilities of the Allied countries to mobilize.'[6] He makes the point that NATO is in a less favourable position than the Western allies were in World War II. They could afford to adopt a more passive posture by concentrating their resources on direct defence by means of a convoy-and-escort strategy, because the requirement to get reinforcements and resupplies across the Atlantic was less urgent in terms of time and less demanding in terms of the hulls available overall. 'Militarily we simply do not have the merchant fleet to sustain the war of attrition that would result ... [from a more passive posture] ... Success in the maritime theaters, without which there can be no success in the land theaters, is impossible without a forward strategy of manoeuver, initiative and offense.'[7]

Support for forward operations largely depends on a greater confidence today that the carrier battle-group can, after all, cope with nuclear and diesel submarines and the attention of the Soviet naval air force. As Robert Weinland has observed: 'The acquisition of new defensive systems and the prospect of revising our *modus operandi* to give increased emphasis to both coordinated multi-carrier operations and the mutual support of land-based and sea-based air have all acted to reduce significantly the hesitancy previously felt about operating carriers in high threat environments.'[8]

Advocates of this policy now tend to argue that previous exercises in exchange analysis often exaggerated the real strength of Soviet forces in the area. For instance, too little attention was paid to the extreme climatic conditions that Soviet forces would have to contend with in any sustained air campaign in the North. This would particularly apply to the Kola airfields, and it seems reasonable to speculate that this is one of the reasons why, for example, naval *Backfire* bombers are not deployed permanently in the area.

The argument about the place of carriers in forward operations is simply a variant of the much wider debate about the vulnerability and general validity of the strike carrier in the US navy, which has been addressed by academics and naval professionals for the past several decades. It suffices here to point out the relevance of the carrier debate to strategy in Northern Waters.

Doubts about the place of carriers in forward operations in the North remain. Sceptics argue that the US navy should not hazard some of its most precious assets in an area where geography alone gives the Soviet Union so many obvious advantages. Might it not be the case that, by yielding to the temptation to engage in such operations, the US navy would be playing the game according to Soviet rules? Might there not be other, less risky, ways of achieving the same objective? One alternative often canvassed is the use of long-range naval cruise missiles fired from submarines, aircraft or even surface ships like the *New Jersey*. Thus, when responding to a Congressional question about how he would propose dealing with the 'number one threat' (the *Backfire* bomber), Admiral Hayward recently remarked: 'The best way to counter the threat, of course, is by offensive action to destroy the *Backfires* at their bases, and that is why *Tomahawk*, with its very high accuracy, is so important'.[9] Others doubt whether conventional cruise missiles pack sufficient punch for the suppression of airbases or the destruction of naval forces in harbour.[10]

There are also critics who worry about what the Soviet Union would do if such attacks were, after all, successful or looked like being so. The Congressional Budget Office, for example, has called them 'dangerously provocative in a nuclear armed world', not least because they would increase Soviet incentives to use nuclear weapons against such forces. In peacetime, too, an apparent readiness to contemplate operations like this might be thought unacceptably destabilizing. Thus one recent commentator has argued: 'Exercising restraint in conventional operations on the Northern Flank may not be the ideal way to conduct a conventional war. But it is preferable to the nuclear escalation that more offensive operations might provoke.'[11]

The complexity of the arguments about forward operations and the place of carriers in them, and the extent to which any conclusions are dependent on the precise details of the scenario, render firm judgements on the matter impossible. Clearly no naval commander would engage in forward operations until and unless the local air and submarine threat had been reduced to manageable proportions. There is therefore little prospect of a simple repetition of out-of-the-blue carrier strikes like those at Taranto and Pearl Harbor in World War II. Forward carrier operations would depend on the success of preparatory forward operations by aircraft and submarines; and the extent to which these are possible depends, in turn, on the resource demands of other necessary operations elsewhere. At the same time, no naval commander would wish to forgo the option of employing NATO's sea power in this way. Carriers do operate north of the Arctic Circle for that very reason: not just to acclimatize themselves, but, no doubt, to remind the Soviet Union that such possibilities exist.

To recapitulate, sea control operations in Northern Waters would very likely consist of four elements: the struggle for inshore waters; early attrition campaigns by the local air and naval forces of Northwest Europe against Soviet forces entering the area; barrier operations; and forward operations. Although in theory it is necessary to win sea control *before* it can be exerted, in practice the struggle for the capacity to use the sea and actual attempts to use it are often conducted simultaneously within some larger enterprise against sea communications or the enemy's coastline. As Admiral Gorshkov has said: 'Combat actions, the aim of which is to secure dominance at sea in selected areas or in particular directions, may either precede the solution of the main tasks or be conducted simultaneously.'[12] Because sea control is simply a means to an end, the effort that each side devotes to contesting it will reflect the value of the uses of the sea that are made possible by success. Three of these possible uses merit closer examination.

Strategic nuclear deterrence

The Soviet navy deploys an increasing proportion of its SSBNs in the Northern Waters of Europe and Asia. Most analysts believe that the Soviet Union regards these SSBNs as a strategic reserve that would not be used in the early stages of a conflict but kept back as a force capable of devastating its adversary in the final stages of a general war. Such a force would help the Soviet Union in any bargaining that might take place over the conduct or conclusion of the war: it might be the final decisive means to politico-strategic victory, enabling the Soviet Union to secure an advance won on the ground in Europe, or it might mitigate the consequences of defeat.[13] These functions clearly require that Soviet SSBNs be able to operate safely for a sustained period of time.

One school of thought argues that the importance the Soviet Union has attached to the naval contribution to strategic nuclear deterrence (as evidenced by the scientific/industrial effort required to produce its advanced SSBNs and the heavy doctrinal stress on the need to protect them) in itself provides the main incentive for NATO to threaten it. The prospect of losing the capacity these submarines represent would have a deterrent effect on Soviet behaviour in peacetime and so help to prevent a war from taking place. Should war come anyway, such threats would create a defensive need which the Soviet navy would feel obliged to meet with assets that might otherwise be used against NATO's interests elsewhere. The greater the threat, the more the diversionary consequences. Finally, although in the current or foreseeable state of ASW technology a totally effective disarming strike against the Soviet navy's SSBN force does not appear feasible, those who value damage-limitation strategies tend to argue, along Soviet lines, that destroying something that might otherwise incinerate several cities has much to be said for it, irrespective of any theoretically destabilizing effects such a 'defensive' act might have.

Nevertheless, anti-SSBN operations need, like any others, to satisfy the demands of cost-benefit analysis. One of those costs might be that by threatening Soviet survival, Western successes might force the Soviet Union to use its SSBNs, even though by so doing it would effectively be giving up its second-strike capability, a prospect attractive to neither side. Another calculation would be the balance, and the opportunity costs it represents, between Western forces devoted to tracking down and destroying the SSBNs, and Soviet forces assigned to protect them. If all the Soviet SSBNs based at Polyarnyy in the Kola Peninsula and Petropavlovsk in the Far East went to sea at once, the demands on both sides of such an operation would be severe, and it cannot just be assumed that, simply in terms of the diversionary effects that would ensue, it would necessarily be in the interest of the West to attack them.

The first generation of Soviet SSBNs was the *Yankee* class. These have a relatively short-range missile, which means they must pass through the northern gaps to reach their launch position in the Atlantic, and NATO forces would presumably seek to deal with them as they did so. This source of vulnerability doubtless helped persuade the Soviet navy to give considerable priority to the development of the far longer-range *Delta* and *Typhoon* classes, which can launch their missiles from Soviet waters and still expect to hit the United States. The conventional reading of Soviet naval theory and practice is that the need to protect their *Deltas* and *Typhoons* from Western attack ranks very high in their priorities. Soviet surface ships, submarines and land-based air-power combine in an attempt to transform the Barents and Okhotsk Seas into sanctuaries in which Soviet SSBNs may safely roam. This is at almost complete variance with the usual Western practice of allowing SSBNs to slip their leashes and lose themselves in the oceans, relying for immunity on undetectability rather than on the support offered by the rest of the fleet. But as Gorshkov wrote: 'The First and Second World Wars showed the fallacy of the view that the submarine by virtue of its concealment after emergence from its base can itself ensure its own invulnerability.'[14] In Soviet terminology, the rest of the navy has to give the SSBNs enough 'combat stability' for them to 'solve their tasks'.[15] All members of the Soviet maritime team will be engaged in this specialized form of sea control. By the same logic, so might their opposite numbers in any attempt to contest it.

More recently there have been suggestions that the Soviet navy might be moving away from this strategy in several ways. Admiral Train of the US navy (a former SACLANT) has, for example, suggested that the Soviet navy might seek to send its SSBNs much further afield. 'As they use up the sea space available to them in the northern Norwegian Sea and the Barents Sea, it is quite likely that they will start to station some of their *Delta* submarines in the South Atlantic, perhaps in the narrows between Brazil and Africa.'[16] Another possibility which has attracted recent comment is that the Soviet navy will make serious use of the concealment potential of the Arctic ice. Ice-cover helps protect submarines from air detection but is also often thin enough for submarines to surface in order to communicate or fire their missiles. Below the ice differences in salinity and the ambient noise of ice-floes grinding together make acoustic detection difficult. The US navy, recognizing this, is thought to be developing a submarine especially suited for under-ice operations.[17] If the Soviet navy proceeds with such deployments, and if the US navy seeks seriously to contest them, the Arctic could become the scene of an underwater war of great consequence. In all probability, however, the Soviet navy will continue to exercise *all* its SSBN deployment options, if only to make life as difficult as possible for any opponents.

The defence of sea lines of communication

As already mentioned, the Norwegian Sea would be an important arena for the conduct of a new battle of the Atlantic, assuming that the war lasts long enough for reinforcement and resupply to be necessary. Thought should also be given to the defence of *local* sea lines of communication, especially those used to convey reinforcements and supplies to Norway. The vulnerability of troop transports and supply ships to submarine and air attack from the Kola Peninsula area, and the need for quick responses to menacing situations, have increased the military attractiveness of airlifting in troops and of prestocking heavy equipment *in situ.*

Neither of these precautions is likely to obviate the need for normal reinforcement by sea. Although such reinforcements could well be expected to arrive before actual hostilities begin (and, indeed, their very despatch would be a part of the process of deterrence), they would still need to be protected in transit from the UK. The direct route to Tromsø would be faster, would provide better conditions for the location and hunting of submarines, more early warning against air attack and more sea room for evasive manoeuvring. The threat of accidental groundings or of mining would be largely confined to the arrival point. On the other hand, this is just the area where the Soviet submarine and *Badger* and *Backfire* threat would be at its greatest.

The alternative would be to sail over to the southern part of Norway, and then proceed northwards via a coastal route through the Leads. The early part of this alternative route would increase the distance between the reinforcement and resupply shipping and the bases in the Kola Peninsula from which it might be attacked. The coastal environment of the later stages of the route would offer ample concealment from all types of attack, for instance making it difficult for anti-shipping missiles to find their targets amidst the rocks and islands. On the other hand, this route would take longer and there are in fact several places where natural obstacles and bridges could in any case force larger units temporarily out to sea. Either way, the limits and vulnerability of rail and road communications seem likely to encourage the use of the Leads for much north–south traffic, as in World War II.

Should the Soviet Union seek to occupy parts of northern Norway, it would of course be faced with a similar set of operational requirements and policy dilemmas, for NATO's naval and air forces would presumably seek to interdict Soviet sea lines of communication. Conflict in this region would therefore probably involve a campaign of mutual attrition analogous in some ways to the Russo-German struggles of World Ward II in the Black and Baltic Seas. Once again fortune would tend to favour the side capable of exerting most sea control.

Amphibious assault in the North

The strategic advantages the Soviet Union would gain by physically seizing northern Norway have been mentioned. The more territory the Soviet Union seizes, the more the strategic advantage, but the more, too, the costs and risks.

Although Norway maintains small forces well forward, the main point of defence would be in the mountain redoubt centred on Tromsø. Should the Soviet Union seriously seek to come this far, three avenues of approach suggest themselves. Most dangerously for NATO, Soviet ground forces could seek to outflank its position by advancing across the top of Sweden via the Kiruna–Narvik road. But this would involve the Soviet Union in a debilitating war with Sweden as well as with NATO, and so may not seem in practice very inviting. An attack further to the north through the so-called 'Finnish Wedge' is another possibility and one in which both the risks and the opportunities are reduced. But the terrain in Finland is marshy, and therefore not easy. Moreover, the Finnish Wedge feeds into Norway's narrow Skibotn valley, the topography of which would favour the defence. The third, least ambitious alternative would be to advance through Finnmark in the north and then come south, doubtless supported by amphibious attacks and *Spetsnaz* operations ashore.

Common prudence could well persuade the Soviet Union to make at least a limited advance into Norway's far north (as it eventually did in World War II), but anything more ambitious along any of the three routes discussed here would be far more difficult than might appear from the bland large-scale map that so often accompanies discussions on this question. The terrain and the climate can be extremely arduous and tend to favour the defence. The Soviet Union normally deploys the equivalent of only two to three divisions in the Kola area, and these would not be adequate for more than a limited move into Finnmark. Anything more ambitious would require substantial air/land reinforcement from the Leningrad area, a process that would take time and give warning. Moreover, Norway puts considerable stress on early reconnaissance and harassment so as to gain the maximum time for response. The main function of its navy — with its inshore submarines, mines, coastal artillery and fast combatants — is the defeat of amphibious operations. 'Our principal task', its Commander-in-Chief has recently remarked, 'is to prevent a seaborne invasion', particularly in the Tromsø region.[18] Furthermore, this strategy would not cease once the main Soviet force had established a presence ashore. The Norwegian aspiration is represented by the Narvik campaign of 1940, in which the German position won in an initially successful invasion would, if it had not been for events in France, have eventually proved untenable.

Much would depend on the arrival of NATO reinforcements. The only earmarked force (apart from whatever is generated within Norway itself) is the Canadian Air Sea Transportable Brigade, but reinforcements are likely to include elements of the ACE Mobile Force, the UK/Netherlands Amphibious Force and, since 1977, the US Marine Corps, as well as the all-important tactical air support flying into Norwegian airbases. Controlling and protecting this flood of men and material into Norway would be a major undertaking in war and requires extensive practice in peacetime. The UK/Netherlands Amphibious Force trains there for three months a year, and the whole operation is a major feature of a rolling programme of regular naval exercises. The Norway campaign of 1940 demonstrates the ill-advisedness of relying on improvisation in this difficult area, and such rehearsals can also be justified by the deterrent effect on the Soviet Union they can reasonably be presumed to have. The need to reassure Norwegians that the northern half of their country is not regarded as lost almost as soon as the shooting starts is another important justification for these exercises.

Conclusion

In conclusion, Northern Waters would most likely be one of the main areas of conflict between East and West in war, because of their crucial importance to the outcome of events elsewhere. The progress of campaigns in the Atlantic and the Baltic, the capacity to defend the United Kingdom, and even the central strategic nuclear balance would all be inextricably linked to the struggle for control in the North. For this reason, the contrast between the area's situation in war and its normal peacetime tranquillity is likely to be particularly stark.

Notes

1. Quoted in C. Bertram and J.J. Holst (eds), *New Strategic Factors in the North Atlantic* (Oslo: Universitetsforlaget, 1977), p. 37. In 1944 the Russians sought to renegotiate the Svalbard Treaty and to acquire Bear Island.

2. The precise composition of NATO's Atlantic Strike Fleet is very hard to predict; it depends on what the task is and on how many US carriers are available. Each carrier is the centre of a battle-group that would include perhaps two *Aegis* cruisers for air defence, two general purpose DDG-51 guided-missile destroyers and two DD-963 destroyers for ASW, plus supporting submarines and replenishment ships. The US navy would hope to have at least two carrier battle-groups — better three, and ideally four — operating in the same stretch of such dangerous waters as the Norwegian Sea. American efforts would be considerably supplemented by the Europeans, especially the British, who are expected to make available one or two ASW groups centred on their carriers of the *Invincible* class.

3. Quoted in Erling Bjøl, *Nordic Security*, Adelphi Paper No. 181 (London: IISS, 1983), p. 21.

4. Vice-Admiral Ansgar Bethge, 'Land-based Maritime Aircraft in Maritime Warfare', *NATO's 16 Nations*, Special Issue, No. 1 (1984).

5. Admiral Thomas B. Hayward, testimony before the House Armed Services Committee, *Hearings on DOD Appropriations for Fiscal Year 1980* (Washington: US Government Printing Office, 1979), p. 841.

6. Hearings before a Sub-Committee on Appropriations of House Armed Services Committee, *Hearings on DOD Appropriations for Fiscal Year 1983* (Washington: US Government Printing Office, 1982), p. 127.

7. See John Lehman's response to Stansfield Turner and George Thibault, 'Preparing for the Unexpected: The Need for a New Military Strategy', *Foreign Affairs*, Winter 1982/3.

8. Robert G. Weinland, *Northern Waters: Their Strategic Significance*, Professional Paper No. 265 (Arlington, Va.: Center for Naval Analyses, 1979).

9. Admiral Thomas B. Hayward, testimony before the House Armed Services Committee, *Hearings on DOD Appropriations for Fiscal Year 1982* (Washington: US Government Printing Office), 1981.

10. See for instance M.K. MccGwire, 'The Tomahawk and General Purpose Naval Forces', in Richard K. Betts (ed.), *Cruise Missiles: Technology, Strategy.*

Politics (Washington: The Brookings Institution, 1981).

11. See 'Building a 600-Ship Navy' in *Seapower*, May 1982. Also Barry R. Posen, 'Inadvertent Nuclear War? Escalation and NATO's Northern Flank', in *International Security*, Fall 1982, pp.28-54.

12. Quoted in G. Till (ed.), *Maritime Strategy and the Nuclear Age*, 2nd edn (London: Macmillan, 1984), p. 135.

13. See Bryan Ranft and G. Till, *The Sea in Soviet Strategy* (London: Macmillan, 1983), pp. 166-75.

14. S.G. Gorshkov, *The Sea Power of the State* (Oxford: Pergamon, 1979), p. 197.

15. Ranft and Till, as Note 13, p. 171.

16. Admiral Harry D. Train in testimony before the House Armed Services Committee, *Hearings on Military Posture, March 16th 1982* (Washington: US Government Printing Office, 1982).

17. See *Wall Street Journal* and *San Francisco Chronicle*, 19 May 1983.

18. Rear-Admiral B.M. Grimstvedt, 'Norway's Coastal Defence', *NATO's 16 Nations*, Special Issue, No. 1 (1984), p. 77.

6 NEW MILITARY TECHNOLOGIES AND NORTHERN WATERS

David Hobbs

New technology is constantly changing the complexion of military operations. Most often new technology simply improves the performance of established weaponry, but radical progress — or a series of incremental changes — can lead to substantial changes in mission concepts and strategy. This is certainly the case in Northern Waters. New technology is constantly being applied by both East and West, and although this leads to an increase in the complexity of military operations, it seldom results in an overall change in the balance of power. But there are exceptions. For example, the enhanced performance of anti-ship weaponry — along with the numerical expansion of Soviet forces — has forced changes in NATO concepts for reinforcing the Northern Region and for conducting naval operations there.

This chapter briefly surveys some of the principal areas in which technology is affecting operations in Northern Waters. Such a survey is inevitably impressionistic rather than comprehensive, since the effects of technological progress in any theatre are all-pervasive. The main areas examined are space and naval technology. Space technology is increasingly affecting terrestrial military operations, and a number of developments in particular will alleviate some of the traditional problems associated with operations in Northern Waters. Naval technology, too, has implications for operations anywhere, but it has specific consequences for Northern Waters. The effects of new technology on land and air operations will be addressed only when they depend upon space technology; otherwise they will receive little mention, because developments do not affect the North very differently from any other region.

Space-based technologies

Space-based systems already play a major role in terrestrial military operations. To cite just one example, over 70 per cent of all American overseas military communications are relayed by satellite. During the next few years, however, satellites will play an even greater role as new, more sophisticated varieties are employed.

Satellites are used for a host of military purposes, but the tasks which are particularly relevant for operations in the Northern Region are surveillance and reconnaissance, communications, navigation and meteorology.[1] Surveillance is best described as a regular monitoring activity, whereas reconnaissance is a search for specific intelligence, generally of a more urgent nature. Many types of surveillance and reconnaissance satellite are in use, and increasingly the two roles are being combined on single-satellite platforms equipped with a variety of sensors.

Photographic surveillance and reconnaissance satellites use optical, infra-red and, in some cases, radar techniques to obtain detailed pictures of areas of interest. Obviously, such satellites are of enormous value, because they allow the strength and locations of forces to be determined, and even permit accurate measurements of, for instance, the dimensions of a tank's gun barrel.

The United States currently employs four types of photographic spy satellite: Big Bird, and the Key Hole types, KH-08, KH-09 and KH-11. Big Bird can perform both wide-area surveillance and close-look reconnaissance. It uses film cameras coupled to multi-spectral scanners to photograph objects as small as 0.3 metres across. Film is processed on board the satellite and is scanned by an optical system which transmits images to receiving stations on Earth. These images are of poorer quality than photographs, so if fine detail is needed, Big Bird can jettison film capsules, which are recovered in mid-air by specially equipped HC-130 aircraft based in Hawaii.

As its name suggests, Big Bird is a large satellite, about 15 metres long and 3 metres in diameter. In order to obtain high-resolution photographs, it is placed into a very low orbit, dropping as low as 160 kilometres. In this type of orbit, an object would usually decay in about a week because of atmospheric drag. Big Bird, however, is equipped with rocket motors which periodically nudge the satellite back into position, extending its orbital life to about 200 days.

Fewer details are available about the Key Hole spy satellites. KH-08 and KH-09 are known to be film-returning satellites used for photographing high-priority targets. Low orbits are used, which limit their operational time to about 4 months. KH-11 is similar in size to Big Bird but does not use film. Instead a digital imaging system is used, which reportedly can achieve resolutions comparable to Big Bird's, despite KH-11's greater operational altitude. Its imaging system enables information to be made available almost instantaneously, and the satellite's orbital life is about two years. According to some reports,[2] a radar scanner is also carried which is capable of obtaining images through cloud-cover. A new spy satellite — KH-12 — is said to be under development, and, though few details are available, this will probably be able to provide pictures with an even better resolution than its predecessors.

The Soviet Union still relies heavily on photographic rather than data-imaging spy satellites. Orbital lifetimes vary between 14 and 60 days, depending upon the type. These short lifetimes explain why the Soviet Union launches about 35 photo-reconnaissance missions per year, compared with the American rate of around three per year.

Complementing the superpowers' spy satellites is a battery of eavesdropping satellites, which gather electronic intelligence (ELINT). These ELINT satellites — known as ferrets — are used to monitor everything from communications to missile-test telemetry. Ferrets can establish radar 'fingerprints', and enable an adversary's forces to be located and categorized, and can perform essentially similar tasks by monitoring radio traffic. This type of information is obviously useful in assessing an adversary's force dispositions and activities. It also enables known radar sites to be attacked or avoided, and facilitates the development and use of effective electronic countermeasures.

At least two types of American ELINT satellites are known to be in service. One is a subsatellite ferret, which is usually launched along with Big Bird and subsequently boosted into a higher, circular orbit. This type of ferret conducts general surveys, detecting new radar sites and monitoring changes at existing ones. The other type of ELINT satellite is known as Rhyolite. Two are in service in geostationary orbits, one above the Horn of Africa and the other over the Indian Ocean. Despite their huge antennae — the larger of the two is over 20 metres in diameter — their location probably limits their usefulness at high latitudes, but so much secrecy surrounds them that no definitive judgements can be made. Rhyolite is to be replaced by a system known as Aquacade, but beyond the name little more is public knowledge. The Soviet Union employs various sorts of ELINT satellite, including a series of eight ferrets operating in a 650-kilometre orbit at an inclination of 81.2°.

Satellites fitted with ELINT equipment and other sensors are also used for ocean surveillance. The main American satellite system for this purpose is known as White Cloud. The White Cloud system consists of three clusters of satellites spaced at 120° intervals around a 1,100-kilometre orbit inclined at 65.3°. Each cluster consists of three small satellites, dispersed from one parent satellite. The clusters orbit in formation, which allows data from infra-red and millimetre wave sensors on each satellite to be collated. In this way, information can be obtained about surface vessels more than 3,000 kilometres away. Work is proceeding on a successor to White Cloud, which will carry radar, colour scanners, scatterometers and sensitive infra-red detectors. These will provide detailed information about surface vessels and may even enable warm-water trails from submarines to be detected. Research is also in progress to develop satellites capable of monitoring naval vessels, aircraft and missiles.

The Soviet Union makes extensive use of ELINT ocean reconnaissance satellites (EORSATs). These frequently operate in pairs and have low-thrust engines to maintain correct height and spacing. Their purpose is to monitor naval communications and radar emissions. Supplementing EORSATs are radar-equipped ocean reconnaissance satellites (RORSATs). These, too, frequently operate in pairs, and are used to detect and track surface vessels. They are powered by small nuclear reactors which — at the end of a RORSAT's 70-day useful life — are boosted into a higher orbit. On at least three occasions this process has failed and the reactor has re-entered, in one case falling in the Canadian Northwest Territories. EORSATs and RORSATs are known to be used to track American carrier task-forces in particular, but they are also used to monitor 'targets of opportunity', such as the Falklands War.

Assessing the utility of these various intelligence-gathering satellites with respect to the Northern Region is extremely difficult. Satellite operations are among the superpowers' most closely guarded secrets. There is the obvious advantage of assessing, with a high degree of confidence, the nature and numbers of Soviet forces stationed in the Kola Peninsula. In addition, the regular gathering of electronic intelligence would probably provide the most advanced warning of any changes in the level of activity, which are likely to precede a conflict.

In the event of war, intelligence-gathering satellites would probably have the most profound effect on the conduct of naval operations. At present, the dissemination of satellite intelligence is probably too slow to be operationally useful, but that situation is changing as intelligence-gathering and dissemination technologies become both more advanced and widespread. It may soon be possible to locate hostile surface — and perhaps sub-surface — vessels and to relay that data to the relevant friendly forces within an operationally useful space of time. It appears that both super-powers are developing capabilities along these lines, so it is impossible to establish whether any overall advantage will accrue to Western forces or not. It seems certain, however, that naval forces will be detected far more reliably and that engagement distances will increase, since long-range weaponry does exist which could take advantage of the targeting data provided by space-based systems. What can be said, therefore, is that space-based intelligence-gathering systems will undoubtedly make naval operations more complex.

As the complexity of warfare increases, communications become even more essential. Communicating in Northern Waters is extraordinarily difficult, not surprisingly given the size of the area. However, new technology will substantially alleviate the problems involved.

One of the reasons for the relatively poor communications in Northern Waters is that the effectiveness of geostationary satellites decreases as latitude increases. Consequently, satellites have to be placed in orbits which take them nearer the poles in order to plug the gaps in satellite communications networks. At present, the main gap-fillers are three satellites that comprise the Satellite Data System (SDS). These satellites are in highly elliptical orbits passing over the Northern Region. However, the capabilities of these satellites are distinctly limited, and in the event of a conflict they would be used primarily by the USA's Strategic Air Command.

By 1990, however, the Military Strategic-Tactical and Relay (Milstar) system should be operational, which will initially comple-ment and ultimately supersede several existing communications satellite systems. These new satellites will have an enormous communications capacity, and three will be placed in highly elliptical polar orbits, with four in geostationary orbits. In addition, an unspecified number of spare satellites will be placed in very high, secure orbits, to be activated as necessary. Since communications are often described as force multipliers, enhanced communications capabilities in Northern Waters — where forces are precious and existing communications are poor — will be a particularly welcome bonus.

The term 'force multiplier' is also often used in describing another new satellite system — the Global Positioning System (GPS) — whose impact will probably be the most significant so far; undoubtedly it will be the most pervasive. GPS will consist of 18 Navstar satellites placed at regular intervals around three orbital rings, each inclined at 63° to the Equator. Each satellite will transmit signals in two different codes, one for military and the other for civilian use. The military signals will enable a user to establish position to within 15 metres and velocity to within a few centimetres per second. The signals will be encrypted and highly resistant to jamming. User terminals will be sufficiently light and compact to be man-portable. Prototype satellites have already been tested with great success, and the system should be fully operational by the end of 1988.

GPS applications seem almost limitless, and it is already anticipated that the system will service 20,000 users, though this number could ultimately be far larger as new uses suggest themselves when the system is in service. Ships, aircraft, missiles and ground forces will be able to establish position with unprecedented accuracy using passive receivers. This will obviously enable military assets to be employed far more effectively. To cite just a few examples, weapons will be able to be delivered with remarkable precision over any range, so that SLBM accuracies will match those of ICBMs; cruise missiles will be able to navigate without emitting any signals; aircraft will be able to rendezvous for in-flight refuelling without radar or radio assistance; air support for ground forces will be improved; and minesweeping operations will become far more efficient, since swept areas will be mapped more precisely and need not be so large.

However, the benefits of satellite navigation will not be conferred solely on Western forces. The Soviet Union is deploying a constellation of navigation satellites which is almost a carbon copy of GPS. Known as Glonass, it will have both military and civilian users, but since only twelve satellites are planned, its coverage will not be complete. This has led to speculation that Glonass military receivers might be designed to process Navstar's signals, possibly the coarser, civilian frequency. If so, the principle is not new: during World War II, Allied forces opted to use German navigation signals in the Atlantic instead of destroying the transmitters.

Meteorological information is important for the conduct of military operations. Military meteorological satellites have been in use for over 20 years and have evolved quite remarkably. The latest American weather satellites — known as Block 5D — carry various forms of sensor and can transmit data directly to users anywhere in the world. Field and unit commanders — using receivers in a small van — and naval vessels can obtain photographs of their region with a resolution of either 3.7 or 0.61 kilometres. Each photograph covers an area of about 3,000 by 7,400 kilometres. Visible images can be obtained with light levels as low as that from a quarter-moon, while infra-red images are available regardless of lighting conditions. The virtue of the Block 5D system is that no centralized data distribution is necessary: meteorological information is directly available at least twice daily, and possibly more frequently in northern areas.

The Soviet Union operates Meteor 2 weather satellites with a sensor suite broadly similar to Block 5D's. Resolution is believed to be poorer and lower orbits are used, which explains why three are kept operational compared with only two Block 5Ds.

Naval technologies

Progress in terrestrial military technology is also affecting the nature of operations in Northern Waters, and the effect is most profound in the naval sphere. For the Soviet Union, the Kola Peninsula provides easily the most suitable naval basing area. Access to the open sea is denied neither by ice, nor by chokepoints controlled by potential adversaries. Nor does Kola suffer from the logistic difficulties of the naval base at Petropavlovsk on the Kamchatka Peninsula. As a result, around 50 per cent of the Soviet Union's sub-surface fleet and about 30 per cent of its surface fleet are assigned to the Northern Fleet, which also has over 60 per cent of the most modern Soviet SSBNs and almost 70 per cent of the latest surface vessels.[3]

The Northern Fleet has three primary tasks: it provides a large part of the Soviet Union's assured nuclear retaliatory capacity; it threatens NATO's sea lines of communication (SLOCs) between North America and Western Europe; and — along with Soviet ground and air forces — it threatens northern Norway. The introduction of new technology is clearly affecting all these roles, but its influence is most profound on the concept of operations for SSBNs.

Older SSBNs with relatively short-range missiles have to pass through the surveillance systems in the GIUK gap, and must patrol in areas where NATO ASW forces hold sway. However, newer SSBNs fitted with longer-range missiles, such as the SS-N-8, SS-N-18 and SS-N-20, can strike their targets from the Barents and Arctic Seas, where they do not have to run the gauntlet of ever-improving NATO ASW forces, and where they are protected by Soviet naval and air support. This increasing emphasis on operations in the Barents and Arctic Seas is confirmed indirectly by the fact that since 1975 no *Delta*-class SSBNs have been detected passing through the GIUK gap.[4]

To render them even more secure, though, Soviet SSBNs increasingly operate under the Arctic ice, where ASW is hindered by changes in salinity, the background noise from shifting pack-ice, and the physical ice barrier which hampers — or even precludes — the use of surface and air ASW forces. Even so, to launch its missiles an SSBN would have to move into relatively ice-free waters, where it would be easier to detect, track and counter. Consequently, the Soviet Union has developed hardware that allows an SSBN to break through several feet of ice so that missiles can be launched through a patch of open water.[5] This may lead to the adoption of an operating technique known as the 'ice-pick', whereby an SSBN would drift with the ice, practically inert, perhaps for months at a time, ready to forge its way to the surface directly if required.

Naturally, this northward shift in Soviet SSBN operations has not been ignored. US navy hunter-killer submarines now undergo extensive training under the Arctic ice, and new *Los Angeles*-class boats are being modified for under-ice operations.[6] Initial design work has also started on a new class of SSN (submarine(s), nuclear) which will be able to operate more efficiently under ice. In addition, equipment is being developed to detect submarines under the ice by using laser, sonar and other sensors dropped onto the ice.[7]

In addition to the examples described above, a host of new technologies — or refinements of old ones — is being incorporated in naval vessels, both surface and sub-surface. Advances in fields as diverse as data processing, fire control, towed arrays, titanium welding, mines, torpedoes, cruise missiles and propulsion technology are all making their mark. Submarines are becoming faster, quieter and deeper-diving, while their endurance, sensor capabilities and firepower are also improving. Surface vessels, too, are becoming increasingly lethal as the power, efficiency and range of their armaments grow.

These improvements in capability, combined with the numerical growth of the Soviet fleet, have already had consequences for the Northern Waters. Equipment for American reinforcements is now prepositioned, since sea transport appears to be increasingly dangerous. Also, Soviet naval and air assets in the North now appear so formidable that the notion of employing NATO carrier battle-groups north of the GIUK gap is becoming increasingly questionable.[8]

That said, new technology could make southward transit of the GIUK gap decidedly uncomfortable for Soviet surface combatants. Some time ago, the idea was mooted of placing ground-launched, anti-ship cruise missiles on land adjacent to the GIUK gap. A missile like the *Tomahawk*, with a range of about 400 nautical miles, in its anti-ship configuration, could — if well placed — make the GIUK gap extremely hazardous for Soviet forces, though the political costs of such deployments would probably be unacceptable. Nevertheless, the same missile is now being fitted to many American naval vessels, with up to 15 being carried in vertical launching-tubes on new *Los Angeles*-class SSNs, and future SSNs may carry even more. In theory, at least, a combination of surface and sub-surface vessels armed with long-range, anti-ship missiles could pose a major obstacle to Soviet units moving to disrupt NATO's SLOCs. In practice, though, a maritime 'Maginot Line' would be difficult to operate, particularly if submarines — the most survivable weapons carriers — were used as the major launch platforms.

The problem is that, generally speaking, the range of anti-ship missiles exceeds the range of a platform's sensors, and this difficulty is particularly acute in the case of submarines, which have a weapon range that could exceed sensor range by a factor of ten. Not surprisingly, work is in hand to remove this disadvantage in the short term, for surface vessels, by developing long-range radars and helicopter-borne radars. A longer-term, more comprehensive solution entails the networking of target data from such diverse sources as satellites, aircraft and coastal radars. When the technologies needed for this — principally improved communications and data processing — come to fruition, Western navies will be far better equipped to exploit their missile capabilities more efficiently and place Soviet forces more on the defensive.

Targeting difficulties are far less acute for sea-launched, land-attack missiles. Targeting data for ports, airfields and other military facilities can be obtained in advance, so that naval platforms can launch weapons — such as the *Tomahawk* — from safe stand-off ranges. This new capability for naval power projection — both conventional and nuclear — might have major consequences for Northern Waters.

One of the political realities about Northern Waters is that NATO's offensive capabilities are distinctly limited. The nature of its forces in the far north is clearly defensive, and resources for threatening the Kola Peninsula are scarce. However, the very existence of submarines equipped with a powerful, land-attack capability changes the picture dramatically. The threat they pose might cause the Soviet Union to divert still more resources to defensive ASW operations, and the execution of that threat — though hazardous — could substantially disrupt Soviet offensive operations from the Kola Peninsula.

Similarly, ground and air warfare are obviously changing as new technology is absorbed. Few developments, however, are affecting Northern Waters in a different way from any other area. There is, in the North as elsewhere, progress in offensive and defensive systems, but nothing seems likely to alter fundamentally the overall military balance. Certainly some developments give cause for concern, most notably the growth in scale and capability of Soviet amphibious assault forces. In particular, a new Soviet ground-attack aircraft appears likely to enter service. But in the immediate future the threat comes more from Soviet numerical strength than from technological advantage, and the obvious remedy for NATO would be greater numbers, not new technology.

In the more distant future, there are technologies in prospect which may be usefully applied in and around Northern Waters. Some concepts for long-range interdiction using advanced, conventional technologies could help alleviate NATO's numerical disadvantage without the need to pose a politically unacceptable nuclear threat. In addition, there is the possibility that Northern Waters will assume a new strategic significance should ballistic missile defence ever be deployed on a large scale. Such a defence would in all likelihood prompt an increasing emphasis on air-breathing strategic nuclear delivery systems, which could be expected to employ the polar route. It is difficult to assess all the implications of this for Northern Waters, but one consequence might be a substantial increase in Soviet strategic air offensive and defensive deployments. This might form part of a larger strategic balance, but could give rise to a major regional imbalance in the North.

Technology itself is neutral: it favours neither the offensive nor the defensive overall. Technology which confers an advantage on one side in one area generally confers a similar advantage on the other side in another. Progress in missile technology, for example, poses problems for NATO's SLOCs and the reinforcement of the Northern Region. By the same token, it poses problems for the Soviet Union by rendering surface assets more vulnerable and by threatening submarine-launched attacks on the Kola Peninsula. It is impossible to say whether new technology offers more threats than promises in NATO's Northern Waters. All that can be said with certainty is that new technology is increasing the complexity of modern warfare. Most alarming for the West is the erosion of its traditional technological superiority, with the result that numerical comparisons are becoming more meaningful. And in and around Northern Waters, an area often under-emphasized in calculations of the balance of power, numbers increasingly favour the Warsaw Pact.

Notes

1. For more detailed information on the military use of space, see David Hobbs, 'Military Space Systems', in R. Bonds (ed.), *Advanced Technology Warfare* (London: Salamander Books, 1986).
2. R. Turnhill (ed.), *Jane's Spaceflight Directory* (London: Jane's Publishing Co. Ltd, 1984), p. 244.
3. Tomas Ries, 'Defending the Far North', *International Defence Review*, July 1984, pp. 873-80.
4. *Ibid.*
5. Craig Covault, 'Soviet Ability to Fire through Ice Creates New Basing

Mode', *Aviation Week and Space Technology*, 10 December 1984, pp. 16-17.

   6. Nick Childs and Anthony Preston, 'Submarine Developments: World-Wide Review', *Jane's Defence Weekly*, 18 August 1984, pp. 232-9.

   7. As Note 5.

   8. As Note 3.

7 THE CONTROL OF CONFLICT IN NORTHERN WATERS

Elizabeth Young

The concepts

We often talk of 'controlling conflict' but rather seldom define our term. The word 'control' is ambiguous, since in English it means 'command', 'dominate', 'restrain', etc., while in French — another international language — it means 'monitor', 'inspect', and so on. There is a continuity from the French minimum sense to the English maximum which is particularly convenient and which should be kept in mind. 'Conflict' is a simpler concept: 'fight', 'struggle', 'collision', 'clashing', according to *The Concise Oxford Dictionary*. Even in its mildest forms, it prevents cooperation, on which 'control', particularly in the wider sense, depends.

What then are the up-and-coming developments in the Arctic, relating to security or resources, that may 'collide' or 'clash' in such a way as to make 'control' desirable or necessary and which, within the operational time-scale of governments, are likely either to develop inside, or to spread from outside into, the Northern Waters?

Two preliminary points need to be made: first, no single sector in the Arctic, including Northern Waters, can safely be considered as closed or self-sufficient: each sector is part of a complex 'pie' of interpenetrating and interacting systems, natural and man-made. Second, all the Arctic systems are powerfully influenced by, and powerfully influence, much else in the Northern Hemisphere. The experts' temptation is always to abstract individual strands of activity and examine them in isolation. Yet, abstracting events and situations in Northern Waters from their Arctic context will lead to confusion and misconception. It is mainly at the overlaps and interfaces of the various kinds of activity that conflict is likely to threaten.

If these points or areas of clash or collision are to be identified, individual strands of activity must somehow be tagged and, at least conceptually, located; the physical background and its time patterns must be sketched in; the state and non-state human actors

97

must be enumerated; and the pace of developments gauged.[1]

Dyer and Chryssostomidis provide a chart which they describe as 'a first cut approximation at identifying national interests in the Arctic'.[2] It lists seven 'issue areas' in the Arctic: (1) jurisdictional claims; (2) national defence; (3) oil, gas and minerals; (4) transportation and navigation; (5) oceanic and atmospheric research; (6) resources and environments; and (7) native interests.

To these seven, 'development' should be added as an eighth: namely, the kind of development the Soviet Union has embarked upon in Siberia, which is not being pursued elsewhere, but is not negligible for that reason. 'National defence' should be seen to merge into 'international security', which must therefore be added to the second issue area. An examination of these issue areas demonstrates the overlap between resources and security in the region.

Using the headings provided by Dyer and Chryssostomidis, we can identify a number of states as being involved in the Arctic and in that part of the Arctic 'pie' known as the Northern Waters. Even from our sectoral point of view, it is proper to include Japan, because the shortest sea route between Japan and Europe, were it to be openly available to international shipping, would be the Great Circle through the Arctic Ocean.

Ocean nations		Environment nations		Interest nations	
Arctic	Northern Waters	Arctic	Northern Waters	Arctic	Northern Waters
USSR	USSR	Iceland	Sweden	Britain	Britain
Canada	Canada	Sweden	Finland	France	France
Greenland/	Faroes/	Finland		FRG	FRG
Denmark	Greeland/			Japan	Poland
	Denmark			Poland	USA
USA	Shetland/				
	Britain				
Norway	Norway				
	Iceland				

Potential for conflict

Jurisdiction over land is not in serious doubt in Northern Waters, but there are several maritime boundary problems and quasi-jurisdictional and jurisdictional claims[3] which may either lead to dispute or — almost as important — prevent desirable cooperation:

1. Until 1985, the Soviet Union appeared, in its domestic legislation, to be claiming large areas of the Arctic, listing the Kara, Laptev, East Siberian and Chukchi Seas as 'internal' or 'historic' seas. Western objections to these claims were lodged when they were first made. In July 1985, the USSR notified foreign governments of the baselines it was now claiming:[4] these appear not to take in the seas mentioned as internal waters, which is welcome. Nevertheless, the Soviet Union does not always follow normal practice, even in the territorial sea, and this could yet give rise to trouble.

2. Within NATO itself, there is no agreement on the breadth of the territorial sea: the United States, always in theory and sometimes in practice, refuses to admit more than three nautical miles.

3. Soviet-Norwegian boundary disputes and certain kinds of Soviet pressure on Norway, particularly in regard to Svalbard, have so far gone strangely uncommented on by Norway's allies.

4. The Soviet Union's wish to have the Nordic states' independently declared non-nuclear policies converted into a treaty-controlled nuclear-free zone is developing into a kind of quasi-jurisdictional claim, in that the Soviet Union sometimes implies that it has acquired at least a *droit de regard* (a right to supervise) any agreements reached, and even some kind of right to see the non-nuclear policies to which it has become accustomed institutionalized by the Nordic states.[5]

5. The Rockall dispute, though outside the Northern Waters as defined here, has implications for relations between the United Kingdom, Iceland, the Faroes and Ireland.

6. Whether pollution-control zones are a form of national jurisdictional claim, or represent a first step towards the enforcement of international law, is still obscure.

The *security and defence* interests of the various states with a stake in Northern Waters come in many varieties. Superpower national defence interests are different in kind from those of states which are minor parties in an alliance (like Denmark), or which are neutral (like Sweden), or all of whose defence interests are confined within the region (like Iceland's). Within NATO's own councils there is a distinction, which could easily become a difference, between the US view of Soviet activities, actual or potential, in the North Norwegian Sea and the views of the North European Allies.

For the United States, this is an area through which the Soviet Northern Fleet transits to the world's oceans: a 'Blue Seas' event. For the North Europeans, it is an area in which the Soviet Union plays a locally strategic — but not Blue Seas — game of 'grandmother's footsteps'. In the Stockholm CDE negotiations, other concerns have led the NATO allies to insist on excluding Europe's maritime areas from any confidence-building measures the Conference might adopt. As a spokesman from the British Ministry of Defence put it:

> Only those naval activities, such as ship-to-shore combat activities, which form a part of a notifiable activity on land in the CDE Zone are notifiable. The Alliance considered prior to [the] Madrid [CSCE meeting] the balance of advantage in seeking notification of naval exercises but decided that it would be very difficult to develop a concrete, unambiguous and practicable proposal which would be consistent with alliance security, and impose a balanced obligation on NATO and Warsaw Pact Forces.[6]

It might perhaps be thought that an agreement not to conduct exercises without notification in the Exclusive Economic Zone or Fisheries Zone of another country could serve the European purpose.

Meanwhile Soviet naval exercises occur, sometimes to the complete surprise of NATO authorities, around North Norway in what is undoubtedly Norway's EEZ:[7] Soviet weapon tests have been carried out in the disputed area of still undetermined jurisdiction in the Barents Sea; submarines, mini-subs and creepy-crawlies[8] are found, or suspected, not only in Swedish waters but in Norwegian, Greenlandic and Canadian waters too; and exploratory drilling was undertaken just on the Norwegian-claimed median line. These are all activities in pursuit of which more considerate Soviet behaviour might lead to greater confidence being felt by the Norwegians and others.

There is every reason to suppose that Norway would welcome a steadier allied presence in its waters. Until a decade or so ago, a large British distant-water fishing fleet was regularly present in the Barents Sea, together with occasional fisheries research vessels. They are now all gone, and with them certain useful bottom rungs on the ladder of deterrence, which at sea begins with just such a modest but unmistakable national presence.

The superpowers' own relationship in Northern and Arctic Waters is intercontinental, whereas NATO Europe's with the Soviet Union is local and close. The USA's northern position, unlike the Soviet Union's, is hung about with allies, most of which are unwilling to harbour nuclear weapons; even right-wing governments look doubtfully at some of the US military efforts and activities. President Reagan's Strategic Defence Initiative (SDI) evokes little enthusiasm outside interested parties, and neither Canada nor Greenland are likely to provide house-room for SDI-related equipment.[9] Yet it is over the Arctic that the first two layers of defences against Soviet ICBMs would need to spark into action: SDI-related installations could well be submarine- or ice-based in Northern Waters.

Oil, gas and minerals are present in vast quantities under the Arctic, but because the resources of the western Soviet Union are near exhaustion, the USSR is going to be increasingly dependent on Siberian supplies for domestic use and export. Siberia's resources are beyond the range of normal land transport, which means there will be an unprecedented requirement for general shipping, for ice-strengthened and icebreaking shipping and for other, less conventional, forms of transport.[10]

In addition, because drilling in the Barents Sea presents an easier prospect than anything further east, the Soviet dispute with Norway over the boundary delineation there is understandably important.

Arctic transport is an economic necessity for the Soviet Union, and the ever-increasing use of the Northern Sea Route is essential for the development of Siberia.[11] Soviet desires and occasional claims to control the route, though once again understandable, are not compatible with international law. The USSR has already developed a substantial lead in Arctic marine transportation (as outlined in Chapter 4). However, the international community will probably not accept that the carriage of cargoes into and out of Siberia should be a permanent Soviet monopoly, and one that could reach out into other Arctic waters. Given the potential military significance of the kinds of vessel the Soviet Union is acquiring, NATO governments should be taking an interest in these developments.

National defence has regrettably long been the prime mover in *oceanic and atmospheric research,* rather than the kind of international science out of which grew the Antarctic regime. The US navy funds great swathes of Arctic research, not only in the United States. For the Soviet Union, economic concerns and defence interests act in parallel, northern navigation and sciences being vital to both.

Soviet economic and environmental interests may conflict, in that the programme to divert southwards some of the north-flowing rivers may have harmful results in the North. These could be local, altering the ice regime of the Kara and other seas, or have wider consequences that affect the climate of the whole Northern Hemisphere. Institutions both in the United States and in the United Kingdom are studying the foreseeable impact of schemes which even Soviet officials describe as 'controversial'.[12] Research and monitoring should, on such a subject, be fully cooperative; but it is not, for obvious military reasons.

Both superpowers have missile-firing submarines regularly cruising under the ice, where they have seemed safer from the other side's anti-submarine warfare than in the open ocean, or at least likely to present different ASW problems. The upper ocean in the marginal ice zone is a region of extreme accoustic variability and has a high and incalculable ambient noise level due to ice-floe collisions. A Western research effort, MIZEX, is studying the determinants of the position of the ice-edge, and its results will be as significant for strategists as they will be for glaciologists and climatologists.

The symbiotic relationship between national defence, narrowly defined, and the acquisition of information crucially important for understanding and eventually protecting vulnerable global systems, presents problems currently not even addressed. The fact that the drifting ice-stations, set up on ice-floes and from which research of all kinds is conducted, have no status in international law may easily generate disputes as more and more use is made of the Arctic for military purposes.

Resources and the environment can also be a cause of tension in Northern Waters. As well as non-living resources, fish can give rise to conflict, as seen in the Cod Wars between Britain and Iceland. The insertion of the massive Spanish fishing fleet into the

European Community's Common Fisheries Policy is unlikely to be incident-free. The Norwegian electorate's decision to remain outside the Community and Greenland's decision to remove itself were both to a large degree caused by politico-economic conflicts about fish. Despite a record of bureaucratic insensitivity in some European countries to fisheries matters, cooperative fisheries management now seems to be on the way, at least in Northern Waters. Nevertheless, discord between Greenland and Iceland over the management of common stocks and third-party quota allocations appears to be developing.[13]

Whales, which always trigger popular concern, are acoustically vulnerable to submarine noise, and also to being blocked in by ice re-forming in the wake of ice-breakers.

Nuclear-powered ships (submarines, Soviet icebreakers), among which accidents have been reported,[14] are present in the Arctic more than anywhere else and will soon be joined by Soviet nuclear-powered icebreaking merchant ships.[15] International rules governing such ships have not yet been formally established by the International Maritime Organization, given no doubt the small number of civilian ships to which they would at present apply. In any case, naval and certain other classes of state-owned vessels would not be covered by such rules. However, the Soviet Union is completing its first nuclear-powered icebreaking freighters, which would certainly seek business in the international market and therefore entry into other states' waters and ports, as well as passage through the high seas and high seas ice.

The control of pollution within one country's offshore zone can have little overall effect, except perhaps on shipping. Northern Waters are part of the Arctic Ocean, a single physical system which has a steady, rather slow circulation. Most of its pollution has its origins elsewhere: the pollutants responsible for the 'Arctic haze' consist to some extent at least of particulate matter injected into the air as industrial waste in lower latitudes; and other pollutants reach the Arctic via the inflowing Atlantic waters and down the rivers.[16] Little as yet is being done to control it. In June 1985, the Soviet authorities refused British government scientists permission to conduct research in the Soviet EEZ water column into the progress of caesium originating from Sellafield.

The Inuit Circumpolar Conference (ICC), which gathers together the *indigenous inhabitants* of the Arctic Circle, is based in Greenland and might not on the face of it affect security or resources in the Northern Waters. On the other hand, the Greenland home-rule parliament's vote for a nuclear-free zone in their country may well give rise to difficulties between Denmark, not itself a particularly pro-nuclear society, and the United States.[17] The Inuit may come to view the human rights provisions of the Helsinki Final Act as relevant to the rights of the indigenous peoples of the Soviet Arctic, who have not so far been allowed to attend its meetings.

In Canada and Greenland, indigenous economic and cultural interests have frequently clashed with proposals from outside for *development*. This has mostly been intended to be 'expeditionary', i.e., with the workforce moving in to do the job but not settle. Until recently, Soviet policy was to settle the North, but this fell foul of the disinclination of ordinary citizens to move permanently, and the industrialization of Siberia will now perforce depend on permanent installations operated by a transient workforce. Industrialization on- and offshore will mean new sources of pollution reaching the Arctic by river, sea or air. The Soviet record in environmental protection and foresight is not sufficiently encouraging for the other inhabitants of the Northern Hemisphere to ignore what is happening or may happen.

The tools of control

So much for the potential for conflict and for unwillingness to cooperate. What of the possibilities for control? The Arctic and Northern Waters have nothing like the Antarctic Treaty, under which international science flourishes, environmental matters are actively observed, weapons are kept out and sovereignty claims are frozen. The Antarctic is in the public eye, the Arctic is not.[18] The 1920 Treaty concerning Svalbard is one example of the few signs of any international desire to control militarization and environmental matters in the North.

Several existing arms control measures apply in or are relevant to the Arctic and Northern Waters:

1. The Partial Test Ban Treaty (1963) protects the Arctic, as well as the rest of the world, from certain nuclear test explosions in the atmosphere and in the water. The area could nevertheless suffer from the fall-out from peaceful nuclear explosions (PNEs).

2. The Seabed Treaty (1970) applies in the Arctic as elsewhere, but its exclusion of the shelf within twelve miles of the coast creates loopholes in an area where baselines are notoriously difficult to establish with accuracy. The Treaty places no ban on creepy-crawlies.

3. The Treaty Banning Environmental Modification for Hostile Purposes (1976) only bans intentional modifications, and in the Northern Waters careless and unforeseen ones are likely to damage the environment long before intentionally hostile ones do.

4. The Non-Proliferation Treaty (1968) is subscribed to by all the circumpolar states.

In none of the present disarmament negotiating fora is anything being discussed that is specifically relevant to the Arctic or to Western Europe's Northern Waters: indeed, rather the opposite. As already mentioned, confidence-building measures under discussion at Stockholm would not apply, by NATO states' choice, to sea areas as such.

Among the intermediate-range nuclear weapons under discussion at the *Geneva Umbrella Negotiations* between the United States and the Soviet Union, it appears that Soviet shorter-range sea-launched missiles, such as *Shaddock*, which are certainly deployed in Northern Waters, have perhaps for the first time been mentioned.

Proposals for a *Nordic Nuclear-Free Zone*, which go back some quarter of a century, and which would seek to freeze the non-nuclear policies of the four Nordic states, have been damaged by Soviet naval activities in the Swedish archipelago and elsewhere. Nevertheless, such proposals are regularly repeated.[19] Should any kind of movement towards the institutionalization of a nuclear-free zone begin, there can be little doubt that pressures would emerge to extend it into the larger Nordic area, to include Iceland, the Faroes and Greenland.[20] In fact, the 'Nordic Balance' has over time responded delicately and usefully to developments outside and within the area, and, were the independent policy-making of these states to be frozen, Europe would be deprived of a particularly valuable political thermometer.

Suggestions are sometimes made that the superpowers should create '*sanctuaries*' in the Arctic, within which strategic missile-launching submarines would be guaranteed immunity from the anti-submarine warfare activities of the other side. It is even assumed that Soviet SSBN strategy already embodies the idea, though this has been disputed.[21] The characteristics of the latest Soviet SSBNs suggest no such thing, and meanwhile American research into technologies for locating Soviet submarines through any kind of ice continues. For the time being, the idea of SSBN sanctuaries under the ice in Northern and Arctic Waters shows little promise as either a formal or informal arms control device.[22]

Article 234 of the 1982 Law of the Sea Convention would allow the circumpolar states to decide on rules for navigation in ice-covered waters within their EEZs, and cooperation among them in devising such rules could go some way towards providing a single navigation regime for the whole Arctic. Article 123 encourages states bordering on 'enclosed or semi-enclosed' seas to cooperate in protecting them, and this would be to the whole area's interest.

Such cooperation faces two major problems: one is the increasing confrontation across the pole of the superpowers, from which Northern Waters are not excluded; the other is that it is the Soviet side of the Arctic that most needs international attention. It is more used, and for more purposes, than the Western side. But at the CDE in Stockholm, Soviet officials regularly berate the West for its devotion to the idea of 'transparency': 'opacity' is a matter of principle to them in the Arctic, as elsewhere.

Conclusions

Despite the spider's web of relationships that links the 13 nations directly interested in Arctic/Northern Waters matters, there is no underlying framework on which a regime to limit and control conflict can easily be erected. If it is needed, it must be created. Certain usable elements are available — bilateral cooperation agreements, certain provisions in the UNCLOS text, the CSCE and ECE environmental provisions, the arrangements embodied in the Svalbard Treaty, and the peculiar legitimacy of the Inuit Circumpolar Conference, which represents the indigenous community. There is also the Comité Arctique, which — though unofficial — has full circumpolar membership, and whose research projects and conferences address matters of direct interest to all the inhabitants of the Northern Hemisphere. Antarctica's international status, and the regime underpinning it, developed out of cooperative scientific activity: the question for the Arctic is whether the massive research activities going on there can be steered towards fully international cooperation and coordination.

Notes

1. The report by H.D. Smith and C.S. Lalwani, *The North Sea: Sea Use Management and Planning* (Cardiff: The North Sea Research Unit Centre for Marine Law and Policy, University of Wales Institute of Science and Technology, 1984), is a pilot study for a true systems analysis of one small, heavily used, sea. Eventually the Arctic/Northern Waters will need something of the same sort.

2. *Arctic Technology and Policy*, Proceedings of the Second Annual MIT Sea Grant College Programme Lecture and Seminar and the third annual Robert Bruce Wallace Lecture (Washington: Hemisphere Publishing Corporation, 1983), p. 44.

3. See Birnie, Ch. 2.

4. 'Notice to Mariners No. 4450/85' (dated, however, 15 January 1985). Baselines in the Sea of Okhotsk were communicated in 'Soviet Notice to Mariners No. 4604/84'; extensive new claims are not being made in it.

5. See below, p. 105.

6. *House of Lords Hansard*, 2 February 1984, Written Answers, Lord Trefgarne.

7. For instance, the major Soviet exercise carried out in late March and early April 1984, preparations for which had not been observed by the West. In the event, according to *NATO Review*, February 1985, the exercise included 'about half of the Northern Fleet's major service combatants, and a high proportion of the submarine order-of-battle participated. This was the largest exercise of its type yet seen' (p. 20). Another exercise on the same scale was carried out in July 1985. *NATO Review*, December 1976 and February 1985, and its predecessor *NATO Letter*, September 1970, published three series of maps showing Soviet naval activities in Northern Waters. These bring to mind Admiral Gorshkov's statements in his *Sea Power of the State*, (Oxford: Pergamon, 1979), pp. 65-109.

8. Creepy-crawlies are tractored submarine vehicles which can be driven along the sea-bed. They have been used by the Soviet Union most noticeably in Norwegian and Swedish internal waters.

9. For Canadian reactions, see *Aviation Week and Space Technology*, 25 March 1985, pp. 25-6.

10. For example, in 1984 cargo was unloaded directly onto land-fast ice on one of the Svalbard archipelago islands by a 'large tonnage vessel' escorted by two icebreakers, according to Moscow Radio (BBC SWB SU/W/1289/A/10, 28 April 1984).

11. See Elizabeth Young, 'Soviet Arctic Shipping', *Sibérie 1: cultures et sociétés de l'est, 3* (Paris: Institut d'Etudes Slaves, 1985).

12. For example, the Climatic Research Unit at the University of East Anglia. The plans to divert rivers, approved under Brezhnev, are at last being subjected to far stricter cost-benefit analysis, and may not now go ahead.

13. *News from Iceland*, September 1985, p. 24.

14. *Jane's Defence Weekly*, 19 January 1985.

15. *The Daily Telegraph*, 'Nuclear First for Soviet Shipping', 28 May 1985.

16. Immanuel Kant wrote in 1795 about the Arctic Shores: 'The providential care of nature excites our wonder above all when we hear of the driftwood which is carried, whence no one knows, to those treeless shores; for without the aid of this

material the natives could construct neither their boats, nor their weapons, nor their huts for shelter.'

17. See Clive Archer, 'Greenland and the Atlantic Alliance', *Centrepiece 7* (Aberdeen: Centre for Defence Studies, 1985).

18. The British government, for instance, spends on Arctic research a minute proportion of what it spends on Antarctic research, and its newest research vessel, the *Charles Darwin*, is not even ice-strengthened.

19. See Clive Archer, 'Deterrence and Reassurance in Northern Europe', *Centrepiece 6* (Aberdeen: Centre for Defence Studies, 1984), pp. 17-47.

20. See, for example, the European Nuclear Disarmament special report, *North Atlantic Network: The Alternative Alliance* (London: END, 1984).

21. J.S. Breemer, 'The Soviet Navy's SSBN Bastions: Evidence, Influence, and Alternative Scenarios', *Journal of the Royal United Services Institute*, March 1985. See also the letter disputing Breemer's arguments from Commander J.J. Tritten, US navy, in the September 1985 issue of the same journal.

22. The article, 'Nuclear War at Sea', by Desmond Ball, in the Winter 1985/6 issue of *International Security*, is also very relevant.

8 THE UNITED STATES: RESOURCE INTERESTS

Melvin Conant

Northern Waters, as defined in the introduction of this book, are a major area of strategic interest for the United States.[1] Along with defence issues, though, the substantial living and mineral resources found within this zone and on its margins, including most importantly petroleum, deserve special attention. But apart from fishing in the area, the USA has no direct interests, even in petroleum assets, such as they may prove to be; in Northern Waters these lie wholly inside the jurisdiction of other states. However, some of the prospects in offshore Canada may attract the requisite huge investments only if a large share of their anticipated yield is destined for the US market.

Much has been happening, within a broader geographical definition of Northern Waters, that impinges on US concerns, including defence of the US Arctic and the Bering Strait and the security of the logistic systems vital to US exploitation of the resources of its Arctic lands. Consequently there is a greater eagerness to monitor how these waters are used, and by whom.

Only oil and gas are of importance to the USA in the more broadly defined Northern Waters area. Nothing else — fisheries, iron, gold, lead, zinc, silver, copper or coal — approaches the commercial significance of the petroleum reserves already discovered, let alone the additional oil and gas that may yet prove to be economically recoverable. Even so, the United States is highly likely to remain partly import-dependent for its domestic oil and gas reserves; hence the great importance attached to the significant Alaskan discoveries of 1968, which were the largest for the USA since World War II. Nothing comparable to Prudhoe Bay on the North Slope of Alaska has been discovered since, on- or offshore, or in what are described as the 'Lower 48' (states), or in the offshore Canadian Arctic. It is possible that the largest discoveries of oil and gas yet to be made within US territory will be in the Alaskan region.

It is highly probable that Alaskan oil and gas will be generally regarded as destined to meet rising US petroleum needs and will therefore not enter international energy trade. The still declining

US reserves/production ratio virtually guarantees a continuing dependence on oil imports. These have increased since economic recovery began, amounting now to about five million barrels a day, and are likely to rise even more. Moreover, US imports of Canadian natural gas continue and could well increase.

Although there is at present no legal restriction on Alaskan oil exports from sources other than the North Slope (Prudhoe Bay), the public view has tended to be that Alaskan resources constitute a kind of national strategic asset with wide geopolitical significance. It is for this reason that Alaskan energy assets are in a special category and will be closely linked to the defence and security interests of the United States.

Moreover, the US interest in Arctic petroleum could include similarly high-cost Canadian Arctic petroleum reserves offshore, which may only be exploited if the US energy market requires it. It can be argued that there is a strong potential US interest in eventual access to Canadian oil and gas reserves from the region of the Mackenzie delta and the Beaufort Sea.

These prospective US (or Canadian) supplies could be conveyed overland or by a maritime passage whose technical feasibility through ice, if not its economic advantage, is reasonably assured. The US interest in the western hemispheric Arctic energy resources thus extends eastward from its own territory and includes the Canadian northwest Arctic and the eastern Arctic Islands as well.

The major dispute between Canada and the United States which has resource and security implications involves the two nations' different claims concerning the national or international status of key Arctic Island passages. The Canadian assertion of national control is counter to US views. Clearly, the difference between these attitudes has commercial and defence implications. If relations between the two countries were to deteriorate, an unfortunate confrontation would probably be unavoidable, especially over the types of passage permitted to submarines in international law. As for civil maritime passage, the Canadian Arctic Waters Pollution Prevention Act has been generally accepted as a prudent non-discriminatory move, foreshadowed in Article 234 of the 1982 Law of the Sea Convention. It affords a useful (and perhaps essential) constraint on inadequately prepared vessels of any nationality when approaching the region of the Canadian Arctic Islands. Since it is highly unlikely that Canada would apply unreasonable regulations and controls affecting maritime commerce in these waters, serious differences between Canada and the United States over which law governs passage are improbable. Indeed, differences between Canada and the United States over the status of the former's Arctic waters (as internal or international) do not appear to have compromised US military uses of the Arctic, especially submarine operations.

The unresolved dispute between Canada and the United States over the division of the Beaufort Sea acquired importance only with the discovery of Arctic oil and gas. But there is no anticipation of this matter becoming a major issue if widely practised measures are implemented for joint or shared exploitation of resources lying in areas of uncertain ownership.

Of the other Arctic disputes involving resources and security issues, the Svalbard dispute over Norway's claim for control of the continental shelf, with its petroleum implications, is in a very different category and may not be open to compromise because of the extreme defence importance of the region both to the Soviet Union and to NATO. Similarly, although the United States is not a party to the ongoing boundary dispute between Norway and the Soviet Union with respect to the Barents Sea, there are clear defence implications in what might otherwise be viewed as an issue relating chiefly to a division of resources.

What is relatively surprising about US defence interests and energy resources in the Arctic is that the former predates by several decades the discovery of petroleum reserves. Long before Prudhoe Bay, the US and Canadian Arctic played a part in several vitally important detection systems, with the Distant Early Warning (DEW) line monitoring the approach of any Soviet strategic bombers.[2] Now, to defence concerns is added the importance of oil and gas. Very few people would have linked the two until 1968. While there is still no agreed North American continental view of energy, there has been for nearly fifty years a shared commitment by the United States and Canada to their common defence and, of course, since 1949, to their membership of NATO.

Resources

The high importance attached to US Arctic oil and gas reserves reflects the failure over many years to discover fields of supergiant size (five billion barrels of recoverable oil) in the Lower 48 states, on- or offshore. Of the remaining US areas believed to have very good potential, Alaska is given special attention. Although there have been no discoveries to match the 1968 find in Prudhoe Bay, which revealed some 9.6 billion barrels of recoverable oil (the largest single oilfield ever found in the United States), there have been estimates that eastward along the Alaskan northern coast, both on- and offshore, may lie perhaps 12.1 billion barrels all told of recoverable oil. Interest is also being shown in the potential for recoverable west coast oil in offshore basins, notably the Navarin Basin (farthest westward in the midst of the Bering Sea), and St. George and Norton Sound closer inshore.

The surplus of gas in the Lower 48 states continues to stymie the early development of Alaskan reserves (North Slope gas is currently used for injection programmes to maintain oilfield pressures). If the necessary equipment were in place, Alaskan gas would compete with Canadian exports to the United States. Whether the USA reapplies itself to the now deferred Alaska Natural Gas Transportation System hook-up with Canadian pipelines (costing, maybe, $40 billion), or opts for the alternative all-Alaska system (about $25 billion), will depend to some extent on an assessment of the security implications for the United States of the former (overland through Canada) and the latter (with long maritime passages).

It is altogether possible that these expectations of discovering very large Alaskan (and Canadian Arctic) petroleum reserves will not be met.[3] The lack of significant discoveries will have two unavoidable consequences: the USA will become more dependent on ever-higher volumes of oil imports; and, as other non-OPEC sources decline in their production, the USA will increase its dependence on the Middle East. Hence the sense of urgency and the link to security. Thus, a new element in US defence interests in the area could well be the secure passage of crude tankers and even, conceivably, of Liquefied Natural Gas (LNG), if the domestic and international market were of a size which made US Arctic LNG competitive. Never before would transit of these waters have been of significant commercial interest, whether eastbound (via Canadian waters) or westbound around Point Barrow and thence south through the Bering Straits into the North Pacific. Either route is beset with awesome weather and navigational

hazards, with seasonal differences in ice encounters and mountainous seas, especially in the Bering Straits and Sea.

One of the more promising areas in the Bering Sea lies eastward
of the line dividing Soviet and US territories and is inclusive of the
Navarin Basin. The Navarin Basin is therefore yet another addition
to the growing US stake in the resources of the Bering Sea and
passage through it for commercial and naval vessels alike. The
exact location of the US/Soviet boundary line has been subject to
dispute.

In addition, Valdez, on the southern coast of Alaska, is of
importance to energy supply, since it is the terminal for North
Slope crude (a pipeline of 800 miles) and other nearby oil production. In the same vicinity, Cook Inlet, much of which lies north
of latitude 60°N, already has an LNG terminal, and this could be
further developed as an alternative route if North Slope or other
Alaskan gas were to be further exploited. Defence of these facilities, and of the maritime passages to them, is very much a factor
in US security planning. If greater use were not made of Valdez or
Cook Inlet for the movement of additional energy supplies, there
are still other long-term alternatives involving Canadian territory,
for example the entirely overland Alaska Natural Gas Transportation System, on which, as mentioned earlier, agreement was
once reached. Nevertheless, resource and defence interests in the
US Arctic, and its waters, are likely to grow in importance, not just
because of American energy concerns, but because of the likelihood that greater use will be made by the USSR of the Bering
Staits and Sea at the eastern end of its Northern Sea Route.

In addition to the potential commercial passage, there are the
submarine, surface and air patrols through these waters by the
USSR and the United States alike. The area is, for the former, yet
another indispensable gap through which Soviet warships and
seasonal commercial traffic must pass, in this case from the
Siberian Arctic passage past Kamchatka to the Sea of Okhotsk,
and then to Vladivostok in the Sea of Japan and points beyond.
This is another gap the United States must close in the event of
war.

The link, then, between US Arctic energy resources and
defence is best expressed in the observation that for another two to
three years (as in 1984), Alaskan oil production will make up
about 20 per cent of total US domestic oil supply, and that it
moves through a single pipeline to the export facility at Valdez on

the Alaskan southern coast, and from there it goes to the US west coast or to the Isthmus pipeline and the Caribbean. There are no other routes for Alaskan oil. It is, therefore, a resource of great importance. Quite possibly, if further exploration and development take place, and other US reserves are not increased, as is foreseen, the importance of Alaskan oil (and gas) — and Canadian Arctic reserves — to the nation will become even greater.

Apart from the distant prospects of US markets receiving Canadian eastern Arctic Islands gas, and the possibility that its transportation could involve pipeline and maritime systems, there is no other US resource interest in North American Northern Waters that has defence implications. Hence the point has to be reiterated that whereas, in the upper reaches of the Atlantic and moving into the Arctic regions proper, the Western allies have a meld of defence and energy interests, the United States does not, at least directly. There are, as yet, no proven reserves of oil and gas in Northern Waters above 60° latitude that would be of significant interest to anyone, with the single exception of offshore Norway.

Notes

1. See Ch. 9.
2. Report of Secretary of State Harold Brown to the Congress in the 1982 financial year (Washington: Department of Defense, 1981), p. 1212.
3. The failure of the Mukluk operation near Prudhoe Bay was a disappointment, and Prudhoe Bay's production of some 1.5 million barrels a day is expected to decline. For a survey of current activities, see F.E. Niering Jr, 'Alaska: Key to Future Oil Supply', *Petroleum Economist*, July 1984.

9 THE UNITED STATES: STRATEGIC INTERESTS

Steven Miller

In terms of both nuclear and conventional strategy, the North Atlantic and the Norwegian and Barents Seas have, in the past two decades, become the site of intensifying military competition between the great powers. However, the current military context in the Northern Waters region is shaped primarily by the interests and capabilities of the USA and USSR in the area, and although the great powers have vital interests at stake in the northern seas, it is really relative changes in Soviet and American capabilities that have caused the Northern Waters to occupy a more prominent place in Western defence concerns.

Safeguarding the sea-lanes

The Northern Waters are significant in US defence policy for two reasons. First, in this century, US military intervention has been required more than once to preserve the balance of power in Europe, and today it is unlikely that, in the face of Soviet power, a balance could be established in Europe without US commitment. In short, the USA now plays the UK's traditional balancing role, and the North Atlantic has consequently become America's English Channel — providing both separation from and, more importantly, connection to the affairs of Europe. It is through this artery that the United States is able to bring its industrial and military power to bear in Europe.

Overall control of Northern Waters and Europe's Northern Flank is an important factor in the security of the SLOCs in the North Atlantic. Because of the USA's interests in Europe, these sea-lanes have played a traditional part in its security policy. Indeed, twice this century global wars have occasioned great struggles for control of these sea-lanes, as Germany sought to sever the oceanic ties which connected the United States to its European allies.

The challenge this represented to fundamental US interests was often obscured by idealistic and ideological wartime propaganda,

115

but it was clearly recognized by those with good strategic vision. Walter Lippmann, for example, put forward the case in early 1917 for American entry into World War I on the grounds that Germany was threatening to cut 'the vital highways of our world' and thereby prevent normal intercourse with what he called 'the Atlantic Community'. To Lippmann, the inescapable conclusion was that German domination of the Atlantic would be unacceptable: 'The safety of the Atlantic highway is something for which America should fight'.[1] Lippmann returned to this theme during World War II. Writing in 1940, he expressed the belief that 'America's security was vitally connected to Britain's independence and Anglo-American control of the Atlantic'.[2]

This long-standing interest has endured into the nuclear age. Indeed, with the formation of NATO, US security has become more formally and explicitly bound up with Europe than ever before. In 1967 NATO adopted a 'flexible response' strategy which, by emphasizing the possibility of a lengthy period of conventional defence, accentuated the importance of the Atlantic sea-lanes. The strategy seeks to forestall a quick victory by the Soviet Union in central Europe in order to allow NATO's overall material superiority to be brought to bear in the form of sea-borne reinforcements.[3] Should the Soviet Union acquire the capability to seriously disrupt the Atlantic sea-lanes, NATO's objectives would become very difficult, if not impossible, to fulfil.

Because the major threat to the security of the SLOCs is the Soviet Northern Fleet, based at Murmansk on the Kola Peninsula, and because domination of the Norwegian Sea would provide the Soviet Union with a strong position from which it could attack US and NATO forces in the North Atlantic, this whole region must occupy a prominent place in NATO strategy. If another war does occur, it is conceivable that 'the Battle of the Norwegian Sea' could be a decisive one: it has been said that, although World War III will not be won on the Northern Flank, it could be lost there.[4]

NATO strategy calls for sea-borne reinforcement of the Central Front, which requires control of the sea-lanes in the North Atlantic, which depends to a considerable extent on control of the Norwegian Sea, which in turn will be strongly influenced by the outcome of the land battle in Norway. This chain of logic leads to the conclusion that events of great significance could take place in northern Norway, thousands of miles from the primary theatre of action, along a Soviet–Norwegian border far above the Arctic

Circle and presently defended, on the Norwegian side, by the 120 stout-hearted men of the South Varanger Garrison. Although Norway's defences are more formidable than is generally acknowledged, few US defence analysts are comfortable with the thought of such high stakes riding on developments so remote from the reach of US military power.

The first reason, then, that the Northern Waters are significant to the United States is that US grand strategy, as currently embodied in NATO, requires control of the North Atlantic so that America may reinforce its European allies by sea. In safeguarding the sea-lanes, Northern Waters have a prominent role to play.

Strategic anti-submarine warfare

The Northern Waters are also significant for a second important, if more specific, reason: the Barents and Norwegian Seas are deployment and transit areas for Soviet ballistic missile submarines (SSBNs). If the United States is to conduct strategic anti-submarine activities, it must do so in this region.

Increasingly it has been revealed that the USA's operational doctrine for employing its strategic nuclear forces has long called for counterforce attacks against Soviet strategic forces.[5] But the implications of this revelation for US naval policy seem not to have been noticed: not only is strategic anti-submarine warfare consistent with the logic of US strategic nuclear doctrine, but it would surely be required in any significant counterforce operation. This means that it is quite likely that the US navy is deployed in Northern Waters in such a way as to make these operations possible.[6] In wartime, consequently, it is possible that the Northern Waters would be the site of a major US effort to destroy the Soviet strategic submarine fleet — a substantial portion of the Soviet Union's strategic reserve force — and of an intense Soviet effort to prevent that destruction.

Thus, the second reason why the Northern Waters are important in US security policy has to do with the concern of the US navy to carry out, in accordance with the counterforce tendencies in the USA's operational strategic doctrine, strategic ASW against the large Soviet SSBN force deployed in Northern Waters. When combined with the US need to control the sea-lanes of the North Atlantic, this means that the Northern Waters have a potentially large role to play in either conventional or nuclear war between East and West.

Although these US interests in the Northern Waters are long-standing, for many years they did not occupy a very large place in US defence concerns. US naval predominance resulted in confidence that Western interests were not in jeopardy: there was, for much of the nuclear age, no doubt about the ability of the US navy to carry out its assigned missions.[7]

A changed maritime situation

A number of trends evident in the course of the past decade have combined to bring the Northern Waters into the limelight and make them a source of increasing concern. Several improvements in Soviet naval capabilities have substantially increased the threat to Western maritime interests and drawn attention to the Northern Waters as the region most directly affected by the Soviet naval build-up.

The evolving pattern of Soviet naval exercises since the late 1960s has served as evidence that, with its increased capabilities, the Soviet Union will attempt to dominate the Norwegian Sea and may try to interrupt NATO's sea lines of communication in the North Atlantic. Such an effort, if successful, will have the effect of interfering with US strategic ASW operations in Northern Waters and will undermine NATO's strategy of relying on sea-borne rein-forcements from the United States in the event of a long con-ventional war. Concern that the Soviet navy might be able to pre-vent the reinforcement by sea on which Norway depends led the Norwegian government to prepare for reinforcement by air and to sign an agreement with Washington in December 1980 on the prestocking of equipment in Norway for use by US marines.

As a direct result of the Soviet military build-up in the North, the outcome of naval conflict there is no longer nearly certain to be favourable to the United States. Indeed, in ocean areas near to the USSR (such as the Barents Sea and northern Norwegian Sea) the balance of forces probably favours the Soviet Union, and US forces which ventured into these waters would almost surely suffer serious losses. Further away, in the southern portion of the Norwegian Sea for example, the Soviet Union has a weaker grip, but it has still acquired the ability to compete with NATO forces for control. In the sea-lanes of the North Atlantic, the intensity of the Soviet threat depends on Soviet willingness to sacrifice other missions and accept the heavy losses that would most probably result from operating in the midst of powerful NATO deployments, but it is now possible to imagine circumstances in which the Soviet navy could disrupt NATO shipping. The Carnegie Panel on US Security made these same points in reverse when it concluded that, 'as American forces move closer to the Soviet Union to perform missions, their chances of success drop dramatically'.[8]

All this means that several of the missions contemplated for the US navy have become much more risky and demanding. Strategic ASW will become increasingly difficult as more and more Soviet strategic submarines are deployed in heavily defended Soviet waters. Offensive actions by US surface combatants, whether taken to protect the sea-lanes or to aid in the defence of Norway, are likely to be costly and uncertain of success.

The impact of the growth in Soviet naval capability has been heightened by the considerable disarray in US naval policy in recent years. The main cause for concern about the adequacy of US naval power in the past 15 years has been the dramatic decline in the navy's size. In the late 1960s it had roughly 1,000 ships, including nearly 400 major surface combatants. Today the fleet is about half that size. In addition, US naval policy has been hampered by a series of unresolved controversies. For example, the Soviet navy's mission structure is disputed. Although it can bring formidable capabilities to any mission to which it devotes its full resources, the Soviet navy is not capable of pursuing simultaneously all of its potential missions (including the protection of its own sea-based nuclear forces, attacking US SSBNs and striking against the sea-lanes) with full effectiveness. The priority which the Soviet navy gives to these missions has obvious implications for the US naval posture. In particular, although the US navy assumes that attacks on the sea-lanes are given high priority, and justifies much of its procurement on that basis, it is not clear that the Soviet navy does in fact intend to devote a large share of its naval assets to this mission.[9]

How the US navy chooses to defend the sea-lanes (or, put differently, to exercise sea control) is a second basic issue in dispute, and one which involves the choice between a defensive and an offensive approach. These two strategies are not, of course, mutually exclusive, and the struggle to define a middle ground (the most appropriate mix) is an additional bone of contention.[10] A coherent naval policy must resolve such controversies. During the 1970s, however, US policy-makers provided few clear answers to the major questions of naval policy. But with the accession to power of Ronald Reagan, a new, more aggressive naval policy became evident, one with significant implications for the Northern Waters.

Reagan's defence policy

President Reagan and his forceful Secretary of the Navy, John Lehman, have undertaken an ambitious naval programme that aims unabashedly at achieving clear-cut naval superiority.[11] The public symbol of this effort is the goal of a 600-ship fleet (up from fewer than 500 in 1980), which is to include 2 new *Nimitz*-class nuclear-powered aircraft-carriers. Such a fleet, it is said, will enable the US navy to operate with confidence even in 'high risk' areas. Despite the vigorous and confident sponsorship of this policy by the Reagan Administration, doubts persist about the feasibility and desirability of this high-cost approach to fulfilling the nation's naval requirements, and about the wisdom of giving the navy budgetary priority at the expense of other forces.[12]

Although these procurement and budget issues are in themselves matters of no small moment, the strategic preferences evident in the Reagan defence policy are far more important in their implications for the Northern Waters. Four elements of the Reagan strategy are of special relevance to this discussion.

First, the Administration has chosen to place greater emphasis than in the past on preparing for a long conventional war.[13] It is precisely in such a war that the sea-lanes of the North Atlantic, which will bear US reinforcements for the Central Front, will most come into play, and that the Soviet–US naval clash in Northern Waters will correspondingly assume a more vital character.[14] Given the Reagan Administration's concern with a long conventional war, it is not in the least surprising that the navy has profited substantially. As Secretary Lehman has repeatedly pointed out, NATO's dependence on North Atlantic convoys requires 'having a superior force capable of defeating a Soviet move to interdict US sea lines of communication'.[15]

Second, a basic feature of US naval policy under Reagan is its emphasis on offensive missions. This involves, as John Lehman explained at a meeting with reporters shortly after taking office, 'steaming into Soviet strongholds such as the Kola Peninsula near Finland and the Kamchatka Peninsula near Japan to bottle up the Russian navy'.[16] Such an approach is not unique to the Reagan Administration,[17] but it has now been embraced more enthusiastically than by other Administrations in the recent past and, indeed, has been made the central pillar of Reagan's naval policy. This policy results from the belief, as Lehman put it, that the USA's maritime interests can be protected 'only by possessing sufficient offensive naval striking power to defeat and neutralize' the Soviet naval threat.[18]

There can be no doubt that such a policy ensures that, in the event of war, the Northern Waters will be a major theatre of naval operations. Again, it is Secretary of the Navy Lehman who has explained this most clearly: 'I cannot conceive of a NATO war in which we would not be putting not one but several carrier battle-groups into the Norwegian Sea at some point. What we must seek to do is to seek out and destroy the Soviet capacity to interdict our uses of the sea ... We have to go north of the GIUK gap with sufficient power to defeat the threat.'[19] In current US naval thinking, then, a large naval battle in the Norwegian Sea occupies a prominent position.

Third, the Reagan Administration has advanced a concept called 'horizontal escalation', whereby a Soviet military attack in one part of the world might be met by a US counteraction in another where the military situation is deemed less disadvantageous for the effective exercise of US military power. This concept has arisen in relation to (although it is not restricted to) the Soviet threat to the Persian Gulf, as evidenced by Secretary of Defense Weinberger's comment that 'our deterrent capability in the Persian Gulf is linked with our ability and willingness to shift or widen the war to other areas'.[20]

It is relevant here because pointedly included among the ways in which the United States might widen a war is the use of naval warfare. Indeed, Secretary Weinberger has said, 'We have to be prepared to launch counteroffensives in other regions and to exploit the aggressors' weaknesses, wherever we might find them. It is in this context that our need for naval superiority acquires special dimension.'[21] Former Assistant Secretary of Defense Francis West, in an article published shortly before he took office, was even more specific in suggesting that a US campaign against Soviet shipping might be a suitable response to Soviet initiation of conflict in the Persian Gulf.[22]

Thus, the concept of horizontal escalation, when combined with the US navy's offensive strategy, raises the prospect that the United States might respond to Soviet intervention in the Near East by initiating major naval conflict in the Norwegian Sea. This means that the Northern Waters are militarily significant not only in the context of a war between NATO and the Warsaw Pact, but also in connection with possible superpower intervention in the Third World. The notion of a naval counteroffensive against the Soviet Union therefore links Northern Waters and North European security to US global strategy.

Fourth, and finally, the Reagan Administration's much-publicized emphasis on a war-winning nuclear strategy, counter-force operations and protracted nuclear warfare makes it very likely that strategic anti-submarine warfare missions will be desired. It would make little sense to have a nuclear weapon employment policy that sought to destroy all Soviet nuclear forces except strategic submarines. Consequently, the United States has an incentive to monitor Soviet SSBNs in peacetime, to position itself for the conduct of strategic ASW in the midst of conventional war and to carry out strategic ASW missions in the event of nuclear war.[23] All this is perfectly consistent with what we know of US strategic doctrine.

This means that the Northern Waters are a component of the nuclear balance between the superpowers, a fact which increases the likelihood and the danger of conflict in the region in the event of an East–West war. The need to conduct strategic ASW ensures that the Northern Waters would be a major theatre of operation, even in a nuclear war.

These four strategic preferences of the Reagan Administration — emphasis on a long conventional war, on an offensive naval doctrine, on horizontal escalation and on nuclear war-fighting — each accentuate the military importance of the Northern Waters in US strategy. Because the Soviet Union has put a substantial portion of its nuclear forces to sea in the past decade, this region has also grown in importance to Soviet strategy. Moreover, the continuing expansion of Soviet naval power and the renewed US effort to enlarge its navy indicate that increasing levels of forces may be found in Northern Waters in the future.

Notes

1. W. Lippmann, 'In the Defence of the Atlantic World', *The New Republic*, 17 February 1917. See also R. Steel's discussion of Lippmann's thinking in *Walter Lippmann and the American Century* (Boston: Little, Brown & Co., 1980), p. 111.

2. See R. Steel, as Note 1, p. 382. Lippmann provides a more extensive discussion of these points in his *US Foreign Policy: Shield of the Republic* (Boston: Little, Brown & Co., 1943). G. Kennan advances a similar conception of American interests in *American Diplomacy, 1900-1950* (New York: The New American Library, 1951), pp. 10-11. See also B. Brodie's interesting discussion of American interests and the threat to them in 'The Strategy of the Atlantic', Document No. 2 (Princeton: American Committee for International Studies Conference on North Atlantic Relations, September 1941).

3. On these points, see, for example, Admiral Harry D. Train, 'NATO's Maritime Responsibilities', *Naval Forces*, Vol. 3 (1982), No. 1, pp. 14-16; W.H. Bagley, 'Sea Power: Neglected Key to a Revitalized NATO Strategy', *International Defense Review*, No. 4 (1978), p. 509; and G.L. Underwood, 'Soviet Threat to the Atlantic Sea Lines of Communication: Lessons Learned from the German Capture of Norway in 1940', *Naval War College Review*, May/June 1981, p. 47. A recent survey of the NATO/Warsaw Pact balance noted that 'about 97 per cent of the American material the battle in Europe would consume would have to come by sea'. See 'Do you Sincerely Want to be Non-nuclear?', *The Economist*, 31 July 1982, p. 32. For an early discussion of the importance of the North Atlantic to NATO strategy, see F. Uhlig Jr, 'The Atlantic Ocean: Sea of Decision', *US Naval Institute Proceedings*, March 1954, pp. 275-9.

4. See, for example, R.G. Weinland, 'Northern waters: Their Strategic Significance', CNA 80-1839.00 (Arlington, Va.: Center for Naval Analyses, 16 December 1980), p. 2.

5. See, for example, D.A. Rosenberg, 'A Smoking Radiating Ruin at the End of Two Hours', *International Security*, Vol. 6 (1981-2), No. 3, pp. 3-39; H.S. Rowen, 'The Evolution of Strategic Nuclear Doctrine', in L. Martin (ed.), *Strategic Thought in the Nuclear Age* (Baltimore: The Johns Hopkins University Press, 1979), pp. 131-56; and D. Ball, 'US Strategic Forces: How Would They Be Used?', *International Security*, Vol. 7 (1982-3), No. 3.

6. Barry R. Posen points out that US naval deployments on the Northern Flank could cause nuclear escalation by threatening the Soviet strategic reserve force — even in the context of conventional war. See his 'Inadvertent Nuclear War? Escalation and NATO's Northern Flank', *International Security*, Vol. 7 (1982), No. 2, pp. 28-54.

7. For discussion of the extraordinary superiority which the US navy brought into the postwar period, see S.P. Huntington, 'National Policy and the Transoceanic Navy', *US Naval Institute Proceedings*, May 1954, pp. 483-93.

8. Carnegie Panel on US Security and the Future of Arms Control, *Assessing the Balance: Defense Spending and Conventional Forces* (Washington: Carnegie Endowment for International Peace, 1981), p. 129.

9. See Congressional Budget Office, *Shaping the General Purpose Navy of the Eighties: Issues for Fiscal Years 1981-85* (Washington: US Government Printing Office, 1980), pp. 21-2, which notes that 'the Soviet Union has never accorded top priority to ships and aircraft most effective for attacking the sea lanes, though many of its forces could be employed for this mission'.

10. See Ch. 5, by Geoffrey.Till.

11. As stated explicitly in Caspar Weinberger, *Annual Report to Congress, Fiscal Year 1983* (Washington: US Government Printing Office, 1982), pp. 11-12.

12. On the costs of building a 600-ship fleet and the difficulties that the United States may have in achieving it, see Congressional Budget Office, *Building a 600-Ship Navy: Costs, Timing, and Alternative Approaches* (Washington: US Government Printing Office, 1982). On the wisdom of giving the navy highest budgetary priority, see R. Komer's thoughtful essay, 'Maritime Strategy vs. Coalition Defense', *Foreign Affairs*, Summer 1982, pp. 1124-44. Komer argues, 'The kind of 600-ship navy being sought by the Administration and Congress is proving to be so expensive as to be achievable only at the expense of other critical defense needs' (p. 1143).

13. See, for example, G.C. Wilson, 'Weinberger Order: Plan for Wider War', *The Boston Globe*, 17 July 1981. Also, Posen, as Note 6.

14. Conversely, of course, if one thinks that NATO is ill-equipped to fight a long war in central Europe, then that deficiency would need to be remedied before it could make sense to invest heavily in additional naval forces. For an interesting discussion of these points, see L. Martin, 'Future Wartime Missions', in J.H. Veldman and F.T. Olivier (eds), *West European Navies and the Future* (Den Helder: Royal Netherlands Naval College, 1980), especially pp. 65-6.

15. Quoted in 'Navy Secretary Urges Building Balanced Offensive Capability', *Aviation Week and Space Technology*, 31 August 1981, p. 45.

16. 'Unclear Sailing', *Newsweek*, 16 March 1981, p. 24. The article goes on to report the opinion of one nameless defence expert that the likely result of this policy in wartime would be that 'we would get our asses ground to peanut butter'.

17. Indeed, the US navy has had a persistent preference for offensive missions, but budget constraints and the differing policy priorities of civilian leaders have often prevented the navy from fully pursuing its preferences. See, for example, the testimony of Admiral Hayward in the House Armed Services Committee, *Department of Defense Authorization for Appropriations for Fiscal Year 1980* (Washington: US Government Printing Office, 1979), pp. 1254-5. The Carter Administration had alarmed the navy by putting more emphasis on defensive naval missions. See, for example, B. Weinraub, 'Brown Seeks to Cut Involvement of Navy in Non-nuclear War', *The New York Times*, 27 January 1978; 'Navy Protests Limitation of its Long-term Mission', *The New York Times*, 14 March 1978; and O. Kelly, 'US Navy in Distress', *US News and World Report*, 6 March 1978, pp. 24-6.

18. US Congress, House of Representatives, Committee on Appropriations, Sub-committee on the Department of Defense, *Department of Defense Appropriations for Fiscal Year 1983* (Washington: US Government Printing Office, 1982), p. 7.

19. 'Lehman Seeks Superiority', *International Defense Review*, No. 5 (1982), pp. 547-8. See also Posen's discussion of Northern Flank scenarios in 'Inadvertent Nuclear War?', Note 6, pp. 39-49.

20. Quoted in G.C. Wilson, 'US May Hit Outposts in Event of Oil Cutoff', *The Washington Post*, 17 July 1981. For discussion of the idea of horizontal escalation, see C. Weinberger, *Annual Report to Congress, Fiscal Year 1983* (Washington: US Government Printing Office, 1982), pp. I-15-I-16.

21. Quoted in R. Halloran, 'Weinberger Tells of New Conventional Force Strategy', *The New York Times*, 6 May 1981.

22. F. West Jr, 'NATO: Common Boundaries for Common Interests', *Naval War College Review*, January/February 1981, p. 65. Also suggestive is J. Lehman's comment that US naval policy will be 'increasingly countervailing'. See his article, 'Rebirth of a US Naval Strategy', *Strategic Review*, Summer 1981, pp. 13-14.

23. According to recent public statements, the US navy intends to seek out and destroy Soviet SSBNs even in a conventional war: Admiral James Watkins, 'The Maritime Strategy', in *US Naval Proceedings*, January 1986 (supplement on *The Maritime Strategy*, pp. 2-17).

10 CANADIAN MARINE RESOURCE DEVELOPMENT IN THE ARCTIC

David VanderZwaag

A sea of opportunity, a sea of uncertainty

A sea of opportunity describes the Canadian vision of Arctic Waters, for the waters promise a wealth of hydrocarbon reserves, an abundance of hard minerals on adjacent lands and numerous possibilities for marine transportation. The Beaufort Sea/Mackenzie Delta offshore region, in the Canadian Western Arctic, is estimated to contain 1.35 billion cubic metres (8.25 billion barrels)* of recoverable oil and 1,865 billion cubic metres of recoverable gas. Hydrocarbon deposits in the Arctic Islands are estimated to include 686 million cubic metres (4.2 billion barrels) of recoverable oil and 2,257 billion cubic metres of recoverable gas.[1] Beaufort/Mackenzie and Arctic Islands deposits together could comprise approximately 43 per cent of Canada's potential oil and gas resources.[2]

Two lead–zinc mines operate adjacent to Arctic Waters and depend on summer shipping for the transportation of mineral concentrates to European markets. The Nanisivik Mine, located on Strathcona Sound approximately 17 miles from the community of Arctic Bay on northern Baffin Island, began production in 1976. The Polaris Mine, only 90 miles from the magnetic North Pole and the world's most northerly mine, is situated on the coast of Little Cornwallis Island and began sustained production in February 1982. The Northwest Passage, the approximately 900-mile-wide stretch of ice-covered waters separating mainland Canada from the High Arctic Islands,[3] offers a transportation short-cut between the Atlantic and Pacific Oceans. For example, the shipping distance between Yokohama, Japan, and Montreal could be reduced from approximately 16,000 to 7,500 miles.[4]

A sea of uncertainty describes the management framework for Canadian Northern Waters, since the legal/political regime

---

*One cubic metre = 6.11 Barrels British.

remains unstable at both the national and international level. At the national level, Canada's northern territories, Yukon and the Northwest Territories (NWT), continue to push for full province-hood and greater benefits from, and control over, offshore development. Although in Canada's Western Arctic the Inuit settled offshore claims with the federal government in March 1984, land claims in the Central and Eastern Arctic are still subject to negotiation. Canada has yet to formulate a clear Arctic Ocean policy that sets forth priorities and time-frames for marine resource developments, and has yet to create a firm decision-making process for integrating conflicting political visions.

At the international level, the waters of the Canadian Arctic archipelago still have an uncertain legal status. Canadian officials on numerous occasions have stated that the waters are internal and therefore subject to total Canadian sovereignty, which includes the right to prohibit foreign vessel transits. The United States, mean-while, claims that the Northwest Passage is an international strait subject to the right of transit passage, and that the coastal state maintains only minimal controls over it, such as the right to impose traffic separation schemes and the right to prohibit marine scientific research and hydrographic surveys.[5] The maritime boundary between Yukon and Alaska remains unresolved. Both Canada and Denmark claim the uninhabited Hans Island, which lies midway between Greenland and Ellesmere Island, and they have yet to negotiate a boundary in the northern Lincoln Sea.

The following four sections examine, first, Canadian opportunities for Arctic marine-related resource developments, both non-renewable and renewable, and, second, the uncertainties, both national and international, in the management regime governing Canadian Arctic Waters.

Non-renewable resource opportunities

Oil and gas

Only one major producing oilfield exists in the Canadian Arctic, at Norman Wells. Since 1982 Esso Resources Canada Ltd has been in the process of a major expansion of the field, and increased pro-duction, scheduled to begin in 1985, is expected to reach about 25,000 barrels a day (having previously been 2,000 barrels a day).[6]

The only major producing gasfield in northern Canada is

Amoco's Pointed Mountain gasfield near Fort Liard, NWT. The proposed Alaska Highway Natural Gas Pipeline, which would transport natural gas from Prudhoe Bay through southern Yukon into Alberta and on to the United States, has an uncertain future. Construction of the northern section through Alaska and Yukon is on indefinite hold because of depressed markets and low prices for gas in the United States.

The Beaufort Sea/Mackenzie Delta hydrocarbon development project, in which it is proposed to produce and transport oil and gas from the Beaufort Sea/Mackenzie Delta region, has encouraging potential but no assured future as yet. Threshold commercial reserves have yet to be established.[7] Although the companies have proposed shipping oil and gas via pipeline through the Mackenzie Valley,[8] or via tankers through the Northwest Passage or by a western route around Alaska (see Figure 10.1), a Canadian environmental assessment panel in a report in 1984 cast a number of doubts over transportation methods. The panel favoured a small-diameter (e.g. 400 millimetre) buried pipeline for transporting oil from the Beaufort Sea region, and recommended that any large-diameter pipeline (e.g. 1,000 millimetre) should be subject to a comprehensive public review. The panel also recommended that the government of Canada withhold approval of the tanker option pending two evaluation stages: a Research and Preparation Stage would seek to identify wildlife distributions and hearing sensitivities of marine mammals, and would involve upgrading navigation and communication systems, ice detection systems and hydrographic surveys along the proposed route; and a Two Tanker Stage would involve actual construction of two Arctic Class 10 tankers and testing their effects on wildlife and ice regimes.[9]

In the High Arctic Islands, where the first exploratory well was drilled on Melville Island in 1961 and where 158 wells had been drilled by 1981, two major projects have been proposed for transporting hydrocarbons via tankers. The Arctic Pilot Project — which planned to transport liquefied natural gas from Bridport Inlet, Melville Island, by two Arctic Class 7 icebreaking tankers through the Northwest Passage to a terminal site in eastern Canada — is on indefinite hold because of a lack of markets. However, in early 1984 Panarctic Oils Ltd, partly owned by Petro-Canada (Canada's state-owned oil company), unveiled plans to transport oil from the Bent Horn field discovered on Cameron Island in

Figure 10.1: Tanker Routes in Northern Canada

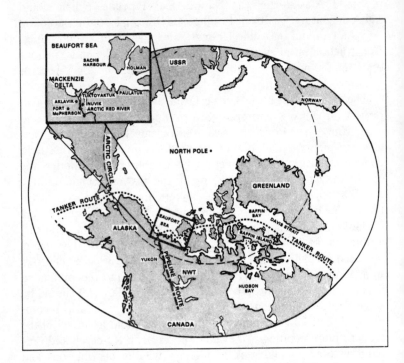

Source: Dome Petroleum Ltd, Esso Resources Canada Ltd, and Gulf Canada
Resources Inc., *Beaufort Sea/Mackenzie Delta Environmental Impact Statement,* Vol. 2
(1982), p. xii.

1974. The Bent Horn Project, given conditional approval by the
Minister of Indian Affairs and Northern Development in February
1985, proposes to produce oil and store it in tanks over the winter,
and to ship moderate amounts of oil through the Northwest
Passage to eastern markets during the summer. (In the past,
Panarctic had used ice-strengthened tankers to deliver diesel fuel
to an exploration base on Melville Island, but the tankers returned
empty.)

To demonstrate the feasibility of the plan, Panarctic's ship *Lady
Franklin* carried one barrel of crude oil from Cameron Island to
Montreal during the summer of 1984. In late August and early
September 1985, Panarctic shipped 100,000 barrels — the first
ever commercial shipload of Canadian Arctic crude — to a

Montreal refinery. Phase two of the project, expected to begin in three years' time, might continue with 400,000 barrels per year carried by one or more ships.[10] Within six to eight years, Panarctic hopes to develop a large oil discovery at Cisco, off the coast of Lougheed Island, which is estimated to contain 300 million barrels of oil.[11] (See Figure 10.2 for major petroleum areas.)

In Canada's Eastern Arctic, offshore hydrocarbon activities have been severely restricted for political and environmental reasons. Drilling in Lancaster Sound, first proposed by Norlands Petroleum in 1974, has been delayed and made subject to extensive governmental and public review. A Lancaster Sound Regional Study Committee issued a green paper, in January 1982, which identified six possible options for the region: (1) no new development; (2) environmental protection; (3) renewable resource economy; (4) Northwest Passage shipping; (5) balanced

Figure 10.2: Major Petroleum Areas in Northern Canada

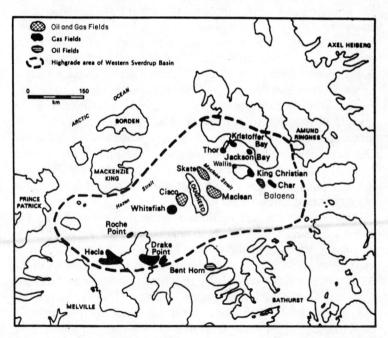

Source: Adapted from *International Petroleum Encyclopedia 1983* (London: PennWell, 1983), p. 27, and Department of Indian and Northern Affairs Canada, *Canada's North* (Ottawa: Supply and Services Canada, 1983), p. 8-19.

development; and (6) non-renewable resource economy.[12] A final report, issued in November 1983, recommended that an integrated land-use plan be formulated for the Lancaster Sound region before any final development decisions.[13]

A proposal by Petro-Canada in July 1977 to drill in North Davis Strait has also been on hold pending a decision on Lancaster Sound. Drilling in South Davis Strait has been limited to three exploratory wells. In 1979 Esso drilled a dry hole. In 1980 Aquitaine, using a drillship, made a significant gas discovery.[14] In 1982 Canterra Energy Ltd also drilled a dry hole.[15]

In Hudson Bay, the first exploratory offshore well was drilled in the summer of 1985 northeast of Churchill, Manitoba, but no commercial grade of oil or gas was discovered. A second well was expected to be completed by the end of October.[16]

Hard minerals

Two northern mines currently depend on part of the Northwest Passage for bringing in supplies and shipping out metal concentrates. The Nanisivik Mine ships about six loads of lead, zinc and silver concentrates to European markets per year.[17] Since ore resources (10.5 per cent zinc, 0.8 per cent lead) totalled 4.4 million tonnes in January 1983 and annual ore production reaches approximately 600,000 tonnes,[18] the mine is estimated to be able to continue operating until around 1990. The Polaris Mine, operated by Cominco Ltd, makes about nine lead and zinc shipments annually, during the short shipping season of August to late October, for sale to European smelters.[19] Estimated ore reserves (14.1 per cent zinc, 4.3 per cent lead) of approximately 23 million tonnes should allow the mine to operate, at a rate of 2,100 tonnes per day, into the next century.[20]

At least three other significant mineral deposits have been identified adjacent to Arctic marine areas, and these could depend on marine shipping in the future. The Bathurst Norsemines site, located 96 kilometres south of Bathurst Inlet in Canada's Central Arctic and jointly owned by Bathurst Norsemines Ltd and Cominco Ltd, contains estimated reserves of about 20 million tonnes of lead, zinc and silver mineralization.[21] Borealis Exploration Ltd estimates total iron ore deposits on the Melville Peninsula in Canada's Eastern Arctic to be 4.3 billion tonnes, but development is currently uneconomic because of current world oversupply of iron ore.[22] At Mary River on northwest Baffin

Island, Baffinland Iron Ltd owns a high-grade iron ore deposit (68 per cent) estimated at 260 million tonnes, plus a lower-grade deposit (30 per cent) of 500 million tonnes.[23] Development is at present precluded by the need to move the ore approximately 100 kilometres overland to Milne Inlet for shipping.[24] (See Figure 10.3.)

Renewable resource opportunities

In at least three respects, Canadian Arctic Waters are not a sea of opportunity for renewable resources. First, at the primary productivity level, the Arctic Ocean is considered the least productive of the world's oceans. For example, the Beaufort Sea produces less than 20 grams of carbon per square metre per year, compared with 121 for the Bering Sea, 150 for the Atlantic Ocean shelf,[25] 90 for the North Sea, 400 to 500 for Georges Bank off New England[26] and 5,475 for the Antarctic Ocean.[27] Second, the number of fish, bird and marine mammal species is relatively low compared with other ocean areas. For example, the Beaufort Sea supports approximately 43 fish species, compared with over 300 species off the east and west coasts of southern Canada.[28] In the Canadian Arctic there are some 25 species of mammals, compared with 126 species in British Columbia, and only six major species — beluga and bowhead whales, ringed and bearded seals, polar bear and Arctic fox — rely on marine food chains.[29] About 80 species of birds — roughly 12 per cent of all the North American bird species — breed in the Canadian Arctic. Third, the rate of biological growth tends to be slow. For example, many Arctic fish do not reproduce until they are five to ten years of age, and then not every year.[30]

However, renewable resources can be very abundant at particular times of the year and in particular areas. The coastal waters of the Beaufort and northeast Chukchi Seas support an estimated two million migratory birds, between spring and autumn,[31] and over 10,000 whales, including 75 per cent (approximately 3,800) of the world's population of the endangered bowhead whale.[32] Groups of 100 to 1,000 or more beluga (white) whales gather in the shallow waters of the Mackenzie River estuary in July and August,[33] perhaps because the relatively warm waters are conducive to calving and feeding and are sheltered from the wind.[34]

Figure 10.3: Mineral Exploration and Mining: Northwest Territories — 1983

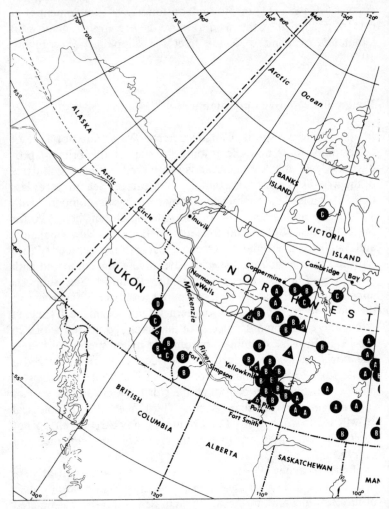

Source: Adapted from Department of Indian and Northern Affairs Canada, *Mines and Mineral Activities 1983* (Ottawa: Supply and Services Canada, 1983), pp. 28-9.

Lancaster Sound, the eastern entrance to the Northwest Passage, is perhaps the most productive marine area in the entire Arctic. A third of eastern Canada's 8.3 million breeding colonial seabirds, such as murres, kittiwakes and guillemots, and tens of thousands of eider and old-squaw ducks, snow geese, loons and shorebirds

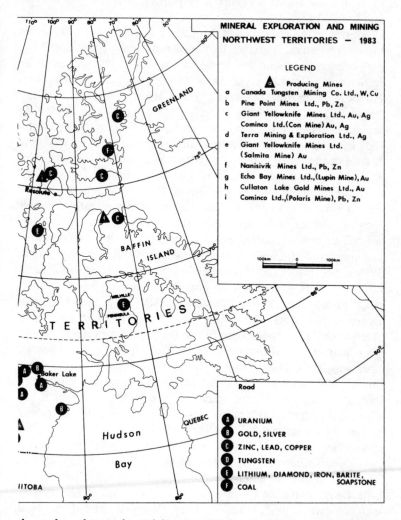

depend on the nutrient-rich waters during the brief summer season from late April until September.[35] Marine mammals in the sound include 85 per cent of North America's narwhals and 40 per cent of the beluga (white) whales, in addition to large populations of ringed, harp and bearded seals.[36] Polynyas — recurring open water areas surrounded by ice — occur at various locations across the Canadian Arctic[37] and are points of aggregation for marine mammals in winter (because they provide access to air) and for birds in early spring (because they provide access to open water and food).[38]

Marine living resources in the Canadian Arctic are not just an important natural heritage; they also represent a critical cultural and economic lifeline for numerous northern communities. Six settlements (Inuvik, Aklavik, Tuktoyaktuk, Sachs Harbour, Paulatuk and Holman) rely on the marine resources of the Beaufort Sea. From 1972 to 1981, the communities landed an annual average of 132.8 white whales,[39] and from 1970 to 1980 they harvested an annual average of 2,488 seals and 7,345 Arctic fox.[40] For the years 1978 to 1981 the annual polar bear quota was 85.[41] In the Lancaster Sound region in the Eastern Arctic, four coastal communities (Resolute, Arctic Bay, Pond Inlet and Grise Fiord) have relied upon wildlife harvests for a majority of their income. For example, Resolute hunters have averaged a yearly wildlife income equivalent to 60 per cent of their total income.[42]

Commercial fishing has not been extensive in Canadian Arctic Waters because of such factors as low biological productivity, ice-covered waters, a small human population and high transportation costs to markets. Small commercial fisheries in the Canadian Beaufort Sea supply local markets, primarily with whitefish and Arctic char, and export some fish to the prairie provinces.[43] In the Canadian Eastern Arctic, commercial fishing by domestic operators in the Davis Strait region did not begin in earnest until 1979,[44] and major species taken in recent years include Greenland halibut, Northern shrimp, roundnose grenadier and wolf-fish.[45] Canadian total allowable catches in 1984 were set at 12,500 metric tonnes for Greenland halibut, 5,000 tonnes for shrimp and 4,000 tonnes for grenadier.[46] The annual value of the still under-developed shrimp fishery, harvested by 12 licensees in 1984 (10 held by southern enterprises),[47] has been estimated to be potentially Canadian $3.5 million. Other exploitable species include cod, redfish, salmon, char, lumpfish and Greenland shark.[48]

Commercial fishing in the Eastern Arctic has been subject to international cooperation. In 1979 and 1980, Canada and the EC cooperated in managing three transboundary species — Greenland halibut, Northern shrimp, and roundnose grenadier.[49] The 1980 Canadian–EC fisheries agreement set total allowable catches (25,000 tonnes for Greenland halibut, 8,000 for grenadier and

29,500 for shrimp), established national allocations (Canada received 3,500 tonnes of halibut, 800 of grenadier and 2,500 of shrimp), organized reciprocal licensing arrangements and provided for logbook keeping and for the exchange of catch statistics.[50] EC-licensed vessels were permitted to fish in Canadian waters for 2,500 tonnes of shrimp, and Canada was allowed to fish in Greenlandic waters for 2,000 tonnes of shrimp. This arrangement was very attractive to Canada, since heavy ice on the Canadian side of Davis Strait had limited the fishing season to five or six months, but access to the Greenlandic zone extended the season to 10 to 12 months. The Northwest Atlantic Fisheries Organization (NAFO) — formerly the International Commission for the Northwest Atlantic Fisheries — provided scientific information and management advice for the three transboundary stocks.[51]

However, in 1981 Canada and Denmark/Greenland could not reach agreement on a total allowable catch for Northern shrimp, and the breakdown of negotiations led to unilateral management approaches for the Davis Strait region from 1981 to 1985. Canadian fishermen have been excluded from Greenlandic waters and EC fishing vessels have been excluded from Canadian waters.[52] Total allowable catches, set independently by Canada and the EC for transboundary stocks, have exceeded scientific recommendations by 18 per cent for shrimp and 30 per cent for Greenland halibut and grenadier.[53]

Nevertheless, some cooperation has been possible for managing North Atlantic salmon. The Convention for the Conservation of Salmon in the North Atlantic Ocean was signed by the EC, Ireland, Norway, Sweden, the United States, 'Canada, and Denmark (for the Faroe Islands) and entered into force in October 1983. It established the North Atlantic Salmon Conservation Organization (NASCO), whose purpose is to facilitate scientific research into salmon distribution and stock enlargement, to recommend regulatory measures and to coordinate efforts to minimize foreign catches of salmon originating in the rivers of another party.

Greenland's withdrawal from the EC in 1985 raises new possibilities for future fisheries management. Denmark on behalf of Greenland has become a party to NASCO, as pledged in the EC–Greenland agreement on fisheries, and has joined NAFO because of the advantage to be gained from obtaining scientific and managerial advice.[54] Numerous possibilities exist for increased

Canadian–Greenlandic cooperation in fisheries management, including joint agreement on total allowable catches and national allocations for transboundary stocks, agreement on licensing for third-party vessels, provision for cooperation in surveillance and enforcement and the creation of a marketing strategy for sealskins. The establishment of a Canadian consul in Greenland might also facilitate intergovernmental communications. However, fisheries discussions between Canada and Greenland that were scheduled to occur in the summer and autumn of 1985 were postponed.

Marine mammals also display transboundary distributions, and more formalized international cooperation for their management is required. Bowheads, belugas, narwhals, walruses and harp seals migrate from West Greenland waters to Canadian waters in the spring and summer,[55] but with the exception of the regionwide Convention on the Conservation of Polar Bears, cooperative arrangements have been rather *ad hoc* and informal. For example, during the peak of concern about the Arctic Pilot Project, Canada and Greenland/Denmark established a Working Group to consult on such environmental issues as the effect of vessel traffic noise on marine mammals. In 1981 Canadian Beaufort Sea operators cooperated with several Alaskan oil companies to carry out a major population study of bowheads in the Canadian portion of the Beaufort Sea.[56] And in 1983 US, Canadian and Danish/Greenlandic scientists cooperated in investigating the noise effects of icebreaking ships in the Baffin Bay/Northwest Passage region.

National uncertainties

The future extent and pace of marine resource development in the Canadian Arctic remains uncertain because of several national factors. First, the whole decision-making process is fragmented and contains numerous approval points which may hinder or hasten offshore development.[57] An environmental assessment review process, administered by the Federal Environmental Assessment Review Office of the Department of the Environment, applies to any major projects that may have a significant impact on the environment. Projects involving the export of oil or gas, or the construction of an interprovincial or international pipeline, are subject to National Energy Board approval. The Department of Indian Affairs and Northern Development retains power of approval for works which have the potential to deposit waste into Arctic Waters. The Department of Fisheries and Oceans possesses broad review powers for projects which may disrupt fish habitats. Transport Canada regulates shipping and retains approval power over obstructions to navigation, which may cover the siting of marine terminals. A land-use planning process, still in the formulation stage, may soon apply to offshore areas of particular ecological and developmental concern, such as Lancaster Sound and the Beaufort Sea/Mackenzie Delta region.

Second, the extent of territorial powers over the offshore region also remains uncertain. The government of the Northwest Territories has pushed for an offshore revenue-sharing and management agreement similar to the agreements concluded between Newfoundland and Nova Scotia and the federal government.[58] The Minister of Indian Affairs and Northern Development has indicated an openness to consider the resource management and revenue-sharing proposal and has agreed to put it to the federal cabinet.[59]

Third, land claims with an offshore component remain unsettled for the Central and Eastern Canadian Arctic.[60] The Tungavik Federation of Nunavut (TFN), the umbrella Inuit negotiating organization, continues to push for a greater decision-making role in offshore activities, particularly hydrocarbon exploration/development and shipping.[61] On 4 July 1985 David Crombie, Minister of Indian Affairs and Northern Development, announced the appointment of a five-member task-force to review the federal comprehensive claims policy, which includes such issues as the suspension of development activities during negotiations and native participation in offshore management and in resource revenue-sharing.

Fourth, Canadian northern policies remain in a state of flux. The National Energy Program — the policy commitment by the Trudeau government to hasten oil and gas exploration in frontier areas by means of such mechanisms as petroleum incentive grants that pay up to 80 per cent of exploration costs for companies with a high Canadian ownership rate — is in the process of being dismantled by the new Progressive Conservative government of Brian Mulroney. Energy Minister Pat Carney has announced plans to replace the Petroleum Incentives Program (PIP) with an alternative approach such as tax incentives, and to do away with the controversial back-in provision, whereby the federal government retained the option to take a 25 per cent interest in petroleum production (an option the oil industry considered to be equivalent to expropriation without compensation). Such moves could encourage foreign investment and foster development, but exploration activities might be redirected to areas of less financial risk, such as Alberta.

Finally, although numerous marine areas in the Arctic have been identified as requiring special protection,[62] no clear policy or procedure exists for establishing a comprehensive network of protected areas.[63] Furthermore, the Canadian government has not made a clear policy commitment to develop Arctic offshore resources and shipping, and numerous gaps remain in northern management abilities in such areas as hydrographic surveying, search and rescue capabilities, navigation and communication aids, and vessel traffic services. Vessel traffic control in the north is still not mandatory, and vessel routes are still being formulated.[64]

International uncertainties

A number of major jurisdictional uncertainties loom over Canadian Northern Waters. First, the US–Canadian maritime boundary in the Beaufort Sea remains unresolved. Second, the legal status of the Northwest Passage and the waters of the Canadian Arctic archipelago remains unclear. Canadian officials have on occasion indicated that the waters are internal and thereby subject to complete Canadian sovereignty. Support for such a claim may be drawn from such doctrines as those pertaining to historic waters and straight baselines.[65]

On 10 September 1985, External Affairs Minister Joe Clark reasserted and formalized Canada's sovereignty claim by announcing in the House of Commons the establishment of straight baselines around the perimeter of the Canadian Arctic archipelago (effective from 1 January 1986) and the plan to construct a Polar Class 8 icebreaker. He also indicated a desire to initiate talks with the United States on future cooperation in Arctic Waters, and announced the immediate withdrawal of the 1970 reservation to Canada's acceptance of the compulsory jurisdiction of the International Court of Justice.[66]

The United States, meanwhile, has claimed that the waters are subject to the regular Law of the Sea regime and that the

Northwest Passage, in particular, is an international strait subject to the right of transit or innocent passage. The USA first demonstrated this point of view by not officially requesting permission for the transit of the US Coast Guard icebreaker that was accompanying the *Manhattan* through the passage in 1969, and by refusing Canada the privilege of examining voyage data.[67] The United States was prepared to push the issue again in the summer of 1985. It sent the Coast Guard icebreaker, the *Polar Sea*, to resupply the US air force base at Thule, Greenland, and the ship then proceeded westward through the Northwest Passage to the Beaufort Sea. Permission for the voyage was not requested, but Canadian observers were aboard and the United States and Canada agreed to disagree over the status of the waters.[68]

A third jurisdictional uncertainty concerns the extent of Canadian control over the Alpha Ridge, which extends from off northern Ellesmere Island to the Soviet Union. If the ridge is continental in origin, Article 76 of the Law of the Sea Convention may allow Canada to claim continental shelf jurisdiction beyond 350 nautical miles, as opposed to 350 nautical miles for an oceanic ridge not of the deep ocean floor. Results from the Canadian Expedition to Study the Alpha Ridge (CESAR), which gathered geological and geomorphological data in the spring of 1983, indicate that the ridge is oceanic in origin.

The last two major jurisdictional questions involve relations with Denmark/Greenland. A December 1973 agreement between Canada and Denmark on delimiting the continental shelf between Greenland and the Canadian Arctic Islands (see Figure 10.4) left two jurisdictional hiatuses. Because Hans Island, a small uninhabited island less than one mile in length, straddled the median line between Greenland and Ellesmere Island, Canada and Denmark/Greenland decided to leave territorial ownership unresolved by drawing the continental shelf boundary up to the low-water mark at the southern end of Hans Island and resuming the boundary from the northern end.[69] The countries also left undecided the boundary in the Lincoln Sea, and neither side seems anxious to insist upon negotiation, since resource potential in the area is not regarded as significant.[70]

In spite of legal uncertainties, Canada has taken numerous initiatives in international cooperation. For example, since 1976 Canadian and US officials have held meetings to exchange information on offshore activities in the Beaufort Sea.[71] A Joint

Figure 10.4: Delimitation between Canada and Greenland/Denmark

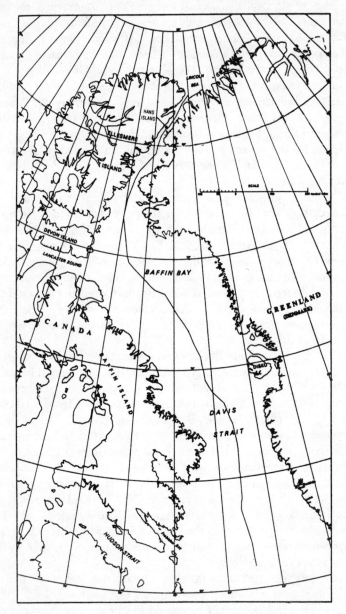

Source: Adapted from XIII *International Legal Materials* (1974), p. 511.

Canada–United States Marine Pollution Contingency Plan for the Beaufort Sea establishes procedures for the two national Coast Guards to respond jointly to pollution incidents that threaten to have transboundary effects. A March 1982 memorandum of understanding pledged the US Coast Guard and the Canadian Department of the Environment to cooperate in pollution control research, for example, research into the behaviour of Arctic oil-spills and the development of pollution response equipment. On 25 April 1985, Transport Canada and the US Department of Transportation signed an agreement to cooperate in research projects on the development of arctic ship design, regulation criteria and construction standards; in the development of ice navigation procedures; and in improving the safety of arctic ship operation.[72] On 26 August 1983, Canada and Denmark signed a Marine Environment Cooperation agreement covering the Nares Strait, Baffin Bay and Davis Strait region. The agreement established joint contingency plans for shipping or hydrocarbon exploration/ exploitation pollution incidents, called for cooperation in scientific research, provided for cooperation in identifying vessel routes outside territorial waters, and formalized the duty to consult on the initiation of any activities that might create a significant risk of transboundary pollution. On 16 April 1984, Canada and the Soviet Union signed a Protocol of Canadian–Soviet Consultations on the Development of a Programme of Scientific and Technical Cooperation in the Arctic and the North. The agreement provides a framework for exchanging information and for cooperative research in four areas: Geoscience and Arctic Petroleum; Northern Environment; Northern Construction; and Ethnography and Education.

Whether Canadian Arctic Waters become a true sea of opportunity will probably depend not only on the development of national managerial abilities, perhaps through a clear sea-use planning process with full Inuit participation, but also on further development of international cooperation. Such cooperation could involve a regionwide Arctic Ocean Action Plan for managing all facets of Arctic developments (including land-based, atmospheric and vessel-source pollution), or new bilateral agreements, such as a Beaufort Sea Boundary agreement to establish a joint resource development zone, and a Northwest Passage agreement to clarify the legal status of the passage. The time is ripe for creative evolution in Canadian ocean law and policy as it relates to the Arctic.

Notes

1. R.M. Proctor, G.C. Taylor and J.A. Wade, *Oil and Natural Gas Resources of Canada 1983*, Geological Survey of Canada Paper 83-31 (Ottawa: Supply and Services Canada, 1984), p. 3. Figures given represent average expectations.

2. For discussions of Canadian hydrocarbon reserves, see Economic Council of Canada, *Connections: An Energy Strategy for the Future* (Ottawa: Supply and Services Canada, 1985); National Energy Board, *Canadian Energy Supply and Demand, 1983-2005* (Ottawa: Supply and Services Canada, 1984); and Department of Indian and Northern Affairs Canada, *Canada's North* (Ottawa: Supply and Services Canada, 1983).

3. The Northwest Passage actually consists of at least five possible basic routes. For a description of the routes, see Donat Pharand, *The Northwest Passage: Arctic Straits* (Dordrecht: Martinus Nijhoff, 1984), pp. 6-21.

4. G.R. Harrison, 'The Arctic Sea — A Sea of Opportunities', in *New Opportunities in Canadian Maritime Ventures* (The Fourth National Marine Conference, Vancouver, British Columbia: November 3-5, 1981), p. 50.

5. Convention on the Law of the Sea, UN Document A/CONF. 62/122, 7 October 1982, Articles 40-2.

6. *NWT Data Book 1984-85* (Yellowknife, Northwest Territories: Outcrop Ltd, 1984), p. 84.

7. Economic Council of Canada, *Connections: An Energy Strategy for the Future* (Ottawa: Supply and Services Canada, 1985), p. 49.

8. At least four overland pipeline systems have been proposed; see Pharand, as Note 3, p. 74; *Beaufort Sea/Mackenzie Delta Environmental Impact Statement*, Vol. 2 (Calgary, 1982), pp. 6.1-6.12; and Department of Indian and Northern Affairs Canada, *Communiqué* 1-8430, 19 July 1984.

9. Federal Environmental Assessment Review Office, *Beaufort Sea Hydrocarbon Production and Transportation*, Final Report of the Environmental Assessment Panel (Ottawa: Supply and Services Canada, 1984), p. 3.

10. 'Panarctic Tanker Ships First Oil', *Arctic Policy Review*, January 1985, p. 2.

11. 'Panarctic Eager to Lift Arctic Islands Oil', *The Globe and Mail* (Toronto), 7 June 1984, p. 36.

12. *The Lancaster Sound Region: 1980-2000, Issues and Options on the Use and Management of the Region* (Ottawa: Department of Indian and Northern Affairs Canada, January 1982).

13. Peter Jacobs and Jonathan Palluq, *The Lancaster Sound Regional Study, Public Review: Public Prospect* (Ottawa: Department of Indian and Northern Affairs Canada, November 1983).

14. *APOA Review* (the Review of the Arctic Petroleum Operators' Association, Calgary), Vol. 4 (1981), No. 1, p. 17.

15. *APOA Review*, Vol. 5 (1982-3), No. 3, p. 10.

16. 'Hopes are Drying Up in Search for Oil in Hudson Bay', *The Chronicle-Herald* (Halifax), 23 September 1985, p. 19.

17. Pharand, as Note 3, p. 66

18. Department of Indian and Northern Affairs Canada, *Mines and Mineral Activities 1983* (Ottawa: Supply and Services Canada, 1983), p. 24.

19. Cominco Ltd, *Annual Report 1983*, p. 8.

20. Cominco Ltd, *Annual Report 1979*, p. 25.

21. Department of Indian and Northern Affairs Canada, *Mine and Important Mineral Deposits of the Yukon and Northwest Territories, 1982* (Ottawa: Supply and Services Canada, 1983), p. 32.

22. *Canada's North*, as Note 2, p. 8-4.

23. As Note 21, p. 37.

24. *Canada's North*, as Note 2, p. 8-4.

25. Dome Petroleum Ltd, Esso Resources Canada Ltd and Gulf Canada Resources Inc., *Beaufort Sea/Mackenzie Delta Environmental Impact Statement*, Vol. 3A (Calgary, 1982), p. 3.51.

26. E.B. Cohen, M.D. Grosslein, and M.P. Sissenwine, 'An Energy Budget of Georges Bank' (paper presented at a Workshop in Multispecies Approaches to Fisheries Management, St. John's, Newfoundland, November 26-30, 1979), p. 4.

27. R.A. Davis, K.S. Finley, and W.J. Richardson, *The Present Status and Future Management of Arctic Marine Mammals in Canada* (Yellowknife: Department of Information, Government of the Northwest Territories, January 1980), p. 6. This figure 5475 may be the highest recorded but the usual range is from 100 to 500 grams of carbon per square metre per year. (Personal communication, Dr Glen Harrison, Bedford Institute of Oceanography.)

28. As Note 25, p. 3.31.

29. Donald A. Blood, *Birds and Marine Mammals: The Beaufort Sea and the Search for Oil* (Ottawa: Department of Fisheries and the Environment 1977), p. 25. *The Beaufort Sea/Mackenzie Delta Environmental Impact Statement* noted that about 22 species of marine mammals may occur between Prince of Wales Strait and Davis Strait, but most species are seasonal and occur in small numbers: for example, the killer whale, the pilot whale, the fin whale and the blue whale. As Note 25, Vol. 3B, pp. 2.1, 2.9, 2.10.

30. Donald A. Blood, *ibid.*, p. 11.

31. As Note 25, p. 3.5.

32. *Ibid.*, pp. 3.9 and 3.13; North Slope Borough Coastal Management Program Background Report (1984), p. 1-202. The exact number of bowhead whales in the Western Arctic is still the subject of some speculation and controversy. For example, the most recent estimate of the Scientific Committee of the International Whaling Commission is 4,417 whales (Draft Report, Scientific Committee of the International Whaling Commission (Cambridge, July 1985), s. 12.1).

33. Donald A. Blood, as Note 29, p. 67.

34. M.A. Fraker, C.D. Gordon, J.W. McDonald, J.K.B. Ford, and C. Cambers, *White Whale (Delphinapterus leucas) Distribution and Abundance and the Relationship to Physical and Chemical Characteristics of the Mackenzie Estuary*, Fisheries and Marine Service Technical Report, No. 863 (Ottawa, December 1979), p. 5.

35. *The Lancaster Sound Region: 1980-2000* (Ottawa: Department of Indian and Northern Affairs Canada, January 1982), p. 53.

36. *Ibid.*, p. 13.

37. See M. Smith and B. Rigby, 'Distribution of Polynyas in the Canadian Arctic', in I. Stirling and H. Cleator (eds), *Polynyas in the Canadian Arctic*, Occasional Paper No. 45 (Canadian Wildlife Service, 1981), pp. 7-28.

38. L. Johnson, *Assessment of the Effects of Oil on Arctic Marine Fish and Marine Mammals*, Canadian Technical Report, Fisheries and Aquatic Science, No. 1200 (Ottawa: November 1983), p. 10.

39. As Note 25, p. 3.70.

40. *Ibid.*, pp. 3.66 and 3.73.

41. *Ibid.*, p. 3.72.

42. H. Myers, 'Traditional and Modern Sources of Income in the Lancaster Sound Region', *Polar Record*, Vol. 21 (1982), pp. 11, 13.

43. As Note 25, p. 3.74.

44. J.F. Sherwood, 'Canada–Denmark Fisheries Relations in Davis Strait:

Domestic and International Management of a Subarctic Fishery' (LL.M.thesis, Dalhousie Law School, Halifax, Nova Scotia, September 1984), p. 80.

45.   *Ibid.*, p. 16.

46.   *Ibid.*, p. 187.

47.   *Ibid.*, pp. 25, 107.

48.   M.J. Dunbar, 'On the Fishery Potential of the Sea Water of the Canadian North', *Arctic*, Vol. 23 (1970), p. 150.

49.   Personal communication, Department of Fisheries and Oceans, International Directorate.

50.   Copy of the agreement given to the author by the Department of Fisheries and Oceans, International Directorate.

51.   As Note 44, pp. 142-3.

52.   *Ibid.*, p. 155.

53.   *Ibid.*, pp. 147, 155.

54.   Personal communications, Atlantic Salmon Federation, St. Andrew's, New Brunswick, and NAFO Secretariat, Dartmouth, Nova Scotia.

55.   As Note 25, Vol. 3B, pp. 2.3, 2.7, 2.9, 2.12, 2.13.

56.   *APOA Review*, Vol. 7 (1984), No. 2, p. 22.

57.   For a detailed discussion of the uncertain nature of the Canadian decision-making process, see D. VanderZwaag and C. Lamson, 'Northern Decision Making: A Drifting Net in a Restless Sea', in C. Lamson and D. VanderZwaag (eds), *Transit Management in the Northwest Passage: Problems and Prospects* (Cambridge University Press, 1986).

58.   See Proceedings of the Standing Senate Committee on Energy and Natural Resources, 1st Session, 32nd Parliament, Issue No. 17, 2 April 1985 (presentation from the Ministry of Energy, Mines and Resources, Government of the Northwest Territories).

59.   Canadian Arctic Resources Committee, *Northern Decisions*, Vol. 2 (February 1985), No. 70, pp. 136-7.

60.   In 1984 the Committee for Original Peoples' Entitlement (COPE), representing Inuvialuit in the Western Arctic, reached a final land-claims agreement with the federal government. The agreement, which extends to the offshore, promises to grant the Inuvialuit greater participation in resource management through new mechanisms, such as Wildlife Management Advisory Councils and a Fisheries Joint Management Committee: *The Western Arctic Claim: The Inuvialuit Final Agreement* (Ottawa: Department of Indian and Northern Affairs Canada, 1984).

61.   A workshop on offshore aspects of Inuit claims was sponsored by the Department of Indian and Northern Affairs Canada and held in Ottawa, 30 and 31 May 1985.

62.   See, for example, Environment Canada, *Canadian Special Places in the North: An Environment Canada Perspective for the 80s* (Ottawa, 1982); and Department of Fisheries and Oceans Arctic Offshore Development Committee, 'A Classification of Areas in the Canadian Arctic for Use in the Renegotiation of Oil and Gas Exploration Agreements', Working Paper 82-8 (Ottawa, August 1982).

63.   Department of Indian and Northern Affairs Canada, *Report of the Task Force on Northern Conservation* (Ottawa, December 1984), pp. 17-21.

64.   Note, however, that Bill C-75, which would amend the Canada Shipping Act to provide statutory authority for mandatory vessel traffic management in the North, received its first reading in the Canadian parliament in September 1985. For an overview of Canadian shipping activity and management approaches in the North, see D. VanderZwaag and C. Lamson, 'Shipping and Marine Environmental Protection in the Arctic: Present Approaches and Future Options', paper presented at the Arctic Heritage Symposium, Banff, Alberta, 24-7 August 1985.

65. For an overview of the doctrines, see David VanderZwaag and Donat Pharand, 'Inuit and the Ice: Implications for Canadian Arctic Waters', *Canadian Yearbook of International Law*, Vol. 21 (1983), pp. 53-84.

66. Statement in the House of Commons by the Secretary of State for External Affairs, the Rt. Hon. Joe Clark, on Canadian sovereignty (Statement 85/49, 10 September 1985).

67. William E. Westermeyer, 'The Transportation of Arctic Energy Resources', in William E. Westermeyer and Kurt M. Shusterich (eds), *United States Arctic Interests: The 1980s and 1990s* (New York: Springer-Verlag, 1984), p. 125.

68. 'Arctic Authority at Stake', *The Globe and Mail*, 13 June 1985, p. 7; and 'Inuit Fear Voyage of US Icebreaker Harms Sovereignty', *The Globe and Mail*, 10 July 1985, p. 8.

69. Kurt M. Shusterich, 'International Jurisdictional Issues in the Arctic Ocean', *Ocean Development and International Law*, Vol. 14 (1984), No. 3, pp. 248-9.

70. Ted L. McDorman and Susan J. Rolston, 'Maritime Boundary Delimitation in the Arctic Region', in Douglas M. Johnston and Phillip Saunders (eds), 'Maritime Boundary Delimitation in Selected Regions', unpublished manuscript, Dalhousie Ocean Studies Programme, Nova Scotia.

71. John E. Carroll, *Environmental Diplomacy: An Examination and a Prospective of Canadian–US Transboundary Environmental Relations* (Ann Arbor: University of Michigan Press, 1983), pp. 83-4.

72. The agreement was Addendum 6 to the Volpe-Jarmieson memorandum of understanding signed by the Minister of Transport and the US Secretary of Transportation in 1970 to foster research and development cooperation in transportation.

The author wishes to acknowledge the Donner Canadian Foundation for supporting his research into Arctic Marine Management issues.

11 CANADA'S SECURITY CONSIDERATIONS IN THE ARCTIC[1]

Nicholas Tracy

The marriage of long-range aviation with the atomic bomb in 1945 brought the Canadian Arctic into the strategic equation for the first time, and it remained a central part of it until, in the 1960s, the intercontinental ballistic missile altered the nature of the threat. Any treatment of security problems in the Canadian Arctic must begin with the inter-alliance conflict between NATO and the Warsaw Pact. However, as the threat to the security of North America has evolved along with the technology, the arrangements made to meet it have created, and will continue to foster, intra-alliance tensions between Canada and the United States. Consideration of that problem is the second ring of the onion. The new and growing political consciousness in the area provides a third dimension to any examination of security issues. The onion will only remain sound if rot does not become significant in any of the rings.

The East–West dimension

For the military professional, the Canadian Arctic constitutes a quiet sector in the NATO frontier which nevertheless plays a vital part in deterring attack elsewhere. In 1944, in the midst of the Anglo-American bombing of German cities, it was recognized in Washington that the strategic importance of American industrial cities made them an obvious target for Russian bombers in the event of Stalin's seeking to occupy Western Europe despite the presence there of British and American forces. When the atomic bomb had demonstrated its potential and had been incorporated into the thinking about defending Europe against Russian attack, it was feared that the Russians might seek to destroy the American bomber force at its bases.

It had been recognized in the Ogdensburg agreement of 1940 that Canada had an obligation to prevent hostile forces attacking the United States across Canadian territory. Canadian servicemen tended to discount the threat to American industry, and certainly doubted the value of an Arctic line of interceptor bases. However, the provision of strategic warning of attack, so that American retaliatory forces could become airborne, made evident sense. Canada could not afford the cost of constructing the Distant Early Warning (DEW) radar line along the Arctic Ocean coast and across Baffin Island, but the Ogdensburg agreement had established a mechanism by which the United States provided Canada with military assistance. Canada therefore undertook to build a second line, the now dismantled Mid-Canadian line, and facilitated American construction of the DEW line.[2] Canadian air defence forces were pooled with those of the United States, and a joint command organization was established by the NORAD agreement of 1958.

The launching of the Sputnik in 1957, and the subsequent Soviet deployment of ICBMs, gradually reduced the importance of Canada's Arctic glacis to the attempt to make the American nuclear deterrent invulnerable. The American radar systems designed to provide warning of missile launches (BMEWS) are located outside Canadian territory. Nonetheless, Canadian–American cooperation to defend the Arctic sector is still relevant, and recent technical developments may be in the process of restoring all its former importance. The increasing vulnerability of ICBMs to pre-emptive attack, and the American Administration's intention to use 'Star Wars' technology to create an effective anti-ballistic missile defence system, provide an incentive for a return to air-breathing systems which can use manoeuvre as cover. The American development of strategic long-range land-attack cruise missiles has been matched by the Soviets, who have developed air- and sea-launched versions. The Soviets are also developing the new, very heavy *Blackjack* supersonic strategic bomber.

There is not a naval threat in the Canadian Arctic comparable to that coming from the air, although it appears that naval interest in the area may increase. The Arctic Ocean has been described as the Mediterranean of the modern world, the central sea which at once divides and unites the USSR, the United States, Canada and Northern Europe. Nonetheless, as Hudson discovered in the sixteenth century, the ice of the polar basin is impassable to virtually all shipping. The conditions are so severe that there is practically no possibility of using the polar ocean for surface naval assault or strike forces. Only submarines capable of protracted navigation under the ice could have a naval role in the Arctic.

There is relatively little submarine activity in Canada's Arctic coastal waters. The Canadian archipelago presents so many navigational problems that there is little incentive for the Soviet navy to use it in preference to the Norwegian Sea or the Bering Strait, despite the military hazards of those routes. Canadian waters are not very attractive either as deployment areas for cruise-missile-carrying submarines, because of the long flight-time for such missiles between crossing the DEW line and reaching targets in North America. The same is true for the air-launched version. Nonetheless, in view of the operational advantages the Soviets enjoy in the area and the fact that NATO and American anti-submarine efforts tend to focus upon the Atlantic and Pacific, there is a potentially greater need for Canadian involvement in anti-submarine warfare in the Arctic. Limited exercises have been carried out on the fringes of the Arctic, and Canada has recently taken delivery of a Canadian version of the *P-3 Orion* long-range patrol aircraft, the *Aurora*, which has some capacity for operation in the Canadian Arctic.

With the exception of maintenance of the radar network (which is increasingly a Canadian responsibility), some scientific effort and routine overflights, the defence of the Canadian Arctic territories has been handled primarily by what has been called a 'preventive scorched ice' policy. The hypothetical threat of sabotage or attack against the few existing Arctic installations imposes no more than a requirement to have the capacity to re-establish the damaged equipment rapidly. There is, however, a need to be able to deploy combat troops to the far north, even if the chances of their being put to the test are minimal. Accordingly, the Canadian armed forces maintain air transports and periodically train soldiers in the area. The problem of survival is so great that it tends to absorb the soldiers' energies. Rigorous training is necessary. The Northern Command HQ at Yellowknife is responsible for planning exercises in as many of the different terrain and climatic conditions as possible. The Department of National Defence has free access for the purpose to all parts of the area. Scattered among the settlements of the north are Northern Rangers, civilians with limited military training who can provide the armed forces with the local knowledge they need to operate effectively.

Managing US–Canadian relations

The dependence of Canada upon the United States for much of the cost of constructing the DEW line, and doubts about its strategic and political effects, have played a major role in the second aspect of the security dilemma in Canada. Proximity to the American colossus has always had a fundamental effect on Canadian affairs. From the time he signed the Ogdensburg agreement, Prime Minister Mackenzie King was suspicious of American intentions and attempted to limit American military involvement in Canadian territory. In 1946 he wrote:

> I believe the long-range policy of the Americans was to absorb Canada. They would seek to get this hemisphere as completely one as possible. They are already in one way or another building up military strength in the North of Canada. It was inevitable that, for their own protection, they should have to do that. We should not shut our eyes ... [but] it might be inevitable for us to have to submit to it.[3]

With perhaps more balance General Maurice Pope had written in April 1944:

> To the Americans the defence of the United States is continental defence, which includes us, and nothing that I can think of will ever drive that idea out of their heads. Should, then, the United States go to war with Russia, they would look to us to make common cause with them and, as I judge their public opinion, they would brook no delay.[4]

The concern that an American build-up of forces in Canadian territory could provoke a Soviet attack was added to the underlying fear that nineteenth century American rhetoric about 'manifest destiny' might finally become a twentieth century policy. Most responsible members of the Canadian government considered the United States to be a good friend, but, as General Pope wrote, 'what we have to fear is ... a lack of confidence in the United States as to our security, rather than enemy action'.

The voyage of the American supertanker *Manhattan* in 1969 through the Canadian Northwest Passage set the alarm bells ringing in Canada, because it was felt that little respect was being given to Canadian claims to sovereign control of the passage. A Canadian military plane transported a number of members of the House of Commons to overfly the tanker, and a year later the government passed the Arctic Waters Pollution Prevention Act, which unilaterally extended Canadian jurisdiction 100 miles seaward in the Arctic. In 1969 the Prime Minister of Canada, Pierre Trudeau, in a speech in Calgary, declared the principle that the Canadian armed forces should have the defence of Canadian sovereignty as their first task.[5] What was implied by that requirement has never been adequately defined, but it was incorporated into the 1970 Defence White Paper.[6] Clearly it combines the tasks of preventing the infringement of Canadian jurisdiction and staving off the domination of Canadian territory and policy by foreign forces. As such the concern must be more with allied states than with those that have little commercial and no known military presence on Canadian territory. President Reagan's policies towards Central America not only demonstrate that problems may arise if national policies diverge too greatly from those of a powerful neighbour, but they also highlight the success of Canadian diplomacy in the late 1940s and 1950s.

The management of Canada's relationship with the United States is essentially a political problem, but it is one in which the Department of National Defence performs important roles. Definition of the functions of the Canadian armed forces in the Canadian–American relationship is especially difficult and conjectural. From the seventeenth to the beginning of the twentieth century, the military forces of what is now Canada had a defensive function *vis-à-vis* the settlements to the south, and even an offensive purpose. That is not the case now. Not only are Canadians happy in a system of collective security, but the disparity of forces precludes a Gaullist foreign policy. Nonetheless it is necessary to take steps to define Canadian jurisdiction and to discourage intervention. The Canadian armed forces further these purposes by helping to establish a cooperative atmosphere, by actively promoting European defence connections, by providing a politico-military trip-wire and by promoting world peace. These functions are not exclusively related to control of the Arctic.

Latent anxiety about being dominated by allies has tended to reduce Canada's defence budgets. Canada has a political tradition — dating at least from the 1910 Laurier Naval Act, and clearly evident during Mackenzie King's leadership — that national control of foreign policy can only be sustained if Canada does not represent a key element in the defence plans of an imperial or allied government. M. Trudeau's 1969 speech, in which he emphasized the defence of Canadian sovereignty, could be seen as a reversion to that tradition. On the other hand, it could be seen as an attempt to harness the strong political support that exists in Canada for defence efforts directed specifically towards the preservation of Canadian control in the Arctic.

It is evident that Canada's contribution to collective defence is appreciated in Washington. It is also evident that the Canadian government can only hope to influence continental defence strategy if a useful proportion of the defence effort is paid for in Ottawa. Furthermore, as General Pope stated, Canada can sustain its independence only so long as American security is assured. The existence of NATO, because it ties up the bulk of Soviet power in Europe, serves to reduce the need for the United States to develop the defences of North America, much of which would perforce be located on Canadian territory. However, Canada's contribution to NATO is a useful military, and an important political, factor in promoting the continued alliance of North America and Western Europe. Participation in United Nations peacekeeping also protects Canada's ability to control its own territory, because it reduces the chance of a major war in which Canadian interests would receive short shrift.

There is no dichotomy between defence of Canadian sovereignty and collective defence, and neither can fully replace the other. Canada must maintain the means to intervene with military force on its own territory, but it must also seek to provide for the needs of collective defence that have to be met on Canadian territory or off Canada's coasts. The ground forces which are trained to react to foreign invasion of Canada's Arctic territory inevitably also have what might be called a trip-wire function analogous to that provided by the conventional forces on the European Central Front. Any foreign government sending hostile forces into the Canadian Arctic would have to overcome a limited military resistance which would trigger an international political crisis. Meanwhile, Canada's gradual takeover of DEW-line installations,[7] and the establishment of the world's northernmost defence facility at Alert, are reducing foreign involvement in Canada's Arctic. It is possible, too, that the slow development of naval activity on the North American side of the polar basin may lead Canada to develop its submarine arm so as to prevent the obtrusive presence of allied naval forces.

In short, the paradox of a Canadian defence policy which focuses on defence of sovereignty but cannot define the threat because it is posed by Canada's closest friend and neighbour, and the reality of a defence effort which is partly concentrated on Europe and the North Atlantic because the European connection modifies the relationship with the United States, make it difficult for that policy to obtain political support.

The domestic intra-regional dimension

The third aspect of the security dilemma in the Canadian Arctic derives from the rising political consciousness of the native peoples of the Arctic and Sub-Arctic. This development raises questions which are even more difficult to define than those posed by intra-alliance concerns. The moral function of a state may be held to be the creation of an environment within which citizens have some prospect of realizing their potential. Hence political activism amongst the northern peoples is a very positive sign that the state is succeeding. On the other hand, it is never easy to reconcile the immediate needs of a part of the state with the long-term interests of the whole. Such conflicts of interest have led to divisions which have been felt by most countries, including Canada, and which have virtually dismembered the Danish kingdom. The independence of Norway and Iceland, and the autonomy in domestic affairs of first the Faroes and now Greenland, have had their impact upon perceptions of the future for Canada's northern peoples. The long struggle to contain the independence movement in Quebec province, and the legal battles over native lands claims, may only be a prelude to a serious split between Ottawa and the 'true north'.

At present, though, there is no internal security problem in the Canadian Arctic. The frontier society may frustrate the efforts of the Royal Canadian Mounted Police, the primary instrument of law enforcement, but not in any politically motivated way. The struggle for self-realization is pacific and legal. The Canadian armed forces do, however, have an impact on the area. Among a very small population they have a high profile, not least because their skills are appreciated by people living in the wilderness.

Furthermore, in order to carry out their tasks in the north, the Canadian armed forces have to place some reliance upon the Northern Rangers, who are highly respected.

Developing national policies to integrate the northern peoples into the greater Canadian society is a task primarily of the Department of Indian Affairs and Northern Development, and of the Northwest Territories government. Since northern separatism would have a major impact on existing security relationships, especially intra-alliance relations, the implications of the north–south dialogue within Canada cannot be ignored by the Canadian armed forces.

Conclusion

Strategy, a branch of politics, is an art of the possible. The development of programmes to deal with inter- and intra-alliance dangers, and with the problems of national cultural alienation, is constrained by realities of budget and disparate purpose. Following the period of rapid development of aerospace warning-systems in the 1950s and 1960s, there was a period of relative quiescence in defence activity in the Canadian Arctic. The focus was on economic developments. Technical developments, however, including the cruise missile and *Blackjack* bomber, together with the growing political consciousness of the northern peoples, have begun to produce a more exacting security environment in the 1980s. This may require a more active Arctic defence effort on the part of Canada if the intra-alliance tensions are not to be exacerbated.

The development of either a main Arctic base or a number of task-specific Arctic military stations has been a central issue under consideration. Budgetary and strategic reasons have been used to support both alternatives. A project exists for the purchase of a new generation of diesel-electric submarines which could be given a limited under-ice capability by using liquid oxygen or high-test peroxide to run charging engines. A fully developed Canadian anti-submarine warfare capability suitable for use in the Arctic archipelago would at once deter the approach of hostile submarines and avert the incursion of allied forces. A case can also be made for exploiting the central location of the Canadian Arctic in the interests of NATO as a whole. North Devon Island is geographically equidistant from Edmonton, Montreal and the areas in northern Norway to which Canadian soldiers are committed in the event of war. A base somewhere in the Canadian High Arctic could serve as a staging-point and as a politico-military bridge that would enhance the credibility of Canada's commitment to the NATO Northern Flank. NATO is a mutual assistance pact, and its political structure might be strengthened if Norwegian forces trained in the Canadian Arctic in order to assist in the defence of the area. Such a development could also help Canada ease other intra-alliance pressures there.

A greater Canadian defence presence in the Arctic should be tailored to have the most beneficial impact on the problem of northern cultural alienation, and should possibly be accompanied by the development of institutions of higher education. A more intense defence contact with the Norwegian, Danish and Icelandic peoples could also help to satisfy the cultural needs of Canada's north. Certainly it is unlikely that the current 'scorched ice' policy will long endure.

Notes

1. This paper is based on a study carried out by the author for the Canadian Department of National Defence, Directorate of Strategic Analysis (Operations Research and Analysis Establishment).

2. The DEW line also stretches into Greenland; see Ch. 13. Canada and the USA have agreed to modernize the DEW-line systems in Canada.

3. Quoted in James Eayrs, *In Defence of Canada, Volume 3* (Toronto: University of Toronto Press, 1972), p. 351.

4. *Ibid.*, p. 321.

5. Department of External Affairs, Canada, *Statements and Speeches, 69/9* (Ottawa: 1969).

6. Department of National Defence, Canada, *Defence in the 70s* (Ottawa: 1971).

7. See Paul Mann, 'New Air Defense Pact Provides Canadian Takeover of DEW Line', *Aviation Week & Space Technology*, 25 March 1985, pp. 23-4.

12 NORWAY IN NORTHERN WATERS

Willy Østreng

Referring to the postwar developments in the Law of the Sea, the economist J.K. Galbraith once stated that God loves Norwegians. With the establishment of economic zones, Norway's ocean territory has since 1945 grown to three times the size of its land territory. Norway currently administers about 40 per cent, or 2 million square kilometres, of the oceans off its coasts — i.e., the North Sea, the Norwegian Sea and the Barents Sea.[1] The Norwegian continental shelf constitutes one-third of the European total, and large parts of it are potentially rich in petroleum.[2] Furthermore, the Norwegian fishing grounds are among the world's richest: for several decades the northeast Atlantic catches have constituted about 20 per cent of the global total.[3] Also, from a military–strategic perspective, these waters are among the world's most vital.[4]

Norway is therefore a *major ocean manager* as well as a *small state*: a considerable management responsibility is combined with limited capabilities. As long as these management functions involve substantial economic and military interests, the gap between responsibility and capability can be a major national problem; the political challenge here lies in the design and operation of management arrangements that reduce the potential for conflict.

Delimitation and management questions in the waters around Jan Mayen and in the Barents Sea serve to demonstrate the range of challenges that the Norwegian authorities face: in the Jan Mayen area, the management responsibilities are regulated by agreements between two allied countries (Norway and Iceland); in the Barents Sea, efforts to work out corresponding arrangements between the USSR and Norway have so far proved fruitless. In this chapter Norwegian endeavours and policy in these two cases will be examined. A main focus will be on the question of why success has been achieved for Jan Mayen and not for the Barents Sea.

155

The Jan Mayen case

Until the late 1970s, the waters around the Norwegian island of Jan Mayen did not attract much attention in international politics, because most experts believed that the area had no interesting resources. This opinion was evident in the 1961 law relating to Norway's extension of the fishing limit to 12 miles, and in the 1976 law relating to Norway's economic zone. Both laws were enacted but not implemented for Jan Mayen, since regulations were held to be unnecessary in areas devoid of natural resources.

In the autumn of 1978, interest in Jan Mayen arose in Norwegian and Icelandic political circles when a Norwegian vessel netted a large catch of capelin southwest of Jan Mayen. More rich hauls were made in the ensuing weeks. This was the first indication that the experts' assumptions had been wrong. There were large stocks of capelin. The political process was launched: in February 1979, the Norwegian government asserted its right to an economic zone around Jan Mayen, stating that it would be established when appropriate. The Icelandic government rejected the Norwegian position, and maintained that under international law a continental shelf claim could not be made nor an economic zone be established around Jan Mayen. The Icelandic position was founded on the belief that only islands were entitled to ocean and seabed areas, and that Jan Mayen was a rock.

Following numerous informal talks and one year of negotiations, Iceland accepted a Jan Mayen zone. However, this zone potentially overlapped with Iceland's 200-mile zone over an area of 25,000 square kilometres. After more negotiating, the parties came to terms in the *Agreement between Norway and Iceland of 28 May 1980, concerning Fishery and Continental Shelf Questions*, in which Norway renounced its claim to the disputed area and Iceland recognized Norway's right to a zone. The day following the conclusion of the agreement, Norway established a 200-mile fishing zone on the basis of its 1976 law and of the clarification that had taken place in its relations with Iceland.

The agreement has offered Iceland considerable gains. *Inter alia*, of the total capelin quota in the Jan Mayen zone, Norway was to have a 15 per cent share annually until 1984, and a corresponding share was granted to Iceland. The parties jointly set the total capelin quota, but if disagreement should arise, Iceland has the final word. Norway may object to the total quota only when it is clearly unreasonable. In principle, then, under this provision Norway may be bound in its own economic zone by Icelandic regulations.

The agreement applies primarily to fish. The continental shelf was dealt with in only two of ten articles, and those concerned the procedure for succeeding negotiations. Article 9 provided for the establishment of a three-member Conciliation Commission to which each party was to nominate one member, while the chairman was nominated jointly. The Commission's mandate was the 'submission of recommendations with regard to the dividing line for the shelf area between Iceland and Jan Mayen. In preparing such recommendations the Commission shall take into account Iceland's strong economic interests in these sea areas, the existing geographical factors and other special circumstances'. On 16 August 1980, the Commission was set up, and in October 1981 an *Agreement on the Continental Shelf in the Area between Iceland and Jan Mayen* was reached.

The recommendations of the Conciliation Commission stated that the division of the continental shelf between Iceland and Jan Mayen was to correspond to the 200-mile zone delimitation line in the area. It was also unanimously agreed that the two countries should cooperate on exploration and exploitation of petroleum resources in an area of 45,470 square kilometres (larger than Denmark) between 68° and 70° 35′ north, and between 6° 30′ and 10° 30′ west. About 70 per cent (32,750 sq. km) of the area is on the Norwegian side of the delimitation line, and 30 per cent (12,720 sq. km) on the Icelandic side.

This cooperation is to be based on joint ventures, unless the parties agree to another form of contract. In the section of the cooperative area situated north of the dividing line, Iceland is entitled to a 25 per cent participation share in the exploration and exploitation of petroleum resources. Norway has corresponding rights in the Icelandic section. In the parties' respective areas their national legislation applies, including provisions relating to supervision and control, security and environmental protection. Moreover, if an oilfield extends beyond the joint development area into the Norwegian zone, the whole of the field will be regarded as part of the joint development area. If, on the other hand, an oilfield stretches into Iceland's 200-mile zone, Icelandic jurisdiction will apply.[5] Norway is to carry all expenses on seismic and magnetic tests on both nations' shelves in the first phase of exploration.

Both nations' exploration costs in the Norwegian section of the joint development area will be carried by the concessionary company. Iceland, however, is not obliged to achieve a refund of Norwegian costs in the Icelandic section. The agreement also states that Norway may explore without Iceland. If there is then a commercial find, Iceland takes its share, after paying its part of any expenses incurred. Iceland therefore avoids risky investments, while Norway has no corresponding right in Iceland's section of the joint area.

Thus, the result of the unexpected capelin catch of autumn 1978 was formal agreements on fisheries and on the continental shelf. As might be expected, they were well received in Iceland. A poll among the Icelandic elite demonstrated that the Icelanders considered the agreements to be very satisfactory.[6] In Norway, on the other hand, they were criticized.[7] In particular the agreement of 28 May 1980 was attacked both by fishermen and by the political opposition. A number of fishermen even suggested that the Minister of Foreign Affairs ought to be taken to court.[8] What were the reasons, then, for the accommodating Norwegian approach?

Few ocean areas display a greater density of warships than the Barents Sea, which borders the Kola Peninsula, the base of the Soviet Union's Northern Fleet. The US base at Keflavik undertakes the surveillance of this fleet throughout the entire Norwegian Sea. In war the task of forces stationed there would be to destroy or neutralize Soviet vessels attempting passage. This is why Iceland is a particularly important member of NATO.[9]

Following Norwegian mediation and substantial pressure from certain NATO members on the British government, the British–Icelandic 'Cod War' of 1975 was called off. This was the only experience the Norwegian government had to draw on in planning its own negotiating strategy. If Norway had established a zone without considering Iceland's interests, the latter might again have played the 'Keflavik card'. Such a development would have created a dilemma for NATO, but security problems would have been posed for Norway as well.

The uncertainty surrounding the future of the Keflavik base has spawned a debate on potential alternative base areas, and Jan Mayen has been mentioned.[10] The island has an important strategic position: the distance to the Kola bases is a mere 1,300 kilometres, as opposed to 2,100 km from the bases to Iceland.

Moreover, the Barents and the Greenland Seas, since the deployment of the *Delta*-class SSBNs, are now of supreme importance to Soviet strategic retaliatory potential.[11] In the 1960s Jan Mayen was situated west of the 'strategic division line' between the USA and the Soviet Union in the Norwegian Sea. During the 1970s this line was pushed westwards towards Jan Mayen, which currently borders the Soviet stationing and manoeuvring area in the Greenland Sea. No doubt exists about the crucial geographical location of the island in the strategic set-up in the North. This was obvious to Icelanders: the left-wing newspaper *Thjodviljinn* suggested that a perfect solution to the Jan Mayen problem would be to transfer the American Keflavik base to the island, partly because a base there would be favourable to the USA, since the Soviet Union intended to deploy its SSBN fleet beneath the polar ice. The author of the article realized that this proposal would probably be rejected by the Norwegians, who have always shown a special interest in American retention of their base at Keflavik.[12]

There can hardly be any doubt that the advantages of Jan Mayen as a military base are exaggerated: it is clear that it can in no way assume all the functions exercised by Keflavik. Among other things, airport capacity on the island could never approach that of Keflavik.[13] These limitations notwithstanding, Jan Mayen may take on *certain* functions and be one of several bases, should the Americans be forced to abandon Iceland. It is reasonable to assume, however, that the newspaper was correct in supposing that Norway would not be inclined to consider further development of Jan Mayen for military purposes, since this might be regarded as a violation of important principles of Norwegian defence policy.

In the postwar period, Norway's defence policy has been based on two major, partly contradictory principles: *reassurance* and *deterrence*, both intended for Soviet consumption. The principle of reassurance operates by means of self-imposed military restrictions, such as the ban on stationing of foreign troops and storing of nuclear arms in Norway in peacetime. The objective is to indicate Norway's non-aggressive intentions. The aim of deterrence is to prevent an attack on Norway by having a modern national defence and membership of NATO. Further military development of Jan Mayen, however, might be regarded as emphasizing deterrence at the expense of reassurance. This might give Norwegian policy a more offensive and aggressive appearance.[14]

In order to avoid a situation in which Norway would have to consider hosting parts of the Keflavik functions on Jan Mayen, the authorities had to eschew a deadlocked conflict with Iceland. Accommodating Icelandic interests was a means to this end, and it was also realized that Norway 'would not receive the support of other countries in a conflict with Iceland'.[15] Support would come least of all from Norway's allies, who are anxious to maintain the Keflavik base. In an American thesis on Icelandic defence policy, it is claimed that Norway was under pressure from both Britain and the USA to arrive at an agreement favourable to Iceland in the Jan Mayen zone conflict.[16]

Most Norwegians probably share Galbraith's view that an alliance exists between themselves and the Divinity — at least as far as the sea is concerned. The feeling that Norway had benefited greatly from the development of ocean law in the 1970s produced a desire to be generous to Iceland. When it was known that Norway, not least with an eye to its fisheries, was going to insist on its right to both a zone and a continental shelf, some of the Norwegian press accused the authorities of *oceanic imperialism.*

Even if the imperialism concept is misleading in this context, it nevertheless touched upon a basic value in Norwegian foreign policy — that of equality and fair shares in international relations.[17] The ideals of equality and justice have been expressed not least in Norwegian Third World policy; Norway is one of the first nations to have made one per cent of its GNP available to developing countries. Also, at UNCLOS III, Norway consistently advocated the views of the Group of 77, in particular on control of the deep seabed.[18] Relative to Iceland, Norway is a major power, as Norwegian authorities recognized. In authoritative quarters in the Norwegian Foreign Ministry it was maintained that 'in negotiations with Iceland during the Jan Mayen dispute we must live up to what we have always insisted on in foreign policy, viz., considerations for the interests of a small country. On this occasion the small country is Iceland, not Norway. For the first time Norway occupies the role of a major power.'[19]

Accusations of oceanic imperialism prompted the government's desire to show moderation in dealings with Iceland. There is, however, no reason to believe that the imperialism jibe had a decisive influence on the formulation of the government's policy, not least because it came after the basic guidelines for the Norwegian policy had been settled. Its importance lay primarily in the fact that its refutation added legitimacy to the policy already chosen.

The question of *surveillance* capacity may also have influenced the Norwegian deliberations; it was obvious that Norway would not have the necessary resources for surveillance of the vast ocean areas acquired in the 1970s. To the Foreign Ministry the decisive factor was 'that the conflict with Iceland would have made it difficult, or even impossible, to establish a zone around Jan Mayen. It would either have been a paper zone or a disputed zone, if we were to use physical force to ensure compliance with our decision, and this we could not possibly have done.'[20] Only by an accommodating approach could Norway establish a 'peace zone' which would be within the bounds of Norwegian surveillance capabilities.

During the drafting of the Norwegian negotiating position, great importance was attached to preserving amiable and close relations with Iceland. In connection with the negotiations on the agreement of 28 May 1980, Ambassador Jens Evensen declared that: 'The close relations existing between our two nations on historic and ethnic grounds formed part of the somewhat special circumstances which governed the conduct and course of these negotiations.'[21] The mandate of the Conciliation Commission also stated that 'Iceland's strong economic interests in these areas, the existing geographical and geological factors and other special circumstances'[22] should be taken into account.

The Jan Mayen agreements in perspective

Iceland obtained the greater concessions in the two agreements, especially that on the continental shelf. The agreements are the result of a rare diplomatic practice: they do not aim at achieving a balance of give and take. However, they do consider Norwegian interests. After all, Norway has a set of agreements which ensure that Norwegian fishermen have a share in resources they had not previously exploited to any extent; new areas have been placed under Norwegian jurisdiction; and Norway has been guaranteed access to any new oil resources. The imbalance lies in the way that Iceland has gained super-optimally, while Norway has gained sub-optimally.

Norway was, in effect, compensated for its 'loss' in the two agreements by considerations that impinged upon but were not dealt with in the negotiations. By adopting an accommodating approach Norway avoided a conflict with Iceland, which might have jeopardized important aspects of Nordic and Norwegian–

Icelandic cooperation, and thereby avoided further strains on its already deficient surveillance and control capacity. Moreover, the major goal, that of preserving peace and stability in the North, was achieved. As a result of its accommodating behaviour Norway succeeded, in terms of practical policy, in living up to the aims of solidarity and equality in the world community. The authorities weakened the impression that they were pursuing oceanic imperialism. Yet another feature of this approach was the avoidance of breaking with important principles in Norwegian defence policy. A potential conflict with the other NATO countries, all of which have been anxious not to risk the Keflavik base or Iceland's membership of NATO, was averted.

When considered in a wider context, the Jan Mayen arrangements clearly safeguard important Norwegian security and foreign policy interests. The solution was simple in concept but effective: *what Norway gave in on in the agreements was compensated for in other issue areas.* In this way the imbalance could be accepted by both parties.

The Jan Mayen agreements are based on two features: first, the *linking* of several issue areas in order to arrive at an *integrated and comprehensive* solution; and, second, the consideration of 'Iceland's strong economic interests, the existing geographical and geological factors and other *special circumstances*' in setting up the arrangement. The two agreements that emerged from the Jan Mayen dispute were the outcome of a two-stage process, and each of them resulted from separate negotiations.[23] Nevertheless, they were integrated: each refers to the other, and they therefore constitute an interlinked, comprehensive set of agreements on resource development that relate to both mineral and living resources in the area. A wide range of 'special circumstances' were also taken into account, ranging from security considerations to concerns for Nordic cooperation.[24] These two basic features, then, which together included the total range of both parties' interests, may prove to be important ingredients in conflict management and conflict-reducing arrangements in other areas as well. However, as will be seen, this policy differs from that adhered to by the Norwegian authorities in the Barents Sea.

The Barents Sea case

The Barents Sea is a 'border sea' between Norway and the Soviet Union, and thus between West and East. The problem here is that, despite being a 'border sea' in terms of *geography*, no delimitation lines have been settled by *policy*. For years the borders have been matters of dispute between the two nations, and no solution seems to be within reach. The disagreement is about (a) the delimitation of the continental shelves between the two countries, and (b) the delimitation of their 200-mile economic zones.

In addition to these issues, the two governments disagree on the interpretation of the *Svalbard Treaty of 9 February 1920*. This dispute has direct consequences for the legal situation in the ocean and on the ocean floor surrounding the archipelago. The lack of fixed sea boundaries and the legal uncertainty in the area may provoke international conflicts, not least because of the interests at stake there.

Although it constitutes only 0.3 per cent of the surface of the world's oceans, the Barents Sea yields nearly 4 per cent of the total annual global fish catch, and accounts for 50 per cent of the Norwegian and 12 per cent of the Soviet annual catches. It is also believed that the continental shelf is rich in petroleum.

The Barents Sea harbours the Soviet Northern Fleet, one of the mightiest naval fleets of our time. From being a vital transit area the Barents Sea has also become an area for submarine deployment. The Soviet interest here has been aptly described by former Admiral Golovko: 'Without the Kola inlet the Northern Fleet cannot exist — the Kola inlet is necessary to the State.'[25]

The security implications of Norway's geographical proximity to the Soviet Union have had a noticeable effect on the formulation and implementation of Norwegian security policy since 1945. Both the decision to join NATO in 1949 and the subsequent policy of self-imposed military restrictions were measures chosen with this situation in mind. The main objective of the Norwegian government is to find solutions to all unresolved questions in the North, without jeopardizing regional stability and tranquility.

In 1967 the issue of the *partition of the Barents Sea continental shelf* was raised by the Norwegian government. Since 1974 negotiations have been conducted with the Soviet Union, albeit without the prospect of an agreement drawing close. Both parties endorse the *1958 Continental Shelf Convention*, and invoke Article 6 as the basis for negotiation. However, the two nations base their arguments on different sections of Article 6. Norway prefers the median line as the basis for negotiation, while the Soviet Union favours a dividing line 'justified by special circumstances'; that is, it believes the dividing line should coincide with the sector line, drawn along longitude 32° 04′35″ east and 168° 49′30″ west.

The Soviet Union invokes an extended interpretation of the 'special circumstances' concept, and the list of circumstances has acquired considerable proportions. Not only is the sector claim included, but economic, demographic, security and other properties of the region are also claimed to be relevant. Norway rejects the sector principle and points to its controversial status in international law. Moreover, the Norwegian government assumes that the term 'special circumstances' applies to geographical factors only, such as coastline configuration and the existence of islands. Hence, the Norwegian position is that neither the sector principle nor the Soviet version of 'special circumstances' is established in existing international law. Since 1978, however, the Norwegian authorities have recurrently confirmed their disposition to compromise in these negotiations. Thus far this attitude does not appear to have been reciprocated by the USSR.

In the course of the first months of 1977, Norway and the Soviet Union both extended their fisheries jurisdictions to 200 miles and thereby initiated the delimitation problem. Because of the importance of the fisheries in the area that was affected by the deadlocked delimitation talks, both Oslo and Moscow found it necessary to establish provisional rules for these fisheries in the *'Grey Zone' Agreement of January 1978.* The area covered by the agreement does not correspond exactly to the area in dispute in the delimitation talks. Some parts of the disputed area are left out, and adjacent areas to the east and to the west are included in the arrangement. The area to the west of the sector line is larger than the corresponding area to the east of the median line; there is thus a geographical imbalance. The 'Grey Zone' Agreement, however, includes a provision stating that *the agreement shall not prejudice the position of either party in the boundary-line negotiations.* It is in force one year at a time only, and has to be renewed by every July 1 to remain in force. It ensures third-party fishing vessels admission to the zone, provided they are licensed by either Norway or the Soviet Union. Norway has jurisdiction over third-country vessels fishing with Norwegian permission, and the Soviet

Union has jurisdiction over those fishing with its consent. The Norwegian authorities emphasize that this system is not a *joint jurisdiction arrangement*, but a regime of clearly *separate responsibilities*.

When the Svalbard Treaty was signed in Paris on 9 February 1920, the states with a major interest in Svalbard agreed to recognize Norway's full and unrestricted sovereignty over the archipelago.[26] This recognition, however, was not without its quid pro quo. Signatory powers reserved the right to most kinds of economic activity on an equal footing with Norwegian nationals. This right was to apply to fishing, trapping and all kinds of maritime, mining, industrial and commercial activity.[27] No nationality was to enjoy special favours; all were to be treated equally and to have equal economic rights.[28] The right of the Norwegian authorities to collect taxes and duties on the islands was also restricted. Revenues of this nature were to be spent exclusively for the benefit of Svalbard, and were only to be levied to the extent warranted by such requirements.[29] In addition, Norway had to pledge not to establish — or allow the establishment by other nations of — any naval base or fortifications in the Svalbard area. Norway thus received a highly restricted sovereignty over the archipelago. The interpretation problem in this context is whether the restrictions on sovereignty should also be effective at sea.[30]

The issue concerning the *shelf* is whether it should be subject to a regime in accordance with the provisions of the 1958 Continental Shelf Convention or with those of the Svalbard Treaty. In both cases the shelf will remain under Norwegian sovereignty, but, under the Treaty, citizens of all signatory powers will have access to the area and its resources on an equal footing with Norwegians, and Norwegian sovereignty will be more restricted than under the 1958 Convention.[31] The position of the Soviet government is that the Svalbard Treaty is the basis for Norwegian sovereignty, while Norway argues that the provisions of the Convention should apply. The USA and other Western powers have not yet stated their position on this issue.

In the opinion of the Norwegian authorities, the restrictions on sovereignty set out in the Svalbard Treaty cannot be given an extended interpretation. They are final and apply only to the areas explicitly mentioned in the Treaty, and not to the continental shelf and the sea beyond territorial waters, which are not mentioned.

The only reference to the sea is found in Articles 2 and 3, in which, in connection with fishing and maritime interests, the scope of the Treaty is extended to cover territorial waters (4 nautical miles in 1971). The areas beyond territorial waters are therefore subject to Norwegian sovereignty in accordance with the provisions of the Continental Shelf Convention, and not with those of the Svalbard Treaty.

The Fisheries Protection Zone (FPZ) raises similar questions in the application of the Svalbard Treaty. Norway again rejects the view that the Treaty applies beyond Svalbard and its territorial waters. The Soviet Union has refused to recognize the legal validity of the zone, and supports this view by direct reference to the Svalbard Treaty. The zone is non-discriminatory in the sense that foreign fishermen are allowed to fish there provided they comply with the regulatory measures enacted. However, the decision to make the zone non-discriminatory should not be mixed up with the principle of equal treatment in the Svalbard Treaty, which, in the view of the Norwegian authorities, does not apply beyond 4 nautical miles. The corollary of this view is that Norway, whenever circumstances dictate, may convert the zone into a discriminatory or fully fledged economic zone.[32] This has not been considered a realistic approach so far, partly because the objective of the zone — protection of the breeding grounds of important species of fish from overexploitation — can be achieved by means of quotas, rather than by reducing the number of foreign fishermen.

Norway and the Soviet Union thus face three unresolved issues of international law in the Barents Sea: the continental shelf, the fishery protection zone, and the delimitation line. From a legal, technical and formal point of view, all these issues are distinct problems that need to be dealt with *separately*. Some problems concern the administrative and legal status of the ocean floor, others the jurisdictional handling of the water column; some concern the regulation of activities pertaining to minerals, others the allocation of living resources; some have to do with military strategy, others with peaceful exploitation of natural resources. The topics vary both in character and content. Nevertheless, the Norwegian government has realized that the different issue areas make up a complex network of problems woven together with security considerations and spill-over effects. Hence, unfortunate differences of opinion in one issue area may generate impediments to the handling of others, and could damage the general political relationship between the two countries, and potentially between the blocs. The prime goal of the Norwegian government in the North, therefore, is to preserve stability and tranquillity and avoid moves that could engender international conflict.

When, in June 1977, Norway established the FPZ around Svalbard, the government had paid particular attention to the following factors: protection of the living resources in the vulnerable Arctic environment; the interpretation of the Svalbard Treaty; the Norwegian viewpoints with regard to the legal status of the shelf surrounding Svalbard; the conceivable reactions of other governments; and the strategic significance of the area.[33] Likewise, in deliberating on the legal status of the shelf, the government gave considerable thought to the implications of the various policy options before settling on a course. For instance, to counteract a possible suspicion that future activity on the shelf would serve military purposes, the Foreign Minister officially emphasized that such activity would be guided by civilian, peaceful, and ordinary economic principles under firm Norwegian management and control. The government also acknowledges that the Soviet presence on Svalbard, economic considerations apart, is motivated by 'the strategic location of the archipelago and a wish to observe that developments do not run counter to Soviet interests'.[34]

This comprehensive reasoning notwithstanding, the Norwegian authorities insist on handling each issue separately. The Soviets thus far have to all appearances accepted this philosophy and procedure. Soviet diplomats are known, however, informally to have expressed views that can be interpreted as favouring a package deal: that is, an integrated and comprehensive agreement comprising all unresolved questions. If this is really what the Soviets want, they are urging an arrangement that to some extent resembles the one accepted by Norway in the case of Jan Mayen, which combined different issue areas into an overall and integrated solution. The resemblance holds for the second feature of the Jan Mayen solution concept as well, the extended interpretation of 'special circumstances'. Norway partly accepted this in relation to Iceland, but refuses to do so *vis-à-vis* the Soviet Union, which has been advocating an extended interpretation since the mid-1970s. Since they are part of Norway's 'nordpolitikk', both features, and their applicability to the Barents Sea, should therefore be examined in more detail.

The Barents Sea in a Jan Mayen perspective

The integrated, comprehensive agreement envisaged would require that the Soviets temper their resistance to the Norwegian position on exercise of authority over the Svalbard shelf and the FPZ, in return for which they would gain recognition of a dividing line in the Barents Sea closely approximating to the sector line. From the Soviet point of view this outcome has several advantages. A division of the Barents Sea shelf close to the sector line may contribute to alleviating some of the present energy problems of the Soviet Union. It is commonly held that Soviet oil production has all but peaked. Over the last three years the growth in Soviet oil production has been less than one per cent annually, and in 1984 production dropped for the first time. The total demand for oil — from internal consumption, hard currency needs and commitments to Eastern Europe — is nevertheless increasing. So, even with a successful substitution policy the Soviets will no doubt be looking for alternative sources of supply.[35] In the Barents Sea, the disputed area included, the prospects for oil are held to be favourable. If the bulk of this area were secured for the Soviet Union the Soviet economy could benefit to a considerable degree. Such a division line would also secure important fishing grounds in Soviet hands.

Furthermore, given the fact that the Barents Sea is a 'playground' of the Northern Fleet and a stationing area for the *Delta* and *Typhoon* SSBNs, it follows logically that the Soviets prefer any Western activity to occur as far to the west as possible. A division line close to the sector line could satisfy this strategic need. Norway, having for years demonstrated an understanding of Soviet security interests in the North, will, with such a package, be in a position to supervise any foreign presence in the Svalbard waters. The Svalbard Treaty allows nationals of the signatory states unrestricted access to prospect. Only by governing the continental shelf and the FPZ surrounding Svalbard in accordance with international ocean law will Norway be in a position to restrict access and regulate this presence.

On the other hand, lumping together several disputed issue areas means that Norway will have to abandon its policy of refusing an integrated, comprehensive deal. At the moment there is no evidence to suggest that a reappraisal of this policy is being considered in Norwegian political quarters. Nevertheless, a package deal could also benefit Norwegian interests. First, it is evident that the essential precondition for Norway in considering adaptation to Soviet requirements in the Barents Sea is that the Soviets recognize and accept the Norwegian position on the two potentially conflict-laden problem areas concerning Svalbard. Second, the resolution of all outstanding problems is by itself a contribution to preserving the stability and peace of the region, the ultimate goal of Norwegian policy. As long as conclusive dividing lines are not drawn, legal uncertainty may provoke conflicts. Third, as long as the dispute remains unresolved, the parties, Norway in particular, will need to consult and negotiate in order to avoid episodes that may increase tensions. This may result in a bilateralization which will enable the Soviet Union to influence developments in the Norwegian part of the Barents Sea as well. Such an outcome benefits the stronger party only, and is contrary to Norway's postwar policy of avoiding a bilateralization of the Svalbard issues.[36] Last, the parties will have reached a compromise solution between the median line and the sector line. Thus viewed, the package is within the bounds of what Norway could find acceptable.

Norway will indeed, if this outcome materializes, have ceded considerably more of the disputed area than the Soviet Union. This geographical imbalance will, however, be compensated for by the Soviet recognition of Norwegian provisions on the shelf and in the FPZ surrounding Svalbard. A significant aspect of this solution is that it does not require Norway to accept the sector line, while at the same time it appears to meet the assumed Soviet desire to have the boundary drawn as far to the west in the ocean as politically feasible.

The second feature of the Jan Mayen-type solution has to do with the interpretation of 'special circumstances'. As demonstrated in the Soviet–Norwegian negotiations, Norway currently defines this concept in a restricted way, in accordance with the old Law of the Sea — the Continental Shelf Convention of 1958. The extended interpretation applied in connection with Jan Mayen is more in line with the new Law of the Sea as defined in the *1982 Convention of the Law of the Sea.* The criterion for delimitation of continental shelves between adjacent states has mutated from a *specific* into a *diffuse* mode: from the *median line principle* and *'special circumstances'* into *equitable solutions*, the spirit of the 1982 Law of the Sea Convention (LOSC-82) being the new guiding principle. The new delimitation criteria are couched in the following terms (Articles 74 and 83 of the LOSC-82):

1. The delimitation of the exclusive economic zone/ continental shelf between States with opposite or adjacent coasts shall be effected by agreement on the basis of international law ... in order to achieve *an equitable solution.*

3. Pending agreement as provided for in paragraph 1, the States concerned, in a spirit of understanding and cooperation, shall make every effort to enter into provisional arrangements of a practical nature and, during this transitional period, not to jeopardize or hamper the reaching of the final agreement. *Such arrangements shall be without prejudice to the final delimitation.*[37]

This development leaves the settlement of criteria for the stipulation of boundaries to the negotiating parties, while at the same time the scope for consideration of regional characteristics is enlarged. 'Special circumstances' now denote not only geographical factors, but also the political, legal, demographic and economic features of the regions in question that may be taken account of. In the Jan Mayen settlements, Norway took a long step towards accepting this extended interpretation, one important reason being that such flexibility would contribute to an acceptable solution that took account of both parties' national interests. In the Barents Sea, the same approach may be viewed more gloomily through Norwegian eyes, the general apprehension being that when a small state and a superpower define the content of a joint package, the superpower will have the final word. This worst-case perspective can only be corrected if the Soviets show their goodwill and intention to reach an agreed and balanced solution. If this is signalled, the chances are that the Norwegian interpretation may become more favourable.

To what extent, then, is it feasible that Norway and the Soviet Union will orientate their negotiation strategy towards a package deal? As already stated, the Norwegian authorities have not publicly made such intentions known. It is, however, taken for granted that they want an outcome within the political confines they have themselves defined, that is, a compromise between the median and the sector lines. This is a precondition if a package deal is to materialize. Further, it can be taken for granted that the paramount concern is not the *mode* of achieving an agreement, but the *actual attainment* of it, the content being the more important feature. If the authorities come to consider that a shift of policy will yield substantial results, and if national prestige does not gain the upper hand during negotiations, such a shift is definitely feasible. It will not come about, however, if Oslo perceives no counterbalancing gain from the policy change — there will be no changes for the sake of change.

The Soviet Union has not officially revealed any interest in the idea that an alternative arrangement of the negotiations might get the deadlocked talks moving. As previously stated, however, Soviet diplomats have in informal contexts expressed views that can be interpreted as favouring a package deal. Officially, they have advocated the extended interpretation of 'special circumstances' for years. Both parties appear to have something to gain from a conclusive solution, and both have to ease off in order to reach a compromise. It is noticeable that it is primarily the Soviet Union that is pressing for Norwegian–Soviet cooperation in the Barents Sea; it is also the Soviets that most urgently need to get on with exploring for oil. Such factors surely increase the readiness for compromise.

Notes

1. Norway has three separate zones: the mainland zone comprises 875,000 sq. km.; the Svalbard zone up to the ice-edge at 82°N covers 743,000 sq. km. (if Norway establishes a full 200-mile zone beyond the ice-edge, the Svalbard zone will be 836,000 sq. km.); and the size of the Jan Mayen zone is 348,600 sq.km. This makes up a total area of 1,966,600 sq. km. (or 2,059,600 sq. km.). These figures have small margins of error and are based on median-line delimitations wherever final agreements have not been reached.

2. See Ch. 3.

3. Willy Østreng, '*Utlandet i norsk havforvaltning. En studie av utenlandske interessers representasjon i norsk havforvaltningspolitikk*' (Oslo: Fridtjof Nansen Institute Publication Series, No. R:28), pp. 31-3.

4. See Ch. 4.

5. *Report and Recommendations to the Governments of Iceland and Norway of the Conciliation Commission on the Continental Shelf Area Between Iceland and Jan Mayen* (Washington: June 1981), Section V, p. 54.

6. As Note 3, pp. 62-85.

7. Finn Sollie, 'Jan Mayen sonen — Forhandlingene med Island', *Internasjonal Politikk*, No. 3 (1981), pp. 383, 406.

8. Knut Frydenlund, *Lille land — Hva nå?* (Oslo: Universitetsforlaget, 1982), p. 59.

9. Willy Østreng, *Sovjet i nordlige farvann. Atomstrategien, Nordflåten og norsk sikkerhet* (Oslo: Gyldendal Norsk Forlag, 1982).

10. *Ibid.*

11. Ellmann Ellingsen, 'Jan Mayen i norsk sikkerhetspolitikk', in *Aschehougs Leksikonservice*, No. 2 (1977), p. 53. See also Ch. 5.

12. The main content of this article is reproduced in 'Keflavik til Jan Mayen?', in *Aftenposten*, 12 July 1979.

13. As Note 11, p. 53.

14. The Soviet press pointed out that the Jan Mayen dispute could cause a breach of the Norwegian base policy. See 'Sovjet-kommentar til konflikten Island-Norge', in *Aftenposten*, 8 August 1980.

15. As Note 8, p. 59.

16. John Fairlamb, *The Evolution of Icelandic Defence Decision-making 1944-1981* (University of Southern California, 1981). See also his 'Icelandic Threat Perceptions', in *Naval War College Review*, No. 5 (1981).

17. See Helge Ole Bergesen, 'The Progressive Free-Rider or Devoted Internationalist', in H.O. Bergesen, H.H. Holm, and R.D. McKinley (eds), '*The Recalcitrant Rich: A Comparative Analysis of the Demands for a New International Economic Order* (London: Pinter, 1982), pp. 148-69.

18. Willy Østreng, 'Norway's Law of the Sea Policy in the 1970s', in *Ocean Development and International Law: The Journal of Marine Affairs*, Vol. II (1982), No. 1/2, pp. 69-95.

19. These viewpoints were expressed by Deputy Foreign Minister Thorvald Stoltenberg in a talk at the Council of ANSA. Excerpts are printed in 'Norge i stormaktsrolle', *Aftenposten*, 18 August 1979.

20. See Knut Frydenlund, As Note 8, p. 59.

21. Jens Evensen, 'La Délimitation du plateau continental entre la Norvège et l'Islande dans le secteur de Jan Mayen', *Annuaire Français de Droit International*, XXVII (1982), p. 718.

22. As Note 5.

23. For a more thorough discussion of the Jan Mayen Agreement, see Willy Østreng, 'International Exploitation of "National" Ocean Minerals: The Case of Jan Mayen', (Oslo: Fridtjof Nansen Institute Publication Series, No. R:007, 1983). Also published in Mark J. Valencia (ed.), 'The Geology and Hydrocarbon Potential of the South China Sea and Possibilities of Joint Development', in a Special Issue of *Energy, The International Journal*, Vol. 10 (1985), No. 3/4, pp. 551-71.

24. The use of linkage strategies has its pros and cons. As for the former, Tollison and Willett have, in an excellent article, demonstrated the increase in cooperation potential that can be gained this way: 'Our theory stresses issue linkage as a means of overcoming distributional obstacles to international agreement where direct side payments among countries are not a politically feasible alternative.' Fisher, on the other hand, sounds a note of caution: 'The joining of issues as leverage of bargaining currency, even when constructively looking toward a negotiated agreement, tends to shift the focus away from the merits of a problem and to put relative bargaining power at issue.' Robert Tollison and Thomas Willett, 'An Economic Theory of Mutually Advantageous Issue Linkages in International Negotiations', *International Organization*, Vol. 33, Autumn 1979. Roger Fisher, 'Fractionating Conflict', in R. Fisher (ed.), *International Conflict and Behavioral Science: The Craigville Papers* (New York: Basic Books, 1964).

25. A.G. Golovko, *With the Red Fleet: The War Memories of Admiral Golovko* (London: Putnam & Co., 1965), p. 40.

26. Article 7 of the Svalbard Treaty. The states were the USA, France, Italy, Japan, Denmark, Britain, the Netherlands, Sweden and Norway.

27. *Ibid.*, Articles 2 and 3.

28. *Ibid.*, Articles 2, 3, 4, 7 and 8.

29. *Ibid.*, Article 8.

30. For a further discussion of the content of this sovereignty, see Willy Østreng, *Politics in High Latitude: The Svalbard Archipelago* (Montreal:

McGill-Queens University Press, 1978), Ch. 4.

31. See Jens Evensen, 'Oversikt over oljepolitiske spørsmal', in *Betenkning utarbeidet etter oppdrag av Industridepartementet*, January 1971, and *Stortingsmelding*, No. 39, 1974-5 (concerning Svalbard).

32. See Carl August Fleischer, 'Grensene i havet', in Håkon Børde (ed.), *Svalbard oq Havområdene* (Oslo: 'By og bygd' series).

33. *UD-informasjon*, No. 25, 13 July 1977.

34. *Ibid.*

35. J.P. Stern, 'Western Forecasts of Soviet and East European Energy over the Next Decades (1980-2000)', in the Joint Economic Committee of the US Congress (Washington: Government Printing Office, 1980).

36. As Note 30.

37. Emphases added. The wording in the two articles is exactly the same, except that Article 74 refers to 'the exclusive economic zone', and Article 83 to 'the continental shelf'. Paragraph 2 has been omitted from the quotation.

13 GREENLAND AND THE FAROES

Jørgen Taagholt

For one thousand years the North Atlantic islands — Greenland, the Faroes and Iceland — have been politically connected to Europe. Iceland has been independent since 1944, but Greenland and the Faroes are autonomous parts of the Danish kingdom. Their surrounding waters have played an important role in local and European whalehunting and fishing. Yet, from an international perspective, they have been seen as very remote and uninteresting regions with no political or strategic importance. Since World War II the situation has changed.

Greenland is the largest island in the world, covering about 2.2 million square kilometres, or approximately one third of the area of the United States. It spans 24 degrees of latitude (i.e., some 2,670 km from south to north, with the northern part being the most northern land of the world, only some 700 km from the North Pole) and approximately 60 degrees of longitude (with a maximum width of roughly 1,200 km). Only a small fraction of it, some 350,000 square kilometres, is not permanently covered by ice. The 50,000 inhabitants live mostly along a 1,500 km coastline in Southwest Greenland.

The Faroe Islands are located between Iceland and Scotland and consist of 17 inhabited islands that cover in total some 1,400 square kilometres. They have a population of approximately 45,000.

A brief survey of the historical development of these societies throws some light on current political and security conditions in the North Atlantic Danish islands.

Historical perspective

Greenland was first inhabited by Eskimo tribes, followed by Vikings from Scandinavia. In the ninth century AD, Norsemen settled in the Faroes and Iceland as well as Greenland. Thus the Vikings bound together all the larger North Atlantic islands into a huge extended empire. Subsequently, Eskimos predominated in

174

Greenland after a new immigration wave and the apparent decline of the Norsemen.

In the seventeenth century large whaling fleets brought renewed contact with Europe in their wake and some racial intermingling. A combination of trading and missionary interests brought about Greenland's close attachment to the Danish–Norwegian kingdom and then to Denmark, and the 1814 Treaty of Kiel placed the North Atlantic islands under the Danish crown. The Royal Danish Trade Departments established trade monopoly in Greenland and the Faroes, but this ended in 1856 in the Faroes, where two political movements later arose, one working for cooperation with Denmark, the other seeking independence, and both strongly affecting politics in the islands from 1900 until 1940.

The Danish administration in Greenland, for the two centuries prior to World War II, pursued a policy of positive isolationism designed to preserve the indigenous hunting culture while introducing formal education and allowing racial mixing. Exploration of Greenland was facilitated by the Danish navy's role in scientific expeditions.

Greenland since 1940

During World War II the North Atlantic area and even the Arctic became strategically important. Aircraft were not capable of crossing the Atlantic without refuelling stops *en route*. Meteorological observations from the North Atlantic and Greenland were vital for ship and air transport and even for the war front in Europe. With the German occupation of Denmark in April 1940, the connection between Denmark and its North Atlantic islands was severed.

In Greenland the Danish administration decided, together with the Danish Embassy in Washington, that the United States should take over the supply service to Greenland. This arrangement was later clarified by the Washington Agreement of 9 April 1941. While the USA recognized Danish sovereignty over Greenland, it was permitted to establish military bases and weather stations. Several air bases were built, of which 'Bluie West One' — now the Danish civilian airport Narssarssuaq — was the most important. Some 28,000 aircraft passed through Bluie West One on their way from the USA to Europe. During the war the number of synoptic meteorological stations in Greenland increased from 5 to 26.[1]

Not long after Denmark became a member of NATO in 1949, a new *Danish–American Defence Agreement* was signed on 27 April 1951. This led to improvements at Søndre Strømfjord (Bluie West Eight), and to the establishment of Thule air base in 1952, the Ballistic Missile Early Warning System (BMEWS) and the Distant Early Warning (DEW) radar chain, which stretched from Alaska over Canada and Greenland to the United Kingdom. In Greenland the Danish Greenland Command was established in 1946, and has been located since 1951 at Grønnedal.

The construction of the defence installations in Greenland showed that it now seemed possible — technologically at least — to build a modern society in the far north, a possibility which in turn led to further interest in the utilization of Arctic resources.

After World War II the Danish government took over the running of all the pre-war weather stations in Greenland and most of the new ones established by the USA during the war. Denmark continued to meet its obligation to supply weather information in agreement with the convention of the World Meteorological Organization. Today weather information is supplied by means of automatic synoptic stations (19 stations since 1984), from which data are transmitted every third hour via polar orbiting satellites to a Danish satellite tracking station at Søndre Strømfjord.[2]

For the Greenlanders the war resulted in rising expectations and a desire to open up their country, so that the whole island could enjoy the advantages of the technological development they had witnessed during the war. When the Danish Prime Minister, Hans Hedtoft, visited Greenland in 1948, he was shocked to see the living conditions there. As a result of this visit, the Danes initiated major development projects during the 1950s and 1960s with the agreement of the local Greenland council (Landsraadet).

A *new Danish constitution* was adopted by referendum on 28 May 1953, under which Greenland became a province within the kingdom of Denmark, enjoying equal status with the rest of the country and having two representatives in the Danish parliament. The incorporation was endorsed by the United Nations General Assembly in 1954, partly on the basis of a recommendation from a Greenlandic delegation.

In many respects political reforms were more feasible in Greenland than in Alaska or Northern Canada. Most of the Greenlanders had settled along the coast, where there is year-round access to the sea for approximately half the population.

Contact with Scandinavia resulted in a slow, harmonious development and provided an improved educational system which laid the necessary foundation for Greenlandic political autonomy. Over the previous century Greenlanders had gradually become involved in administrative and political activities. This was initially the result of the work of H.J. Rink and the establishment of the Forstanderskab (superintendency) in 1857, and later the creation of the two Greenlandic councils in 1908, one for North and one for South Greenland. Unlike other northern ethnic groups, Greenlanders have also always been in a majority; today they make up over 80 per cent of the total population.

Social and economic conditions have also changed radically in postwar Greenland. The relatively mild climate in the century up to about 1960 offered opportunities for large-scale fishing, and kayaks were replaced by fleets of vessels. The establishment of factories to process fishery products resulted in the concentration of the population in towns near open water, so that now more than 70 per cent live in towns with more than 1,000 inhabitants. Many settlements have disappeared, and the Greenlanders have seen their society transformed from a barter into a money economy, with consequent changes in their living conditions. Apartment buildings have shot up and the concentration of people has made it possible to introduce modern sanitary facilities. Mortality has dropped from a very high level to one corresponding to that in Denmark itself, while the birth-rate has remained high. Children and young people make up nearly half of the present population in Greenland (43 per cent were under 20 years old in 1980). The total population has increased from 23,600 in 1950 to 52,347 in 1984, of which about 9,217 were born outside Greenland.[3]

Nationalist and separatist political trends stemming from the social changes of the 1950s and 1960s evoked a response especially from young intellectual Greenlanders. A desire emerged for a greater Greenlandic influence in local matters. Municipal reform came in 1975, together with the initial preparation for *Home Rule*, which was finally introduced on 1 May 1979.[4]

The Greenlandic executive authority (Landsstyret) and the Greenlandic assembly (Landstinget) have taken over responsibility for areas ranging from education, land planning, commercial fishing, trapping and hunting to the activities of the former Royal Greenland Trade Department. Foreign affairs and defence policy, however, remain under Danish control.

The Home Rule Act established that the resident population of Greenland has fundamental rights to the natural resources of Greenland. In order to safeguard the rights of the resident population regarding non-living resources and to protect the interest of the realm, it was stipulated that the preliminary study, prospecting and exploitation of these resources should be regulated by agreement between the Danish government and the Greenland assembly. Both have a right of veto in these questions.

As political awareness has increased in Greenland over the past ten years, political parties have been created. However, only three parties were present in the Landsting after the election in 1984: Siumut (Forward) with 11 seats, Attasut (Mutual) with 11 seats, and Inuit Ataqatigiit (Inuit Brotherhood) with 3 seats. Both Siumut and Attasut favour Home Rule and integration with Denmark. The Inuit Ataqatigiit, having rejected Home Rule in their programme and called for Greenland to secede from Denmark, today cooperate with Siumut and help to form the present Home Rule government.

In 1973 Denmark became a member of the EC. Since Greenland at that time (unlike the Faroe Islands) did not have Home Rule, it entered the EC in spite of an overwhelming local objection to membership. After Greenlandic Home Rule was introduced, the Greenland assembly decided to hold a referendum on Greenland's EC membership in 1982.[5] Approximately 52 per cent of the electorate voted against continued membership and, after difficult negotiations between Denmark/Greenland and the EC, it was agreed that Greenland would withdraw from the Community by 1 January 1985, though this was delayed to 1 February 1985. Greenland achieved Overseas Countries and Territories status and free access to the Community for Greenlandic fishery products, in exchange for a satisfactory agreement on access to Greenlandic waters for Community fishermen. In addition, the Community will pay Greenland financial compensation at the rate of 26.5 million European Currency Units annually.

The regional financial support from the EC for Greenland amounted to approximately 40 million Danish kroner in 1973, a sum that increased to roughly 176 million kroner in 1983.[6] But Greenlandic politicians hope to obtain the financial support for trade and industrial development that has so far been received from the EC from other sources, such as payments for fishery licences.

Among the countries that traditionally fish in Greenlandic waters are Denmark, the Faroe Islands, Norway, West Germany and the Soviet Union. The Soviet Union's presence on Svalbard is maintained for political rather than economic reasons, since coal production on Svalbard runs at a loss for Norway, and the Soviet Union's deficit must be even greater. For similar reasons the Soviet Union may be willing to pay highly for a legal presence in Greenlandic waters. The Western world, including the EC, has to be ready to step in to prevent an unwanted Soviet presence around and in Greenland. Following Greenland's withdrawal from the EC, negotiations with third countries, for example with Norway, have led to free trade agreements.

There is today a trend towards closer contact between the ethnic groups of Alaska, northern Canada, and Greenland, reflected in the signing of the *Inuit Circumpolar Conference* (ICC) charter in 1980. In Greenland and Denmark, the ICC is seen as an expression of close cultural cooperation between neighbours and kinsmen which ought to combine fruitfully with Danish–Greenlandic cultural cooperation. The ICC has, however, harmed its own interests by expressing foreign policy viewpoints that are more idealistic than realistic, and it is thereby risking the growth of doubts as to its nature and purpose.

Greater contact has been established between the so-called *North Atlantic societies*: the Faroe Islands, Iceland and Greenland. In both the Faroes and Greenland, small minorities want separation from Denmark. It is sometimes said that it was unfortunate that the 1814 Treaty of Kiel did not result in an association with Norway, since the lifestyles of Norway and Greenland have more in common: for example, fishing, sheep-farming and reindeer-breeding. However, the characteristic Danish recognition of their lack of knowledge of Greenland, combined with their respect for Greenlandic expertise in trapping and hunting, has resulted in a cooperation based on trust that imported superior Norwegian knowledge could hardly have promoted.

Greenland is to take over not just responsibility for, but also execution of, the many complicated tasks which a modern society must undertake. Vital economic and professional assistance from Denmark will continue, but it will be necessary to maintain a balance so that Greenlanders do not feel that they are under the guardianship of any external power. For the Western world it is important that Greenland keeps its status as a part of the Danish kingdom, and an effort should be made to increase the awareness that it is possible to be a Greenlander and a Dane at the same time.

Although the amount of *fish* caught off Greenland has decreased dramatically since 1967, because of climatic changes and, possibly, overfishing, Greenlanders now have the right to catch as much as they have the capacity for. Although total harvesting has declined, the Greenlandic share has increased.

Significant variations in the *climate* have been observed in the Arctic within recent times. Broadly speaking, a heating up in the first part of the century, with a temperature climax in the 1930s, was followed by a cooling in the 1960s and 1970s. This variation was most pronounced in the Barents Sea, but also affected marine living resources in Greenlandic waters. Human activity, however, mainly in the form of industrial development and the profligate use of fossil fuels (coal, oil, gas), is among the factors scientists expect to have an impact on the earth's climate in future, generally causing higher temperatures, with the most pronounced effect in the Arctic. For societies that depend on marine living resources, climatic changes are of great importance. Although climatological measurements in Greenland are essential, it is difficult to separate observations of man-made impacts on the climate from the natural fluctuations that are observed but still not understood.

For societies whose income is primarily based on marine living resources, the negotiations at the United Nations Conference on the *Law of the Sea* have been important. Greenlandic and Danish politicians and officials work together at such international negotiations to further the interests of Greenland. This is an important dimension of Danish–Greenlandic cooperation.

Between 1976 and 1980, Denmark extended the fisheries zone around Greenland and the Faroe Islands to 200 nautical miles. The delimitation of the fisheries zone towards Norway (the islands of Jan Mayen and Spitsbergen), Iceland and, to a certain extent, Canada, still remains unresolved. In the Kennedy Channel, sovereignty over a tiny island, Hans Island, is disputed between Denmark and Canada.

Greenland is the focus for increasing Danish and international *research* activity. Government and private industry are involved in a wide range of investigations that relate to exploitation of renewable resources, in addition to pure research. Although the

Greenland Fishery and Environment Research Institute has so far worked in cooperation with research institutes from other countries, it now increasingly works alone. With a 200-mile fishery zone around Greenland, other countries retain only an academic interest in fishery research in Greenlandic waters. The consequent reduction in research may affect future international negotiations concerning fish quota agreements, since such agreements require documented research data.

The Greenland Geological Survey is responsible for the general geological mapping of Greenland, and is increasingly involved in governmental exploration into Greenlandic energy resources. Both the Greenland Fishery and Environment Research Institute and the Greenland Geological Survey have consultative and controlling functions in the granting of exploitation concessions to private companies.

Roughly a hundred scientific expeditions visit Greenland each year, of which more than half are foreign. Much of this research has great importance for Greenland. All research in and around Greenland has to be approved by the Ministry for Greenland, and it is coordinated through the Danish Commission for Scientific Research in Greenland, which was established in 1878. Greenland is an open country, and both the Danish government and the Home Rule authorities place as few impediments in the way of scientific research as possible.

Greenland's minerals play a significant role domestically as well as internationally, and perhaps its *energy resources*, too, will be equally important in the future. The primary occupations — fishing and hunting — cannot continue to support the ever-increasing population, and for this reason alone new jobs must be introduced, if unemployment is to be avoided.

Greenland's resources include coal, uranium, several metals, such as lead, chromium, molybdenum and tungsten, and maybe oil and natural gas as well. Although the chromium deposits are modest compared with global reserves, it is nevertheless likely that they are larger than any other deposits within NATO. The importance of the chromium is further demonstrated by the fact that more than 90 per cent of the other available reserves — outside Warsaw Pact countries — are in South Africa and Zimbabwe, countries which in the longer term can hardly be considered a guaranteed source of supply.

Hydroelectric power generation has long been considered

possible in Greenland. In recent years there have been comprehensive glacier-hydrological, geological and meteorological investigations under Danish state management to establish the technical and physical feasibility of setting up hydroelectric plants. Exploitation of the hydroelectric potential seems feasible partly for the supply of local communities and partly for industrial utilization, especially in such high energy-consuming activities as aluminium production based on the deposits of anorthosite and in the production by electrolysis of ammonia-based fertilizer.

In accordance with the agreement over mineral resources of the Danish–Greenlandic Joint Committee, the Danish government has signed a new 1985 Jameson Land concession for oil and natural gas exploitation in an area of some 10,000 square kilometres in East Greenland, just west of Scoresbysund between 70°N and 74°N. The concession was awarded to the Atlantic Richfield Company (ARCO), Arktisk Minekompagni A/S, and a new public corporation in which ownership is split equally between the Danish state and the Greenland Home Rule authorities.

Whether or not Greenland's resources are utilized, they exist and hence are significant in strategic terms. If West European energy supplies reached a crisis point, and Greenland vetoed any proposal to extract its own resources, the Danish–Greenlandic relationship would be put to the test, and a disagreement between the Greenlandic executive authorities and the Danish government could provoke other nations into contemplating intervention.

The extraction of Greenland's resources, however, demands enormous investment of money and manpower, and dependence on imports. An agreed and controlled development of Greenland's resources is the most probable outcome, in keeping with the Greenlandic feeling of solidarity with the rest of the world. Dependence on energy imports, in the long term, makes little sense when combined with restrictions that make exploitation of its own resources impossible. But if utilization of the not yet proven oil resources, and the subsequent increased income, promote separatist movements, Greenland and Denmark may face political problems. A sovereign Greenlandic state with large energy resources would be a tempting target for the superpowers, and the USA, for example, would in all probability never accept another European state's control over Greenland.

Before World War II, the North Atlantic (and especially Greenland) was, because of its remoteness, of no *strategic interest.*

The primary aim for Denmark was to secure sovereignty over the whole of Greenland, and the only serious threat to that was the Norwegian occupation of part of northeast Greenland in July 1931. This conflict was resolved peacefully at the International Court in The Hague, which in 1933 confirmed the Danish right to sovereignty over the whole of the island.

Since World War II Greenland has received growing attention, partly because of its strategic position in the North Atlantic at a time when the Soviet Northern Fleet has been expanding, and partly because of its endowment of natural resources and the technological developments necessary to extract them.

Strategic issues in any region of the world are not solely concerned with foreign policy, military alliances, forces and equipment. Increasingly, a wider range of factors, among them resources (human, material, and financial), scientific and technological development, transportation and communication, and domestic political situations (trade relations, social and economic trends) have to be assessed. Although the Greenlanders have throughout their history struggled against a hard and merciless climate and environment, they have never been at war, and security/political issues are in Greenland very abstract, far from the centre of daily political debate.

Danish defence forces have been active in Greenland for more than 250 years. To meet their obligations — surveillance, maintenance of sovereignty, search and rescue — the forces, under the Greenland Command at Grønnedal, have several inspection cutters and ships with helicopters, and an air force squadron at Søndre Strømford with either *C-130 Hercules* or *Gulf Stream III* aircraft. The forces play a more integrated part in Greenlandic daily life than in Denmark because the Danish forces have traditionally supported scientific expeditions, and today they provide logistic services for the local communities.

Some local politicians have proposed that all young Greenlanders should be enlisted to support the civilian aspects of the work of the Greenland Command. At one time Greenlanders could volunteer for military service in Greenland but, because of financial constraints, this no longer is the case. However, military service in Denmark with the same rights as the Danes is still possible.

In northern Greenland the Danish state also exercises its sovereignty by means of the Sirius Sledge Patrol. Every year, patrols cover a coastal area from Scoresbysund via the northeast corner to Nares Strait in the northwest — a stretch of about 3,000 km, uninhabited except for a few scattered Danish stations.

The military defence of Greenland is only possible because of the *bilateral agreement between Denmark and the USA*. The USA does not, however, maintain defence forces or equipment there or, in accordance with Danish foreign policy, nuclear weapons. Instead, Danish–American defence areas have been established under the agreement, which allows the two governments to set up installations as required for the defence of Greenland and other NATO countries. These commitments to NATO cannot be altered by the Home Rule authorities and cannot be put to a referendum. Current US defence installations in Greenland comprise the BMEWS radar site near Thule air base, a US air force satellite control facility located at Thule air base, and four DEW radar sites, which are linked to Søndre Strømfjord air base and form part of the DEW line across Alaska, Canada and Greenland to Iceland.[7]

During his visit to the USA in 1980, the chairman of the Home Rule executive, Jonathan Motzfeldt, stressed the importance of military installations in Greenland, as being primarily for surveillance but also serving Greenlandic society by providing an important gateway for civilian air traffic. The airport at Søndre Strømfjord is today part military, part civilian and, together with Thule air base and Narssarssuaq, it is served year-round by the Scandinavian Airlines System (SAS) with up to eleven weekly flights between Copenhagen and Greenland during the summer. The total number of transatlantic passengers during 1982 was 65,988.

During the debate on EC membership, Jonathan Motzfeldt and other influential politicians stated that the secession would have no impact on the Greenlandic relationship with NATO or the Danish–American Defence Agreement. Even Inuit Ataqatigiit state that the defence installations in Greenland are of importance to their ethnic relatives in Arctic Canada and Alaska. Meanwhile, although the Home Rule authorities are extending their control over still more matters, foreign and defence policies remain the responsibility of the Danish realm, and a Greenlandic *separation* from Denmark is not the subject of any serious discussion.

Greenlanders are rightly proud of their country and heritage: the hunting trade represents a very highly developed culture, which has reached its present level over the course of centuries. It is a culture which is reflected, for instance, in matters concerning hunting dress, dog sledges and kayaks.

As stated by Greenland politicians, ties of friendship with ethnic kinsfolk to the west of Greenland will probably endure. Similarly, the family ties with Denmark, created by peaceful colonization, cultural impact and the mixture of the races for more than 250 years, cannot be severed. There is a growing understanding in Greenland that Greenlanders can choose their form and degree of dependence; independence itself is not a matter for choice.

Finn Lynge, formerly Greenlandic member of the European parliament, has mentioned the following four possible prospective partners or sources of economic and human support for the new Greenland under Home Rule: Denmark, the EC, North America and the Soviet Union. He gave a strong hint of the answer to the question when he said: 'The Greenlanders have their friends in North America and their family in Denmark. As a member of a family grows, it is natural that differences arise. But in an open and trustful family atmosphere, such differences will eventually contribute to strengthening the family ties.'[8]

The *political situation* in Greenland, in terms of its security and strategic importance in the decades to come, depends in the main on foreign political trends, technological progress and domestic political developments. Greenland itself has little influence on the first two conditions, but domestic political stability, which is controlled by the Home Rule authorities, is essential. It is difficult to create stable conditions in a society involved in a rapid process of transformation, and one in which the democratic system frequently leads to unrealistic expectations, attempts to obtain the unobtainable, and encourages often emotional demands to take over administrative burdens. None of this is realistic; today the politician needs to be rational and balanced.

Denmark contributes to domestic stability by continuing its financial support for the Greenlandic society of about 2,000 million kroner a year (40,000 kroner per capita). This is in accordance with the 1953 Danish constitution, which gives the Greenlanders the right to enjoy equal status with the rest of the country. The investment per capita in Greenland since World War II is roughly equal to that in Denmark over the same period and has created a modern infrastructure: health, education services, housing and industrial activity.

Another important ingredient for stability is domestic responsibility, that is, giving local politicians not only influence but also accountability. The task for the Home Rule authorities — who are responsible in a huge geographic area for trade that ranges from Arctic hunting to modern industrial mining, while there is an increasing unemployment problem and unfortunate climatic cooling — may seem hopeless, but there are after all certain qualities in the Greenlandic mentality which form the basis for optimism. By nature the Greenlander is peaceful and socially conscious; he is not normally aggressive and has a well-developed sense of humour — all qualities which are essential when dealing with reality. However, a great cause for concern is the growing consumption of alcohol in Greenland, a result of the past 25 years of development and alterations in the living conditions. As a consequence, violence has become a part of the community, and it is a problem the Home Rule authorities try to contain by means of local information and restrictions.

Frustrated expectations cause some Greenlandic criticism of Danish management and of local Greenlandic politicians and officials, but in the end the Home Rule authorities have the support of loyal and orthodox Greenlanders, irrespective of which party forms the local government.

The Danish people must understand that the Landsting cannot be expected to solve the multifarious and often complicated problems it faces without making mistakes. It is very important that errors are tolerated. One should also cherish the hope that the Greenlanders, who now number about 50,000, will be able, in the face of inevitable technological development, to preserve due respect for their Inuit heritage, and balance newly acquired technical capabilities with traditional skills.

The Faroes since 1940

In April 1940 the Faroe Islands were occupied by British forces. The Faroese Lagting (assembly) lodged a formal protest which stressed the wish of the Faroese that they be kept outside the struggles of foreign powers. However, relations between the British forces and the population became very cordial, and throughout the war the local fishing fleet made a significant contribution to Britain's fish supply, during the course of which the Faroese lost a third of their fishing fleet and relatively more lives than other active western allies.

Meanwhile, the local Lagting took over legislative power, and Faroese ships began using the local Faroese flag, which was acknowledged by the British government as an allied flag. However, a proposal for secession from Denmark was rejected. In 1946 Denmark took over the British Radio Navigation Station in the Faroes, and in May 1961 the Danish Faroe Command was established at Torshavn.

In 1948 *Home Rule* was introduced within the framework of national unity. Under the Home Rule Act the democratically elected Lagting is the legislative authority in certain spheres, mainly related to internal affairs, especially economic matters. It has the right to take over other matters, but questions relating to foreign and defence policy remain within the scope of national unity under Denmark. The Faroes still elect two members to the Danish parliament.

Originally, the chief economic activity in the Faroes was *agriculture* (including sheep-farming), which today employs only 1.6 per cent of the population. Most of the area is rock or pasture, and only some 2 per cent of the land is cultivated.

Fishing is now the most important trade and includes fish catches in near and distant waters and fish-processing. Since World War II fishing has undergone rapid development through investment in modern cutters and trawlers and in fish-processing plants.

In the negotiations over *accession to the EC* (1970-2), Denmark as well as Norway (and to some extent Britain and Ireland) tried to obtain changes in the Common Fisheries Policy in order to safeguard the interests of those peripheral societies overwhelmingly dependent upon fisheries, such as the Faroe Islands, Greenland, northern Norway, the Shetlands, etc. These endeavours only succeeded to such a modest degree that not one of these societies voted in favour of joining the EC. As to the Faroe Islands, it was stated in the Treaty of Accession that the Faroes within three years could ask the Danish government to let the Treaty come into force in the islands. In 1974 the Lagting unanimously agreed that the Faroe Islands should not be included in the Treaty. Instead, a kind of free trade arrangement came into force in 1974.

The introduction of the *200-mile fisheries zone* regime in the North Atlantic had a drastic impact on the Faroese economy. The major part of Faroese catches had come from distant waters. The 200-mile regime meant the exclusion of Faroese vessels from most of their traditional fishing grounds. Faroese regulative power over their own 200-mile fisheries zone will be an advantage for the islands in the long term, but this advantage is overshadowed, in the short and medium run, by transition difficulties. In order to ease this transition and to obtain optimum utilization of the fishing fleets and the fish stocks, bilateral agreements with other countries in the North Atlantic have been necessary. Such agreements have been made with the USA, Canada, the EC, Iceland, Norway, the Soviet Union and the GDR.

In most of these negotiations the Faroe Islands are in a *demandeur* position, because Faroese fishing in foreign waters is more important to the Faroese economy than fishing in Faroese waters is to foreign economies. The Faroese authorities have felt that it has been difficult to obtain sufficient political understanding, except from Iceland, for the special and difficult Faroese situation. In particular, they have noted a lack of understanding in the EC, notably from Britain. Accordingly, in order to compensate for the loss of areas where they can take catches, especially in EC waters, they have increased the level of exchange of mutual fishing rights with the Soviet Union.

The delimitation of the Faroese 200-mile fisheries zone *vis-à-vis* Iceland and the United Kingdom has still not been agreed. Both of these countries use some very small uninhabited rocks for calculating the median line with the Faroe Islands. The Danish government has contested this as being contrary to international law.

The Faroe Islands, together with the Faroe/Rockall Plateau to their southwest, form a so-called micro-continent, which is separated from the neighbouring countries — the United Kingdom, Ireland and Iceland — by steep drops in the ocean floor. The Danish government is of the opinion that this plateau belongs to the continental shelf of the Faroe Islands, but the UK, Ireland and Iceland also lay claim to it.

Danish *defence* is responsible for surveillance, fisheries protection, and search and rescue services in the islands and their surrounding waters. The activities of the Danish defence forces are conducted from the Faroe Command at Torshavn. The same types of protection vessel and aircraft are used as in Greenland. Although Russian ships have not been frequently observed in the

Greenlandic area since the introduction of the 200-mile zone in 1977, vessels from Eastern Europe can often be seen north of the Faroe Islands, and in recent years Soviet naval activity has advanced towards the south and west in the North Atlantic area, thus approaching the waters around the Faroe Islands.

The relevance of the Faroe Islands in terms of security policy must be seen in the light of the decisive role which the North Atlantic plays in the NATO alliance, especially in its sea lines of communication. The critical line is the so-called GIUK gap, which forms a bottleneck through which any deployment will have to take place. Consequently, the Faroe Islands, which are located almost on this line, are an important element in the NATO defence system. They therefore host a number of NATO *communication and warning installations*. However, the people of the Faroe Islands have no military traditions, and apart from these installations and the Faroe Command at Torshavn there are no military facilities on the islands. The Danish navy maintains the necessary presence of inspection units, but in peacetime the islands have no operational forces.[9]

Notes

1. H.C. Bach and J. Taagholt, *Udviklingstendenser for Grønland* (Copenhagen: Nyt Nordisk Forlag, 1976), p. 205.
2. A. Johnson and J. Taagholt, 'Ionospheric Effects on C³I Satellite Communications Systems in Greenland', *Radio Science*, Vol. 20 (1985), No. 3, pp. 339-46.
3. L. Lyck and J. Taagholt 'Greenland today — Economy and Resources', *Arctic* (in press), Table 3.
4. I. Foighel, 'Home Rule in Greenland', *Meddelelser am Grønland: Man & Society*, No. 1 (Copenhagen, 1980).
5. H. Rasmussen (ed.), *Greenland in the Process of Leaving the European Communities* (Copenhagen: Forlaget Europa, 1983), p. 6.
6. Ministeriet for Grønland, *Grønland 1983* (Copenhagen: Ministry for Greenland), p. 59.
7. H.C. Bach and J. Taagholt, *Greenland and the Arctic Region: Resources and Security Policy* (Copenhagen: The Information and Welfare Service of the Danish Defence, 1982), pp. 52-5.
8. F. Lynge, *Tanker i et bulldozerspor* (Godthåb: Det Grønlandske Forlag, 1977), p. 156.
9. A.C. Sjaastad and J.K. Skogan, *Politik og sikkerhet i Norskehavsområdet* (Oslo: Dreyers Forlag, 1975).

14 ICELAND: UNARMED ALLY[1]

Nigel de Lee

Iceland is a paradoxical country. It is a young Republic peopled by an old and highly cultured nation. The people are of mainly Nordic origin, but are more akin to the Irish in philosophical outlook.[2] The Republic is sovereign, but has no armed forces. It is the least military country in the world, but was a founder member of NATO, and is in close cooperation with the USA. The standard of living is high, but the economy is extremely vulnerable to economic, political and natural forces. At times, the economic interests of the nation have been in direct conflict with the security policy of the state.

Iceland achieved Home Rule in 1918, after a century of peaceful but vigorous agitation against Danish control. The Icelandic government immediately declared a policy of perpetual unarmed neutrality. This was regarded as proper and practical since Iceland had no armed forces, had escaped involvement in World War I, and had faith in the League of Nations. By 1939 strategic and technical developments had made Iceland of compelling interest to both Britain and Germany, and in 1940 British troops occupied the country.[3] The USA took over the occupation in 1941, while still a non-belligerent. In 1944 the Icelanders dissolved their residual links with Denmark and proclaimed a Republic. They looked forward to a return to demilitarized neutrality at the conclusion of hostilities. American requests for long-term bases were strongly rejected, and by 1947 the last combat troops had departed.

Events in 1948 convinced the government that disarmed and isolated neutrality under the protection of the United Nations was not a safe policy. In 1949, with Scandinavian encouragement, Iceland became a reluctant and restrictive founder member of the North Atlantic Alliance.[4] Communist aggression in Korea convinced the government that it had to accept a military presence in order to obtain security. As a result of the 1951 Defence Agreement, the USA acquired bases in Iceland, and promised to defend the Republic with the US-manned Icelandic Defence Force (IDF).

Membership of NATO and the Defence Agreement remain the

twin pillars of Icelandic security policy, but they have been challenged. In 1956 the government sought to remove the IDF, but was dissuaded by the crisis in Hungary. In 1973-4 Iceland threatened to leave NATO in protest against British conduct of the fisheries dispute, but Britain conceded. Membership of NATO and the presence of the garrison remain topics of political controversy.

The strategic importance of Iceland derives from its geographical position. In peacetime it is vital to NATO's surveillance of Warsaw Pact naval and maritime air activity in the North Atlantic. In time of emergency or war, NATO would rely upon forces based in Iceland to prevent the Soviet Northern Fleet from breaking out into the Atlantic, to secure the sea lines of communication from the USA to Europe, and to maintain the reinforcement airbridge. If NATO were to adopt a more forward defence in the North Atlantic, Iceland could be an excellent base from which to mount attacks on Soviet installations in the Kola Peninsula.

The political background to security policy

Icelanders are nationalists, deeply concerned with their origins, proud of their unique culture. It is this culture, based on language, literature and historical experience, which is regarded as defining and animating the nation.[5] Any threat to the cultural heritage is seen as a threat to the survival of the nation.

The obsession with national origins and cultural purity has encouraged a defensive xenophobia and conservatism, and a desire to isolate the nation from the world. This explains the sensitivity to any factor or event which might impinge upon the sovereignty or independence of the Republic, and the sentimental regard for a policy of neutrality. Basic social values are derived from a consideration of the past: the ancient tradition of individualism mitigated by voluntary mutual assistance means that Icelanders are libertarian.[6] They are impatient of central authority, moralistic and legalistic in political outlook. Individuals may be guided by moral principle, but often have a cynical view of politics. The attitude to law is instrumental and argumentative, resulting in 'exact and pedantic and supple and subtle interpretation'.[7]

During the Age of Settlement, Icelanders frequently resorted to armed violence to settle disputes or discharge moral obligations, but they never formed an army. This ignorance of military service, the association of armies with the era of Danish rule, and the general lack of discipline makes them profoundly unmilitary and anti-military in outlook. Armies are regarded as being *per se* absurd and dangerous, and most Icelanders would consider them inconsistent with their own commitments to pacifism and human rights. The use of armed force by state against state, or government against people, is considered wrong.[8] By extension, this leads to a suspicion and fear of military alliances. Even the most conservative Icelanders look forward to the time when force will be replaced by arbitration, negotiation and the rule of law under the auspices of the UN.[9] Some Icelanders are attracted to Marxism by its anti-colonialist rhetoric and commitment to 'peace and freedom'. In the past, to be Marxist was fashionable and a distinct advantage in academic life; recently, however, young Icelanders have turned from Marxist ideas, partly because of the record of the USSR on human rights, and partly because of an increased commitment to individual freedom. The notion that the USSR was a friend to small nations struggling for independence was discredited by the Vietnamese invasion of Cambodia and the Soviet intervention in Afghanistan.

Most Icelanders know nothing of strategic matters,[10] so public opinion on security issues is vague, emotional, contrary and fearful of change. The result has been a consistent level of unenthusiastic support for the official policy.[11] Opinion polls show that 80 per cent of those with an opinion support NATO membership, while some 64 per cent favour retention of the IDF. However, both are seen as necessary temporary measures, not permanent, natural, or desirable in themselves.[12] There is a general ignorance of how military alliances work, and of how Iceland's security is connected to that of the West in general. Many Icelanders wish that Iceland could escape from the frightening and dangerous bipolar world, and retire into unobtrusive neutrality, protected by strategic insignificance, demilitarized status, harmlessness and international guarantees. Some consider that refusal to be a pawn in the strategic game between the superpowers is practical, prudent and morally imperative, and that abstention from alignment would be the safest policy. They believe that close association with the USA is dangerous because Iceland, being a small nation, could lose political and economic independence and risk cultural distortion as a result of the influence of its ally.[13]

Rational consideration of national security is also prevented by an intense emotional horror of all things nuclear, and a refusal to admit that the safety of the Republic might depend upon nuclear weapons. There is a superstitious conviction that the existence of nuclear weapons makes war more likely, and that only nuclear installations or weapons would attract nuclear attacks. This in turn leads to the belief that conventional defence is irrelevant, because any war will rapidly escalate to full nuclear exchange; so, alliance to a nuclear power may well guarantee destruction rather than security. The Icelandic Peace Movement, which emerged in 1980-1 and is based on the church, doctors, and feminist groups, concentrates its efforts on general anti-nuclear propaganda and encounters little opposition. Some 66 per cent of the public support the movement, and 79 per cent of NATO supporters favour the establishment of a Nordic nuclear-free zone.[14]

Although a significant and vociferous minority of Icelanders, adroitly led by the People's Alliance, has persistently attacked the official policy, a solid if inert mass of support for the status quo has emerged. This majority appears to be influenced by some notion of the strategic importance of Iceland, concern to show solidarity with Norway, and unease at the behaviour of the USSR, but most of all by a strong prejudice against radical change.[15]

The impact of party politics

The inhibitions imposed by public opinion have been complicated by the constitution and politics of the Republic. The legislature, the Althing, consists of 60 members elected by proportional representation. There are four main parties, and none has ever commanded an absolute majority, so all governments are coalitions. The members of the cabinet are responsible to the Althing individually, but not collectively. Ministers often adopt policies which impede or contradict the intentions of each other. When coalitions are being formed, highly contentious matters are usually set aside by mutual agreement. In this way party leaders can take office without alienating electoral support by publicly abandoning their commitments. In the past, parties to a coalition have agreed to maintain the status quo in security policy, and not to treat it as a live issue. The political manifesto of the latitudinarian coalition that formed in 1980 made no direct mention of security.[16]

The main parties are the Independence Party (IP), Progressive Party (PP), Social Democratic Party (SDP) and People's Alliance (PA). In 1983 the SDP split, with the splinter calling itself the Social Democratic Alliance (SDA), and the Women's List (WL), a feminist organization, gained entry to the Althing.

The IP is the largest party, and usually wins 35-40 per cent of the vote and at least 20 seats. It draws support from the business community in Reykjavik, but also has a wider national appeal. It is under-represented in the Althing because the electoral system is biased against the urban constituencies. The IP describes itself as a party of patriotic reform, inspired by cultural heritage and ancient values, committed to preserving sovereignty and independence, but not doctrinaire, fanatical or reactionary. The IP has been the firmest and most consistent supporter of NATO and the IDF. IP leaders are suspicious of the intentions of the USSR, because of the scale of its diplomatic effort in Reykjavik, its propaganda in Northern Europe, and its frequent use of force. They believe that the IDF is indispensable to the security of Iceland and to the maintenance of stability in the North Atlantic. In 1980, the IP began to press for a more active approach to NATO membership, in the belief that such a policy was essential to the security of Iceland and would bring political and economic advantages. The party also favoured the improvement and modernization of facilities at Keflavik, but only to maintain the capacity of the IDF, not to expand or change its role.[17]

The PP is the second largest party, and usually wins 20-25 per cent of the vote. The main sources of support are farmers and fishermen, and their Cooperative Federation, the Samband, which is the largest single enterprise in Iceland. The traditional policy of the PP was to support NATO firmly, but oppose the presence of the IDF in peacetime. The PP did support the Defence Agreement of 1951, but by 1955 had concluded that the Cold War was over and that the IDF was redundant. The atmosphere of detente and the fisheries dispute with Britain inspired the PP to press once more for evacuation of the garrison in 1973. But by 1980 the strongest PP leader, Olafur Johannesson, had changed his mind and decided to give firm support to the IDF. There is still opposition to the IDF within the PP, especially from the rural areas, but most have accepted it. The party has approved the more active approach to NATO, but is anxious that it should not lead to any enhancement of the strategic importance of Keflavik. Any such development would conflict with its growing interest in promoting naval arms control in the North Atlantic.

The SDP is based on the Reykjavik trades unions, and usually wins 15-20 per cent of the vote, although its support fluctuates. In 1983 it split, but the SDP and SDA are in agreement on security issues. The party has always supported NATO membership. In 1956, it favoured evacuation of the IDF, but since that year has been a staunch supporter of the garrison, with the reservation that it must never be used for offensive purposes.

The PA is a collective of nationalists and radicals, and usually wins about 20 per cent of the vote. It is the most persistent critic of official security policy and the only party to propose an alternative. The present leader, Svavar Gestsson, studied in the GDR, and once led the 'League Against the Base', a movement dedicated to the evacuation of the IDF.[18] But the membership of the PA is nationalist and pacifist rather than communist. After the Czech crisis of 1968, the leaders severed all public connection with the USSR; the idea that they were being influenced by a foreign power offended their nationalist feelings, and the action taken against the Czechs made the Soviets profoundly unpopular. Many members are bitterly critical of the USSR; some believe that the superpowers are equally malignant and dangerous; others believe the USA is a more immediate threat because it has troops in Iceland, and they can perceive no threat from Russia. PA policy is that Iceland should return to unarmed non-alignment, guaranteed by the UN, USA and USSR. This would pave the way for a progressive demilitarization and neutralization of the entire North Atlantic, making it a zone of peace.

The PA claims that membership of NATO is a violation of the policy adopted with Home Rule in 1918, and of the national tradition of resolving political questions by peaceful means. They believe that the obligations incurred interfere with independence. The presence of the IDF is regarded as an insult and threat to sovereignty, and as a reckless provocation of the Soviet Union. PA leaders say that the base was forced on Iceland, in defiance of the special terms of the Republic's adherence to NATO. They believe that it serves American, Norwegian and Danish interests, but not those of Iceland. The most popular and effective criticism of the IDF was that it was a source of cultural pollution and social disruption. This charge found great sympathy among supporters of all the political parties. The USA was compelled to respond by sealing off the base, and this policy of seclusion has been successful.[19]

In the late 1970s, the PA moderated its line on security policy, in order to conform to changed circumstances. In 1974 an opinion poll revealed that over 50 per cent of the electorate wanted the IDF to stay. This, and a desire for office, led the PA to enter coalitions in 1978 and 1980 without demanding that the new government commit itself to seek the evacuation of the IDF. The old PA line always blamed NATO for the presence of the garrison, and sought to damn the first with the cultural sins of the second. The new line is to argue that NATO and the IDF are separate, and that the garrison has tied Iceland closely to the USA, thereby preventing a more natural European orientation within NATO.

Because the cultural argument is no longer effective, the PA now concentrates its criticism of the IDF on specific military issues. In particular, it alleges that the base is not designed to protect Iceland, because without it the Republic would be militarily insignificant and would need no defence. Further, the base is intended to support American forward operations against the USSR, so its presence guarantees an early attack on Iceland in wartime. The most serious charge, in Icelandic terms, is that Keflavik is a nuclear base, or part of a worldwide system based on nuclear weapons. Most Icelanders would consider that any connection with nuclear weapons would make the base morally repugnant and highly dangerous. This element of the PA line has been supported by the Soviet media.[20] Although the PA can no longer hope to eject the IDF, it does all in its power to impose a freeze on development at Keflavik, to prevent or delay any changes or improvements.

The Women's List, which won three seats in the 1983 elections, has a radical feminist view of security. The balance-of-power system, alliances and military activity are all regarded as an immediate threat to all humankind, which can be contained only by policies based on human and female values. Members are not concerned with strategy or military affairs, since such things are seen as irrelevant and dangerous. They intend to dismantle the old system of world politics by psychological means: feminist and peace movements are to exert moral pressure on the leaders of the USA and USSR, isolate them emotionally, and then make them freeze deployments. In smaller countries nuclear-free and demilitarized zones are to be set up by popular acclamation, to 'hedge in' the superpowers and deprive them of room for manoeuvre, until they are induced to dissolve their respective blocs and disarm.[21]

The IP and PP are traditional coalition leaders, and reluctant to combine. Between 1944 and 1980, only two governments, lasting five years in all, contained both.[22] In 1983 the economic emergency united them in support of a policy of austerity. The coalition survived a strike against this policy in the autumn of 1984, but the economic interests of the urban IP still conflict with those of the rural PP. Because of the shift in the PP's attitude to the IDF, there has been no friction on security policy.

Until 1983, the fragility of coalitions and the volatile condition of public opinion, often exacerbated by the agitation of the PA, restrained Icelandic governments from taking initiatives in the security field, except in extreme and pressing circumstances. Official policy has been stable, minimalist and unobtrusive. Defence is regarded as a branch of foreign policy, and military considerations have had very low priority. The approach to military force has been restrictive; the priorities have been to cut the size and activities of the IDF to the irreducible minimum, promote arms control and disarmament, and keep nuclear weapons away from Iceland. Official statements always emphasize that the IDF is a minimum, non-nuclear, purely defensive garrison: a necessary, but regrettable and temporary measure for self-defence, and a contribution to stability in the North Atlantic.[23]

Threat perceptions

There is considerable dissonance between the threat perceptions of the Icelanders and those of the rest of NATO. Icelanders do not regard the military power of the USSR as the most direct and immediate threat to their vital interests. A majority discount the possibility of involvement in any armed conflict within the next five years. They do not perceive a major threat to their territory. Their idea of what must be protected is distinct. They wish to preserve their culture, upon which their sense of national identity is founded; their rich but vulnerable economy; and their sovereignty and independence, as well as national territory.[24] They perceive threats to all these, and labour under a general anxiety that the small size of the nation, some 240,000 souls, renders it vulnerable to being overwhelmed by larger powers, or by the uncontrollable tides of global political, economic and cultural movements. For many Icelanders, close association with the USA and NATO has seemed to generate more visible threats to the culture, political status, economic welfare and physical safety of the Republic than the military strength and intentions of the USSR.[25] Conservative Icelanders have, like Asgeir Asgeirsson in the 1950s 'mistrusted the moral and cultural influence of the Americans ... feared the great political influence of the Russians and their henchmen'.[26]

It was a perceived threat from the USSR to the independence of small nations that drove Iceland to abandon its preferred state of unarmed non-alignment and join NATO. The issue was contested with bitterness and violence. Opponents of NATO maintained that membership would destroy the sovereignty and independence of the Republic, and create a risk of unnecessary involvement in war against the USSR. The government calmed the storm of objection by imposing restrictive conditions on membership: the Alliance must accept that Iceland would only provide similar facilities to those available in World War II in the event of an emergency, and by mutual agreement; the Republic would not raise any armed forces, and would not allow troops on its territory in peacetime. The worthy and pacific motives of the government were emphasized: the wish to protect peace, freedom and democracy, and the anxiety to act in conformity with the UN Charter.[27]

Opponents of NATO regarded the arrival of the IDF as proof that NATO was merely a stalking-horse for the US desire to acquire a base in Iceland for its own national purposes, and that the USA would make and break solemn assurances for reasons of expediency. Once in place, the IDF was regarded as a source of cultural, social and moral disruption, and a cause of unhealthy economic distortion. Successive governments pressed for reductions in the size of the garrison, and in 1974 it was sealed off to make it invisible. An experimental relaxation of this seclusion in 1978 provoked condemnation from all quarters.

Iceland has often perceived threats to its economic survival and progress from the behaviour of NATO partners, most notably in fisheries disputes with Britain, West Germany, Denmark and Norway. Recently there was a strong adverse reaction to the US decision to give an American merchant shipping concern, Rainbow Navigation, a monopoly of shipping business to the IDF, to the detriment of Icelandic lines.[28] The discomforts of coexisting with allies can appear more important than the remote and abstract Soviet military threat.

Icelanders have ambivalent attitudes towards the Soviet Union. The great expansion of Soviet military capabilities is given little attention by the media,[29] and is ignored by many on the grounds that since they cannot assess the threat, the best thing to do is disregard it. They see war as a natural cataclysm, not as an instrument of policy, and some believe Soviet policy to be less adventurous than that of the USA, and so less dangerous. The USSR is an important trading partner, a large and reliable buyer of fish products, and the main supplier of petroleum. But there are signs that the USSR is becoming more unpopular and suspect. Soviet attempts to use the commercial relationship to influence Icelandic policy are strongly resisted. Many Icelanders resented the Soviet Union's clumsy attempts to embarrass the relationship with NATO by offering support during the Cod Wars and the Jan Mayen dispute.[30] The large size of the Soviet Embassy, with a staff of 37, creates unease, and the government is keenly aware of the increasing Soviet naval and air activity around Iceland. Some IP leaders believe the USSR aims to dominate the North Atlantic, and would attempt to seize and use Keflavik in a crisis.[31]

Icelanders are not favourably impressed with the Soviet performance in arms control and nuclear disarmament. The USSR has consistently proposed a nuclear-free zone in the Nordic area, but Icelandic ministers have been careful to note that no such scheme would work unless it included Soviet bases on the Kola Peninsula. In contrast to the USSR, the USA has taken great care in dealing with the nuclear issue. The Icelandic government imposed an absolute ban on the presence of nuclear weapons in 1964, and has regularly confirmed the permanence of the ban to counter anti-IDF propaganda from the PA. The USA has abandoned normal practice to support the Icelandic government, and given repeated assurances that it understands and will respect the Icelandic policy.[32]

Icelandic resources and economy

The only significant natural resources available to Iceland are fish and energy. The sources of energy are not threatened, but some Icelanders fear they may attract multinational concerns whose activities will damage the environment and way of life. The fish stocks, the basis of the economy for most of this century, are vulnerable, and a principal concern of foreign policy since 1949 has been to conserve them and secure preferential or exclusive use of them. To achieve their objectives, Icelandic governments have made use of international law, moral suasion, alliance diplomacy and force. They have been prepared to employ any means necessary, including threats to abandon their security policy, because they have believed that they were right in terms of justice, if not strictly in terms of current law, and that the very survival of Iceland was at stake.

In 1948 the government was anxious to conserve coastal fisheries, but also not to violate international agreements. By 1952 it was considered necessary to act unilaterally against the Anglo-Danish Convention of 1901 and, in the face of objections from Britain, to impose a 4-mile Exclusive Fishing Zone. Misgivings about the illegality of the EFZ were overridden by reference to US claims to the right to conserve resources of the contiguous sea in 1945, and the 1951 decision of the International Court of Justice (ICJ) on the Anglo-Norwegian case, which referred to the special needs of coastal communities. Above all, the Icelanders believed that the need to conserve threatened spawning grounds and stocks for the future was urgent.

The unilateral extension to 12 miles in 1958 was justified on the same grounds, and by the additional argument that Britain's opposition was based upon an obsolete standard, because the UN Conference on the Law of the Sea at Geneva had given tacit support for a 12-mile limit. The Icelanders made forceful use of their Coast Guard to police the new EFZ. They used implied threats to the base at Keflavik to persuade the USA to ensure that the use of the British navy was restrained and ineffective. As a consequence, the Coast Guard was able to make fishing in the EFZ unprofitable. The dispute was ended by an agreement with Britain in 1961, which committed Iceland to referring future disputes to the ICJ for adjudication.

In 1972 Iceland made a further unilateral extension, to 50 miles, and refused to accept that the ICJ had jurisdiction. Icelanders have been at pains to justify this defiance of international legal authority. The arguments used have included reference to the intolerable delays in the progress of UNCLOS, to the detriment of vital national interests; the notion that all international law and jurisdiction is based on consent, a principle violated by British use of duress to extract the 1961 agreement; and the claim that acceptance of the ICJ's jurisdiction would have been a derogation of sovereignty. Iceland had claimed sovereignty over the continental shelf in 1969, and went on to place increasing reliance on this vague concept to justify more extensive claims to control. The dispute with Britain was decided in a similar way to that of 1958, with the Icelanders threatening to leave NATO and claiming that their existence as a viable community was in peril. The final extension to 200 miles was made in May 1974 and accepted by Britain — after mediation by NATO and Norway — in the Oslo Agreement of 1976.[33]

Since then Iceland has continued to support the award of extensive rights over fish and seabed resources to coastal states, and has defended its interests against foreign powers. A dispute with Norway over the fishing and seabed resources around Jan Mayen was settled by a condominium arrangement agreed in October 1981. More recently, Iceland has been in dispute with the EC over the exploitation of capelin off East Greenland. The government is also determined to maximize the scope of its claim to resources in the vicinity of Rockall. Iceland refuses to accept British annexation of the Rockall area as valid, and has proposed that questions arising from its resources be settled by multilateral negotiations between Iceland, Britain, Eire and the Faroes. Iceland's own claim rests upon the notion that the Hatton/Rockall bank is a natural extension of the Icelandic continental shelf. In 1984 an Althing commission called on the government to claim rights on the continental shelf out to a limit of 200 miles, or to median lines, and to incorporate the Hatton/Rockall Plateau into the Icelandic economic zone.[34]

Since 1980 it has become clear that securing fishing grounds and other marine resources from foreign exploitation will not be sufficient to ensure the prosperity of Iceland. After 1976 there was massive investment in the fishing industry. The catch peaked in 1981, and began to fall. The failure of the catch is particularly serious in the most valuable species. The decline of stocks is attributed principally to overfishing, although changes in the environment are also blamed.[35]

Exporting fish has also become less profitable and more difficult. Demand and prices for the old staples — fish oil, meal and salt fish — are in decline. Icelandic fish face increasingly strong competition, some of it subsidized, in traditional markets in the

USA. Between 1982 and 1983 marine product exports fell from 75 to 68 per cent of the total by value. Meanwhile, profitability has been undermined by an increase in costs. The difficulties of the fishing industry are primarily responsible for the economic predicament of the country, which is currently burdened by a foreign debt of 60 per cent of GNP, a falling GNP, and a reduction in the standard of living. All parties are agreed that fishing must be revived and diversified, by improvements in marketing, exploitation of new species, fish farming, and concentration on fully processed high quality commodities. They are also agreed that the economy must diversify, to reduce dependence on fishing. There is some disagreement about how the economy should be restructured.[36]

Recent developments in security and resource policy

The present government, following the IP policy, favours large-scale development of energy-intensive industries, using the abundant reserves of hydroelectric and geothermal power. In contrast to previous governments, it is in favour of offering easy terms to large foreign concerns in order to attract them to the country. The other parties are not certain that large-scale foreign involvement in such projects will be good for Iceland. Members of the SDA and PP are not convinced that foreign multinational corporations will provide employment for the future or be amenable to local control. Members of the PA and WL are convinced that the activities of such firms will be harmful; that they will distort economic, social and political developments and create serious risks of pollution. At present, the government is going ahead unchecked, and is planning a rapid expansion of manufacturing, led by the high-energy sector.[37]

The government of 1983 has also taken a firm initiative in the field of security, with a policy of 'increased participation'. This has emerged because of the lack of friction between the IP and PP on security issues, and partly because of efforts to improve the general level of strategic knowledge.

During 1974-8 the SDP proposed the creation of an Institute of Foreign Affairs to study all aspects of foreign and security policy. This was not accepted, but the Althing was perturbed by the general ignorance of security affairs among the Icelandic government and people, and in 1980 founded the Oryggismalanefend, a commission of eight members, two nominated by each of the main parties. Its terms of reference were to consider the following areas of interest: national security; alternative security policies; the position of Iceland in relation to world conflict; the current world situation and its effects on Icelandic security; the future of the base if the IDF were to be evacuated; terrorism; demilitarized zones; peacekeeping; surveillance; and the security of other small states. Despite early fears that the PA would use the Commission to ferret out information of a sensational nature in order to embarrass NATO and the IDF, its members have managed to work in a spirit of academic impartiality, and have undoubtedly done much to raise the level of strategic debate in official circles. In 1980, the members of the political parties on the Oryggismalanefend had no real understanding of the North Atlantic security environment, or the significance of the GIUK gap, or the issues of reinforcement strategy. The work of the Commission has not changed basic attitudes and policies on security, but it has done much to educate the Althing and the public in basic strategic ideas.[38]

The commission has concentrated its attention on nuclear strategy, arms control, and the maritime balance in the North Atlantic, all areas of specific interest to Iceland. Research staff have published major reports on the theory of nuclear deterrence, the GIUK gap, the attempt to create a demilitarized zone in the Indian Ocean, and the concept of a Nordic nuclear-free zone. Their approach has been to explore and evaluate the abstract concepts of security policy in a primarily philosophical style. There has been no serious examination of the nature and conduct of conventional operations, or of the practical problems of alliance policy-making and warfare. It must be noted that this stems not only from the lack of historical military experience, but also from the small size of the Commission staff. Their output of published work has, nonetheless, been prodigious.

In considering the current strategic situation of Iceland, the Commission's chief research officer has come to the conclusion that the country and the GIUK gap are becoming less important and attractive to the USSR, but of more interest to NATO. He argues that the deployment of *Delta* SSBNs means that the Northern Fleet will no longer have to secure passage of the gap in order to secure strategic deterrence. He believes that there is no hard evidence that the Soviets would attempt to attack the Atlantic

SLOCs, because they would only become important in a long war; the Soviets favour short wars, and the Northern Fleet lacks the types of ship and the necessary numerical superiority to make such an attack successful. On the other hand, the USA is interested in using Iceland to secure the reinforcement airbridge, defend the SLOCs, and support a forward strategy the aim of which would be to contain the Soviet SSBNs and SSNs and attack their bases on the Kola Peninsula.[39]

The 1983 government has decided to put its new knowledge to active use, and has adopted a policy of 'increased participation'. This is to apply at two levels; at NATO HQ in Brussels, and at the IDF base at Keflavik. In Brussels, the method will be to take a greater interest in the deliberations of the political and military bodies of the Alliance, and indeed Icelandic observers began to attend sessions of the Military Committee in May 1984. By this method, Icelanders will gain expertise and experience in security matters and be able to take a more active part in serving the national interest during the formulation of Alliance policy. There are signs that this greater interest has already attracted the good-will of Alliance partners.[40]

The government took a positive line on military developments in Iceland in the summer of 1984, while emphasizing, as always, that the functions of the base at Keflavik are purely defensive — for the protection of Iceland and surveillance of the sea around it — and that any changes planned are to maintain its existing role and capacity. The radar coverage is to be modernized, with new equipment at Keflavik and Stokksnes, and the revival of disused sites in the northeast and northwest to help deal with the increasing Soviet air activity. The government has emphasized that these developments will also improve civil air-traffic control. The 12 *Phantoms* at Keflavik are to be replaced by 18 *F-15s*, and these are to be protected by hardened hangars. New fuel storage tanks and a new air terminal are being prepared. The government has also considered the possibility of having Icelanders trained to operate the radar, and of using the Coast Guard to assist in maritime surveillance.[41]

The policy of increased participation was debated in the Althing in the spring of 1984, and encountered no serious opposition. The PA opposed certain specific developments at Keflavik on environmental or military grounds, but could make no headway against the solidarity of the IP, PP and SDP, which all support the new line. It appears that the new policy is politically safe for the fore-seeable future, and it would certainly be difficult to make a U-turn and withdraw from it, now that it is underway.

The development of the security policy may be regarded as a protracted and reluctant adjustment of attitudes, from utopian isolationism to a painful recognition of unwelcome external realities. Because defence requirements are incompatible with a number of cherished national values, and because there is a very limited knowledge of military affairs, security has proved to be the most contentious and emotionally charged issue in Icelandic society and politics. The present government is making an onslaught on the traditional general ignorance of strategic issues and has adopted an active security policy. But even if it succeeds in the field of security, it may fail if its economic policy breaks down — the usual reason that a coalition disintegrates. A successor government may be less positive in approach to security, or more inhibited by political and social constraints.

Conclusion

The only serious potential threat to the new policy lies in the current American debate over plans to use Iceland for forward operations in wartime. The notion of attack being the best form of defence would be most difficult to promote in Iceland. If the US defence establishment continues to discuss such plans in public, it could undermine the credibility of the IP leadership in Icelandic public opinion, and strain an increasingly close working relationship.

Notes

1. Much of the information in this article is derived from interviews conducted by the author in spring 1980 and summer 1984 with the following Icelanders: Bjorn Bjarnasson — journalist and member of the Oryggismalanefend; Olafur Ragnar Grimsson — Parliamentary Chairman of the People's Alliance; Gunnar Gunnarsson — Research Officer of the Oryggismalanefend; Hordur Helgasson — Icelandic Foreign Office; Gunnar Karlsson — University of Iceland; Magnus Thordarsson — Atlantic Committee; Thor Whitehead — University of Iceland; Stefan Benediktsson — Social Democratic Alliance; Olavr Egillsson — Icelandic Foreign Office; Kjartan Gunnarsson — Independence Party; Einar Haraldsson — People's Alliance; Haraldr Olafsson — Progressive Party; and members of the Women's List.

2. According to an International Gallup Poll of Attitudes and Values reported in *News From Iceland*, December 1984.

3. This is described in Chs. 1 and 2 of D.F. Bittner, *The Lion and the White Falcon: Britain and Iceland in the World War II Era* (Connecticut: Archon Books, 1983).

4. Gunnar Gunnarsson, *Icelandic Security Policy* (Reykjavik: Oryggismalanefend, May 1984), p. 9.

5. Speech by President Vigdis Finbogadottir, reported in *News From Iceland*, October/November 1984.

6. *The Policy and Pursuits of the Independence Party*, Reykjavik, July 1984, pp. 2-3.

7. Sir A. Gilchrist, *Cod Wars and How to Lose Them* (Edinburgh: Q Press, 1978), p. 17.

8. Women's Alliance, *Policy Statement*, Reykjavik, 1984, p. 14.

9. *Statement of HE Geir Hallgrimsson to UN General Assembly, 38th Session, 26 September 1983* (Reykjavik: Icelandic Foreign Ministry, 1983), p. 273.

10. J.R. Fairlamb, *The Evolution of Icelandic Defense Decision Making 1944-81*, Ph.D., 1981 (Ann Arbor: University Microfilms International, 1984), p. 112.

11. Gunnar Gunnarsson, 'Icelandic Security Policy', *Cooperation and Conflict*, Vol. XVII (1982), No. 2, p. 266.

12. Public Opinion Poll by University of Iceland, reported in Gunnar Gunnarsson, *Icelandic Security Policy* (Reykjavik: Oryggismalanefend, May 1984), pp. 21-3.

13. For an account of these attitudes, see Nigel de Lee, 'Bastion of the North? Icelandic Security Policy', *RUSI Journal*, December 1981, pp. 47-53.

14. See also J.J. Holst, 'The Pattern of Nordic Security', *Daedalus*, Spring 1984, pp. 209-21, and the Public Opinion Poll by University of Iceland, as in Note 12.

15. Bjorn Bjarnasson, 'Iceland Between East and West, Trade and Security', unpublished paper, October 1983, p. 8.

16. Fairlamb, as Note 10, p. 96. Jon Sigurdsson in *News From Iceland*, April 1981.

17. *The Independence Party in a Nutshell*, Reykjavik, 1983, p. 7; *The Policy and Pursuits of the Independence Party*, July 1984, pp. 2 and 5; *24th Bi-annual General Meeting of the IP*, autumn 1981, pp. 3 and 5.

18. Erling Bjøl, Adelphi Paper No. 181, *Nordic Security* (London: IISS, 1983), pp. 31-2.

19. See Nigel de Lee, as Note 13.

20. Statements by Tass, 6 December 1984, and Moscow Radio, 10 December 1984.

21. Women's Alliance, *Policy Statement*, 1984, pp. 2, 3, 12-13.

22. This is well described in O.R. Grimsson, *The Icelandic Multilateral Coalition Systems* (London: University College, July 1977).

23. Geir Hallgrimsson, *Statement to UN*, pp. 273-5 (as Note 9).

24. International Gallup Poll of Attitudes and Values, reported in *News From Iceland*, January 1985; and Fairlamb, as Note 10, p. 49.

25. Nigel de Lee, as Note 13, and the editorial in *News From Iceland*, January 1985.

26. Sir A. Gilchrist, as Note 7, p. 28.

27. Olavr Egillsson, 'An Unarmed Nation Joins a Defence Alliance', in *NATO Review* No. 1 (1983), pp. 1, 5-8.

28. Fairlamb, as Note 10, p. 57.

29. Erling Bjøl, as Note 18, p. 34.

30. Bjorn Bjarnasson, as Note 15, pp. 6 and 9; *News From Iceland*, December 1984; Sir A. Gilchrist, as Note 7, p. 105. See also Ch. 12.

31. *24th Bi-annual General Meeting of the IP*, 1981, p. 3; Geir Hallgrimsson, in *News From Iceland*, October/November 1984.

32. Fairlamb, as Note 10, p. 59; Olafur Johannesson in *News From Iceland*, May 1982; Geir Hallgrimsson, as Note 9, p. 275, and in *News From Iceland*, October/November 1984; Gunnar Gunnarsson, as Note 4, pp. 12-13; *News From Iceland*, January 1985.

33. Fairlamb, as Note 10, p. 55; Sir A. Gilchrist, as Note 7, pp. 55, 98-9, 104; Icelandic Ministry of Foreign Affairs, *The Fishery Limits off Iceland, 200 Nautical Miles*, October 1975; Hannes Jonsson, *Friends in Conflict: The Anglo-Icelandic Cod Wars and the Law of the Sea* (London: Hurst, 1982), Chs. 4, 5 and 6.

34. *News From Iceland*, November 1981, July 1983, August 1984.

35. Johannes Nordal, *Address to the Annual Meeting of the Central Bank of Iceland*, April 1984, p. 5; National Economic Institute of Iceland, *A Brief on the Icelandic Economy*, No. 2, July 1984, p. 4; Central Bank of Iceland, *Annual Report*, 1983, p. 6.

36. Editorial, *News From Iceland*, March 1985; Central Bank of Iceland, *Annual Report*, 1983, p. 17; National Economic Institute of Iceland, as Note 35, pp. 7-8; Johannes Nordal, as Note 35, p. 3; Steingrimur Hennansson, *News From Iceland*, January 1985.

37. Ministry of Industry, *Power Intensive Industries in Iceland*, 1984, p. 15; Olafur Isleifsson in *Icelandic Review*, No. 2 (1984), p. 72; Women's Alliance, *Policy Statement*, 1984, pp. 9-10; *News From Iceland*, March 1985.

38. Gunnar Gunnarsson, as Note 11.

39. See Gunnar Gunnarsson, *G-I-UK Hlidid* (Reykjavik: Oryggismalanefend, 1981, English summary of conclusions), and as Note 11, pp. 2-7.

40. *News From Iceland*, June 1984.

41. Statement by Geir Hallgrimsson in *News From Iceland*, July 1984, October/November 1984.

15 THE SOVIET UNION AND NORTHERN WATERS

David Scrivener

The USSR has partly surmounted its geographical disadvantages to emerge as the largest single naval power in the Northeast Atlantic. Its large fishing fleet's freedom of access was severely curtailed by the extension of national jurisdictions at sea in the mid-1970s. It closely monitors political trends within and between states potentially hostile in time of war, with a view to defending or promoting its military and economic interests. In the northernmost regions the Soviet Union endeavours to influence the terms for Norwegian security and offshore resource exploitation, while seeking to shape the evolution of the legal and diplomatic framework in which other states may participate in this process. The USSR has amassed considerable experience in working the resources of its most northerly territories and secured an impressive lead in maritime transportation in difficult ice conditions. It now faces the demanding task, however hesitantly, of opening up the assumed hydrocarbon and mineral riches of the vast continental shelf in its western Arctic sector, a task which has wide-ranging security, trade and environmental implications.

Military perspectives

Recent events involving Soviet forces have underlined dramatically the extent of their presence in Northern Waters. In May 1984 missiles stored at Severomorsk on the Kola inlet exploded.[1] A rogue SS-N-3 *Shaddock* cruise missile crashed in Northern Finland after briefly overflying Norwegian territory in late December of the same year. In early summer 1985 a Soviet warship cut the cable of a Norwegian vessel conducting seismic tests in the Barents Sea. The last two incidents were followed by official Soviet apologies. The expansion of Soviet naval operations in the North Atlantic over the past 10-15 years culminated in the large-scale multi-fleet naval exercise in April 1984, apparently designed to test and demonstrate the Northern Fleet's ability to push Soviet maritime defence frontiers further south, and more quickly, than ever before.[2] Soviet submarines have intruded into Norwegian territorial waters on numerous occasions.[3]

The forces based or deployed in the Northern Waters area occupy a central place in Soviet planning for war and in the peacetime projection of power in support of state interests. Geographical conditions give the Soviet Northern Fleet the tasks of executing wartime missions of strategic nuclear strike, strategic defence of the homeland against attacks from the sea, support of operations on the Central Front in Europe and the interdiction of enemy SLOCs across the Atlantic. Forces and installations on the Kola Peninsula also play a vital role in strategic air and missile defence, and provide forward operating bases for strategic aviation.[4]

Recent technological developments carry several implications for Soviet military strategy in Northern Waters. The introduction of long-range, MIRVed SLBMs on Soviet *Delta-* and *Typhoon-*class SSBNs in the mid-1970s and early 1980s respectively, though not removing the requirement for SSBN egress to the Atlantic, has afforded the option of rearward deployment of Soviet SSBNs in the Barents and Kola Seas. This has consolidated a reserve strategic nuclear force for intra-war deterrence, protected by the SSBN-support mission of the rest of the Soviet submarine and surface fleet. Yet the most recent evidence suggests the growing importance of a wider arc of potential Soviet SSBN patrol areas — taking in the Greenland Sea and the more secure Central Arctic Basin — in which the role of the Barents Sea would be more that of a gateway. Such an arc creates an extended opportunity for rearward deployment, in which Soviet SSBNs could patrol under the ice off the Canadian archipelago and northeast of Greenland.[5] The *Typhoon*'s design provides a greater ability to break through thicker ice than that of earlier Soviet submarines and allows it to open its missile hatches for firing, unencumbered by ice chunks.[6] *Delta*-class SSBNs are already believed to patrol in the Greenland Sea, in the deep water beyond Svalbard, possibly transiting from Kola to the east of the archipelago.

The opportunity to evade Western tracking may also affect future deployment trends of Soviet attack submarines using transit routes through the waters of the Canadian Arctic archipelago either to emerge from the Arctic Basin into the North Atlantic in order to attack NATO SLOCs or, in the case of land-attack cruise-missile submarines, to patrol off the North American coast.[7] Soviet hunter-killer submarine patrols in Canadian waters and in the Greenland, North Norwegian and Barents/Kola Seas will probably expand, as will the installation of listening devices.

Western estimates project a sharp increase in the relative weight of the airborne leg of the Soviet strategic triad in the next decade, with a central role for air-launched cruise missiles carried by *Backfire*, *Blackjack* and modified *Bear-H* bombers. The new AS-15 3000-km range ALCM could be fired from aircraft over the Arctic and Canadian archipelago to hit targets in the USA, and strategic aviation would continue to rely on facilities in the Kola area in wartime for forward basing and refuelling.

The vulnerability and scale of Soviet military investments in the Kola area will continue to render their protection vital. To secure the operating and transit areas of Soviet SSBNs in the Barents Sea demands rapid deployment of Soviet naval forces into the Norwegian Sea and the capture or neutralization of North Norwegian airfields. The same is true of the SLOC interdiction mission and the air defence of the Kola. Similarly, the need to locate and destroy US, UK and French SSBNs deployed in the Norwegian Sea will remain for some time. US cruise missiles based on submarines will add to the difficulties of the Soviet strategic air and missile defence network in countering the threat from air-launched long-range cruise missiles, and force upon it a daunting task that will require the extension outwards of surveillance and early-warning operations. The forward naval strategy of the USA, with its emphasis on bottling up the Soviet Northern Fleet in the Barents Sea and early action against the Kola installations, could well merge in Soviet perceptions into the initial signs of a strategic nuclear offensive against the Soviet heartland.[8]

Indeed, official US statements dismissing any concept of bastions for Soviet SSBNs in the Arctic Basin or marginal seas, coupled with much greater interest in ASW operations closer to Soviet shores as part of the forward defence of NATO's Atlantic SLOCs, have prompted a heightened Soviet perception of the vulnerability of their submarine-based deterrent to rapid degradation in the early stages of an East–West conflict.[9] The importance of US SSN operations 'near Soviet shores', combined with known and suspected acoustic detection systems in the Barents Sea, is often stressed by the Soviets. References to Western plans to install acoustic and electronic listening devices covertly in the Svalbard archipelago probably reflect a genuine concern in addition to serving a useful, if little-noticed, propaganda function.[10] The Soviets have themselves in all probability installed seabed acoustic devices throughout the Barents Sea, including the waters of the Svalbard archipelago. ASW protection of Soviet vessels plying the western approaches of the Northern Sea Route will also become a more important requirement in future years.

Renewed Soviet efforts to encourage the creation of a Nordic nuclear-weapon-free zone in the 1980s are both a response to what is described as the 'militarization' of the Northern Flank and a tactical device to exploit domestic unease in Scandinavia over the intensified military competition in European Northern Waters. The Soviets have also endeavoured to gain acceptance for Moscow's interpretation of Norway's 'base and ban' policy as an international legal obligation, especially since Norway's decision, in 1980, to pre-stock heavy equipment for use by US marines.[11]

The Barents Sea

In February 1968 the USSR assumed general continental shelf rights and, in March 1984, declared a full 200-mile economic zone. It proclaimed a temporary 200-mile fisheries protection zone in December 1976, which was enacted in early 1977 and followed in May 1977 by a decree bringing the measures into effect in the Barents Sea, pending future legislation on a 200-mile economic zone that would take into account the outcome of UNCLOS III. This legislation omitted any reference to the delimitation of the Soviet zone relative to those of other states (see Figure 15.1).

During Soviet–Norwegian negotiations on continental shelf delineation in the Barents Sea, the USSR, while sharing Norway's endorsement of Article 6 of the 1958 Continental Shelf Convention, consistently stressed the importance of the provision that allowed 'special circumstances' to be taken into account and chose to elevate this above the median line/equidistance principle.[12] Soviet jurists have argued that automatic application of the equidistance principle in shelf and zone disputes would be unjust and that its employment in the absence of agreement on some other solution would amount to the imposition of a formula unacceptable to one side. In commenting on the UNCLOS process, Soviet lawyers pointed approvingly to the inclusion within the draft texts of the need to take into account 'all circumstances para-

Figure 15.1(a): The Barents Sea

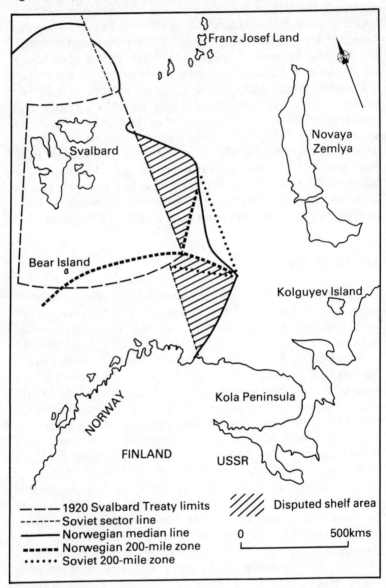

Legend:
- — — 1920 Svalbard Treaty limits
- ------ Soviet sector line
- —— Norwegian median line
- ▬▬▬ Norwegian 200-mile zone
- •••••• Soviet 200-mile zone
- ////// Disputed shelf area

0   500kms

Figure 15.1(b): The Grey Zone

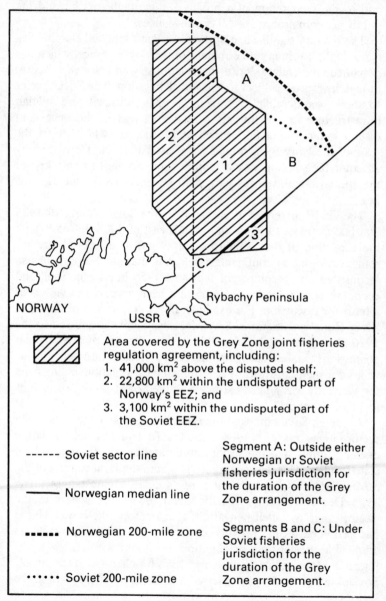

Area covered by the Grey Zone joint fisheries regulation agreement, including:
1. 41,000 km² above the disputed shelf;
2. 22,800 km² within the undisputed part of Norway's EEZ; and
3. 3,100 km² within the undisputed part of the Soviet EEZ.

----- Soviet sector line

—— Norwegian median line

■■■■■ Norwegian 200-mile zone

••••• Soviet 200-mile zone

Segment A: Outside either Norwegian or Soviet fisheries jurisdiction for the duration of the Grey Zone arrangement.

Segments B and C: Under Soviet fisheries jurisdiction for the duration of the Grey Zone arrangement.

mount in the corresponding area' in delimiting continental shelves, and to the recognition of a broader range of factors beyond the purely geographical as special circumstances.[13]

The military significance of the Kola Peninsula and Barents Sea is no doubt a primary determinant of the Soviet stance, which has remained unbending since negotiations with Norway began, though it is rarely subject to specific elaboration. The Soviets refer to their considerable investment in the industrial and human infrastructure of the Barents coastal area and in the near- and distant-water fishing fleet based at Murmansk, which dwarf the scale of the Norwegian presence in East Finnmark. Consequently an equitable solution would require some account to be taken of the special circumstances judged to be operative in the Barents Sea.[14]

The USSR increased its emphasis on the Soviet decree of 1926 that laid claim to all lands and islands east of 32° 4′35″ east (with the exception of the Svalbard archipelago) as a 'special circumstance' relevant to continental shelf delimitation. Moscow has so far insisted on acceptance of the same 1926 line as the shelf and economic zone boundary, and has not been prepared to view it as a basis for discussion. For example, in his description of the 1977 'Grey Zone' negotiations, S.V. Molodtsov, having referred to the 1926 Decree as establishing the 'western border of Soviet polar possessions', states that it was necessary 'to take into account the well-known and historically determined legal situation issuing from the generally recognized existence of the Soviet polar possessions and their frontiers'.[15]

Although Soviet maps of the Barents Sea clearly show the 1926 sector line as the sea border of the USSR, actual Soviet legislation does not imply that the sector coordinates are considered to be a state frontier. This detracts somewhat from the legal validity of the Soviet extended interpretation of 'special circumstances'. The 1926 Decree made no specific claim to ice-free waters in the 'sector' or to the shelf beneath it. Furthermore, the Soviet Union has refrained from formally endorsing the sector principle as admissible in maritime delimitation, no doubt with an eye to its rejection of the sector doctrine as a basis for claims in Antarctica.[16] Soviet lawyers in the past asserted a claim to polar seas within the sector coordinates; more recent writings appear to avoid advancing the case for the special status of polar waters based on an extended view of the Decree or the sector theory. Norway's abandonment of its claim to Franz Joseph Land subsequent to the Decree could not be seen as recognition of the sector theory in general, nor could it be construed as acceptance of the sector line as a maritime boundary. The sector principle remains highly controversial in international law.

The outcome of UNCLOS III technically worked to the advantage of the Soviet legal position on the Barents shelf, since the importance of the median line principle was downgraded to one of equality with the pursuit of equitable solutions in which special circumstance arguments could acquire greater currency. This may have been behind Moscow's reticence in the dialogue with Oslo and will probably discourage any Soviet deviation from the sector line position. Indeed, in June 1976, Moscow reportedly responded to a Norwegian offer to amend the median line with an even stronger insistence on the sector line. This Soviet inflexibility may have been strengthened by the outcome of Norwegian–Icelandic negotiations over the delimitation of fisheries zones and shelf boundaries around Jan Mayen in 1980-1.[17] Norway's abandonment of its initial insistence on the median line for the delimitation of Jan Mayen's economic zone and continental shelf, together with acceptance of joint fisheries management in the Jan Mayen zone and provisions for cooperation in seabed exploitation in an area predominantly on the Norwegian side of the agreed shelf boundary, could quite feasibly be interpreted as a political, if not legal, precedent for the disputed Barents Sea area. Similar Norwegian accommodation of equitable principles in the delimitation of Jan Mayen's economic zone and shelf boundaries with Greenland would, at the least, encourage continued intransigence in Moscow in the expectation of eventual Norwegian concessions to the Soviet version of 'special circumstances'.

Moscow also probably saw the continuation of the shelf dispute as a reliable restraint on Norwegian interest in intensified offshore exploration in the contested area and the Barents at large. The Soviet military will seek to delay significant Western energy operations for as long as possible. That the Soviet Union for the first time took the initiative in calling for a resumption of the stalled negotiations in 1980 probably issued from a more lively awareness of the potential energy riches in the Barents and Kara Seas: any exploitation of those riches would require a political climate that might, if necessary, attract foreign assistance to the Soviet offshore programme.

Following implementation of the 'Grey Zone' Agreement of 1978 (see below), the USSR on the whole refrained from any actions in the waters above the disputed shelf area that might have increased tension and complicated resolution of the dispute. The Soviets had earlier fired missiles into the western part of the area, near the sector line, in a series of tests in late 1976 to late 1977 which effectively denied the region to shipping for a total of 12 weeks. Moscow briefly seemed to have abandoned its restraint in May 1983, when the *Valentin Shashin* drillship, in probing the Varanger Basin structure, strayed approximately 1.5 miles west of the median line. After initially maintaining that this was a training exercise, the Soviets admitted the ship had accidentally drilled inside the disputed area. The incident may well have been unintentional given the difficulties the Soviets have obliquely acknowledged in handling the highly sophisticated Norwegian dynamic positioning equipment on board the three Finnish-built Arctic drilling-ships.[18] In any event, the *Shashin* kept within the two- to three-mile margin of error corridor recognized by Norway.[19] Yet similar incidents may recur if the Soviets again venture close to the median line while investigating the flanks of structures extending into the disputed area. The incident might be seen as putting pressure on Norway to seek a more rapid shelf settlement.

The USSR objected to Norwegian geophysical surveying off Finnmark in 1974, when the vessel concerned approached the sector line, and in 1976 it described surveying by the Norwegian *Seisearch* in the disputed area as occurring in the 'Soviet polar area'.[20] No further incidents occurred involving Norwegian vessels until summer 1985, when a Geco survey ship's cables were cut by a Soviet warship, apparently outside the disputed zone.[21] Yet Soviet sensitivities were no doubt aroused by the contract awarded in 1985 to Geco to survey extensive virgin areas of the Barents Sea between 22° and 32° east (i.e., within 4'35" of the sector line). Indeed, Norway plans to license test drilling on the seabed adjacent to the disputed zone by 1987. Moscow can hardly take offence at Norwegian-authorized prospecting in the undisputed parts of the Barents, since Soviet operations occur quite close to the median line.

Fisheries management

The common need for effective management of the rich yet vulnerable fish stocks of the Barents Sea came to be felt more acutely in the 1970s in both Norway and the USSR. The declaration of a Norwegian EEZ and Soviet FPZ in late 1976 brought the delicate prospect of overlapping fisheries jurisdiction claims, and raised Norwegian concern about potential conflicts over inspection of third-country vessels in the waters above the disputed shelf out to 200 nautical miles. The two governments had agreed earlier in the year, through the Norwegian–Soviet Fisheries Commission, on mutual access, setting of total catches and allocation of quotas in their respective national zones. Negotiations stemming from a Norwegian initiative led to the temporary bilateral fisheries management agreement of June 1977, which entered into force in January 1978.

The 'Grey Zone' Agreement covered an area out to 200 miles of 67,000 km^2 (26,000 square miles), of which 41,000 km^2 lay above the disputed shelf. The Grey Zone embraced 8,900 square miles to the west of the Soviet sector line and 1,200 square miles to the east of the Norwegian median line, northeast of Rybachiy Peninsula. TACs and quotas were to be agreed through the bilateral fisheries commission. Joint policing was avoided by allowing each state exclusive jurisdiction over its own vessels and those of third countries it licensed to operate in the Grey Zone. The arrangement has worked well on a practical level and been renewed annually with relatively few difficulties. Both states clearly have a major stake in enlarging Barents Sea fisheries. Joint fisheries management and cooperation in protecting species previously subject to rapid depletion have facilitated a marked resurgence of such stocks as cod, haddock and herring. Joint fisheries research expeditions in the Barents began in the early 1960s and have proved highly useful to both sides.

The establishment and regular renewal of the Grey Zone arrangement, in addition to meeting a shared Soviet concern to improve fisheries management, works in favour of the Soviet position on shelf delimitation. The inclusion of such a large area west of the sector line is probably viewed as a precedent for future Norwegian concessions on economic zone and shelf delimitation, and may tempt Moscow to regard the western limit of the Grey Zone as a *de facto* boundary.[22] Moscow may take the agreement to indicate a Norwegian readiness eventually to compromise on its insistence on the median line. Molodtsov cites the agreement as a good example of the utility of 'temporary measures' in avoiding tension and facilitating resolution of outstanding boundary disputes. Although he acknowledges that such measures are by nature temporary and do not prejudice the final zone and shelf delimitation, he presents the agreement's existence as a further argument that undermines the equidistance principle.[23] However, the area embraced by the Grey Zone was determined according to fisheries management rather than legal criteria, though the Soviets make no effort to stress this. The western extreme of the zone mostly corresponds with the ICES 30°E statistical boundary dividing the Barents (I) and Norwegian Seas (IIa) fishing areas.

In the absence of agreement on shelf and zone delimitation, the USSR may use the Grey Zone accord to encourage consideration of joint management or consultation processes in other functional spheres (e.g. oil exploitation), with the longer-term aspiration of realizing some form of exclusive condominium arrangement. The Soviets have tried to treat the area of the Baltic disputed with Sweden as closed to third-country fishing, on occasion boarding Danish and West German vessels and presenting for completion forms printed in Russian and Swedish.[24] Similar incidents have been very rare in the Barents Grey Zone; the Soviets boarded a British trawler in Spring 1978, but subsequently explained this as an error on the Soviet captain's part. The terms of the agreement avoided instituting joint enforcement of fisheries regulations through coordinated inspection and thus maintained a regime of separate jurisdictions.

The Grey Zone arrangement met the Soviet interest in conserving joint fisheries stocks in the Barents Sea while being open to interpretation as a precedent for shelf and zone delimitation with Norway. It also shares some similarities with, and implications for, Soviet policy on fisheries jurisdiction in the Svalbard/Bear Island area. Finally, it may contribute to Norwegian–Soviet offshore energy cooperation in a manner that is advantageous to the Soviet position on shelf delimitation.

Offshore exploration

The Soviet Union began extensive seismic surveys in the Barents Sea in 1978, and in 1980-2 it conducted three comprehensive geological and geophysical expeditions in the southern part aboard the research ship *Professor Shtokman*. Three theoretically promising areas were identified west of Novaya Zemlya and in the south-eastern Barents Sea region.[25] In late spring 1982 the Finnish-built ice-class drillship *Valentin Shashin* spudded its first well, on the

Murmansk High Structure (70°N, 42°E). In 1983 two ships operated in the Barents, finishing the earlier well and opening another nearby. A third well was then spudded by the *Valentin Shashin* on a structure near the disputed shelf area (see p. 216). Wells were also spudded in quite shallow water in the Pechora Sea. In late 1984 Soviet officials began hinting at a major oil and gas find in the central portion of the Barents.[26] The Finnish firm Rauma Repola was due to deliver the first two of three Arctic-conditioned Gusto-type jack-up rigs to the USSR in the second half of 1985, one of which was certainly destined for work in the Barents Sea. In May 1985 the *Shelf-4* Arctic-capable semi-sub built by the Soviets at Vyborg was delivered to the waters off Kolguyev Island in the southeast Barents; it is capable of drilling in water depths of up to 200 metres.[27] (Exploration wells were drilled on Kolguyev Island itself in the early 1970s.) Finnish and Norwegian firms have sold over 15 offshore supply vessels to the USSR, at least one of which was working in the Barents in 1983.

The USSR has very little experience in, or technology appropriate for, offshore exploration and development, particularly in harsh Arctic conditions. Only in the early 1980s did the Soviets employ semi-submersible, non-fixed platforms in the Caspian Sea. Two *Shelf* rigs were in operation there in 1985.[28] Most of the equipment used in the joint exploration off Sakhalin Island was provided by Japan. Nor have the Soviets had any practice in coping with blow-outs. Operations in the Caspian were plagued by production delays, insufficiently trained operating personnel and infringements of safety discipline. In addition, the Soviets had considerable difficulty in handling positioning equipment on the three Finnish-built drillships.

Despite falling real prices on the world oil market and growing production difficulties in existing onshore oil-bearing regions, Soviet exports of crude oil and petroleum products to the OECD countries continued to rise in 1984, underlining the crucial role of oil as a major hard currency earner for the USSR.[29] As well as seeking improved recovery techniques onshore, the Soviet Union seems set to embark on an expanded offshore exploration effort, including the Barents Sea. In early 1982 Moscow announced it was considering projects in the eastern Barents in three areas of 100-300 metres' depth to the value of several billion dollars. In 1985 the Ministry of Geology referred, in the 1986-90 Five-Year Plan, to a 100 per cent increase in the volume of offshore drilling on the

Soviet continental shelf at large. In 1983 the Director of the Oceanology Institute urged the formulation of a comprehensive plan for a 'scientific and industrial offensive in the higher latitudes', coupled with the development of Soviet ice-resistant prospecting, drilling and extraction equipment, to allow a rapid acceleration of exploration in the western Arctic seas of the USSR, despite the limited knowledge of the seabed.[30] Although the Kara Sea is the most promising area, the probable predominance of gas deposits there and the extremely harsh ice conditions make the Pechora Sea the first priority, followed by the southeastern and central Barents Sea.

The USSR will remain reliant on Western technology inputs for work in the Barents Sea, but will be trying to improve its own technology and equipment base over the next five to ten years. Furthermore, Moscow will require Western expertise, some degree of participation, and capital in order to offset the investment costs involved in any offshore production in the western Arctic. Soviet observers closely follow the economic and technical uncertainties encountered by other Arctic states, and take note of the specialized equipment these countries have developed for their own use or export.[31]

In 1982 the Soviets first sought to gauge the interest of Norwegian shipbuilding and engineering companies in assisting offshore development of the Soviet Barents, and, following the green light from the Norwegian authorities for Norwegian firms to seek orders for equipment and expertise, commissioned Norwegian Petroleum Consultants to draw up a master plan on Moscow's behalf. The resulting Boconor scheme, handed over in late 1984, included development plans and cost estimates for field exploration embracing fixed platforms and subsea production units, and afforded Norwegian companies some access to Soviet plans and markets in the Barents. The Soviets have been expected to decide, on the basis of the scheme, what equipment and services will be provided by Soviet industry and foreign companies.

Future Soviet orders could well involve more Arctic-capable jack-up and semi-sub rigs and drilling vessels for exploration and development. The USSR seems especially interested in Western (UK, French and Norwegian) assistance in developing Soviet subsea technology. Plans are also well advanced to establish a hyperbaric centre in Leningrad, with a good chance of a British firm as partner, in order to improve Soviet handling of underwater repair operations. In early 1985 the Norwegian oil company Saga Petroleum was contacted by the Soviets through a 50 per cent Finnish-owned North Norwegian trading company (Pomor-Nordic Trade A/S) regarding technical assistance for the Barents shelf. Saga and Pomor-Nordic were encouraged to consider a joint application for an oil exploration licence in the Barents.[32] This may be the first tentative Soviet attempt to draw foreign operators into the Soviet western Arctic offshore programme.

In 1983 Soviet officials began to resuscitate earlier vague proposals for some form of 'major Nordic project' for the joint exploration and development of the Soviet Barents Sea. They presumably hoped such a project would furnish equipment, reduce the Soviet investment burden and assist in marketing recovered oil and gas. The Soviets floated the idea of a joint Norwegian–Soviet pipeline from the Barents, via Finland and Sweden, to west European gas markets. However, financing terms, market difficulties and sensitivity to the intra-alliance politics of technology transfer could act against the clear interest of Norwegian firms in carving a niche in the fledgling Soviet offshore programme, a development which would give cause for official concern in Oslo over the implications for the Soviet–Norwegian continental shelf and economic zone dispute.[33]

The Soviet Union has so far received little interest from Norway in long-term schemes for joint exploration and exploitation in the Barents. Any Soviet hope of using cooperation in exploration to strengthen its sector claim has so far been frustrated by Oslo's determination that Norwegian equipment, expertise and presence will only by offered to the USSR for activities unambiguously clear of the disputed area. The suggestion of joint pipelines seems to indicate a Soviet tactic of incremental moves towards establishing a *de facto* condominium regime for non-living as well as living resources in the Barents. Should major oil-finds occur on the Soviet shelf, the USSR might adopt a more flexible position on delimitation in order to secure a long-term Norwegian input into their development. More intense prospecting by both sides will necessitate some form of understanding on activities that affect fields extending into the disputed area, however little progress is achieved in the shelf delimitation negotiations.[34] Such regular bilateral consultations will provide the Soviet Union with a further opportunity to influence economic developments to the west of the sector line, and perhaps give them occasion to press for a minimum non-Scandinavian offshore energy presence in the Barents Sea as a whole.

The Soviets have yet to express much concern about the ecological implications of energy exploitation in the Barents. Their acceptance of the conservation rationale in the 'Grey Zone' Agreement indicates some potential receptivity to Norwegian interest in bilateral cooperation to avoid damage to shared fish stocks. It is unclear whether Moscow will respond to Norway's announced intention to seek agreement on safety standards and operating procedures on oil rigs in order to avoid environmental damage in the Norwegian and Soviet economic zones.[35]

The pace of Soviet offshore exploration in the Barents and Kara Seas will be determined mainly by investment priority decisions in the 12th Five-Year Plan. The relative weight of export market conditions, availability of foreign technology and finance, and delimitation issues will no doubt be matched by very careful attention to the military implications of the evermore closely interwoven offshore tapestry of the western portion of the Barents. The future pattern of political relations there is also linked to Western and especially Soviet interests in the Svalbard archipelago.

Svalbard

Since the late 1930s the USSR and Norway have been the only permanent exploiters of Svalbard's mineral resources, having bought up the stocks and fields of companies from other countries. The plan of the Soviet company Arktikugol to spud a wildcat in early 1985 constituted the only drilling scheduled for that year. Soviet scientists have played a leading role in marine geological and glaciological surveying, and the USSR has as preponderant a presence as Norway. The Polish station at Hornsund is the only year-round third-party scientific presence. In drawing attention to its special economic interests, Moscow now seems less concerned with the reserves of coal than with the other possible hydrocarbon resources in the archipelago, and appears increasingly preoccupied with the issue of who might seek them out, in view of the marked rise in interest among Western companies in geological mapping and seismic surveying of Svalbard (see Figure 15.2).

Figure 15.2: The Svalbard Archipelago

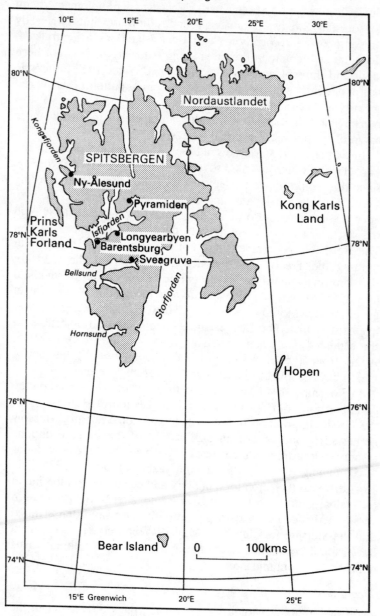

Source: Norsk Polarinstitutt, Oslo.

Sovereignty

Soviet historiography of Svalbard shows Russian diplomacy trying to forestall Swedish–Norwegian annexation of Spitsbergen by pressing for its recognition (with Bear Island) as a neutralized, demilitarized common-use area from which Russia's northern lands and shipping could not be threatened. Since 1917 the USSR has persistently sought, at the least, accommodation of its special security and economic needs there and, at the most, joint Soviet–Norwegian administration of the archipelago in order more assuredly to safeguard national interests.

In January 1923 Moscow advised Oslo against ratifying the Paris Treaty, which awarded sovereignty over Svalbard to Norway, since this would impede achievement of the 'only just and lasting solution' to the legal status and administration of the archipelago. Such a solution could only be determined by agreement between the states which had done most to develop its natural resources. The Bolshevik government had not been invited to take part in drafting the Treaty, which nonetheless preserved the rights of Russians on Svalbard until a recognized Russian government could be invited to sign it. Following *de jure* recognition of the Soviet government, Moscow accepted Norwegian sovereignty over Svalbard — including Bear Island — and voiced no objections to the Mining Code when invited to adhere to the treaty in 1935. Apart from a brief yet telling interlude in 1944-7, the Soviet Union has not sought to challenge Norwegian sovereignty.[36]

In November 1944 Molotov sought a bilateral agreement on the co-militarization of Spitsbergen and the cession of Bear Island to the USSR. In addition to the right to garrison Svalbard, Moscow requested a joint accord on exploitation of the area's economic resources. It justified this request on the grounds of the continuous Soviet mining activity in the interwar years. Although the USSR in 1947 dropped its search for a military and economic condominium on Svalbard and the cession of Bear Island, later Soviet criticism of certain activities in Svalbard permitted by Norway often claimed that the Storting Resolution of May 1947 had endorsed the need for bilateral consultations whenever Moscow saw a threat to its military and economic interests.[37]

Demilitarization

After the failure of Molotov's *démarches*, the USSR assumed the mantle of the most ardent exponent of Article 9 of the Svalbard

Treaty, which states that Norway must never build or allow naval bases or fortifications in the archipelago, 'which may ... be used for warlike purposes'.[38] Understandably, the USSR still fears possible hostile use of Svalbard by Norway and its NATO allies as a base for exercising control over the Barents/Norwegian Seas passage, for strikes against northern Russia, or for covert peace-time submarine tracking and electronic intelligence-gathering. Norway's entry into NATO in 1949, and the subsequent inclusion of Jan Mayen, Svalbard and Bear island within the responsibility of NATO North Atlantic Command in 1951, presented a challenge to what the USSR now chose to claim was the principle of demilitarization and neutralization inherent in the original Svalbard Treaty. Basing its arguments on an extensive and at times bizarre interpretation of the Treaty, Moscow protested Norwegian plans to build a landing-strip at Ny-Ålesund in 1958, and pointed to alleged US intentions to build bomber-capable runways and radar installations on Svalbard. It also objected for many years to plans for a commercial airport at Longyearbyen,[39] and opposed a 1965 Norwegian–ESRO agreement to operate a telemetric station on Kongsfjorden, which it alleged could be employed secretly for electronic surveillance of northern Russia over which Norway would have no control. Today refuelling stops by Norwegian reconnaissance aircraft at Longyearbyen are closely and openly noted. Moreover, any expansion of economic or scientific activity by Norwegian and other Western personnel on Svalbard will probably provoke a return to the more frequent Soviet warnings against 'militarization' that were characteristic of the 1950s and 1960s.

In the 1960s Soviet international lawyers challenged the legal substance and practical performance of Norway's right and obligation under the Treaty to ensure that the archipelago would never be used 'for warlike purposes', a phrase which they equated with the principle of complete demilitarization. They claimed that even installations and devices that merely *could* be employed for military purposes of any kind should be banned, including Norwegian facilities ostensibly designed to help enforce Article 9 of the Treaty. In one notable article, a Soviet author omitted any reference at all to Article 9 as the basis for the arms control regime, dwelling instead on the words 'peaceful use' in the Treaty preamble, which he equated with the phrase 'exclusively for peaceful purposes' found in the 1959 Antarctic Treaty. If the Svalbard

Treaty did not specifically permit the use of military personnel for peaceful purposes, in contrast to the Antarctic Treaty, then even their temporary presence was forbidden. A more tolerant Soviet interpretation viewed the archipelago as a partially demilitarized, neutralized area in which the sovereign power could maintain forces at the level necessary for the area's defence, provided that it forbade foreign military deployments.[40]

Dekanozov argued that the lack of specific international guarantees in the Svalbard Treaty should be remedied by all *the most interested parties* exercising their inherent equal right to participate in ensuring compliance with Svalbard's demilitarized status.[41] Thus, for example, the most effective method of precluding the possibility of Longyearbyen airport's being used for military purposes would be its joint construction and control by Norway and the Soviet Union, especially since they had the greatest interest in regular air links with the archipelago. More adventurously, he suggested Svalbard's inclusion in a Nordic nuclear-weapon-free zone, with attendant international guarantees (presumably Soviet inspection), as an alternative compensation for the current lack of assurances.

Moscow's attempts first to revise the Svalbard Treaty and subsequently to gain the right of supervision over its military aspects in cooperation with Norway reflected its primary desire to block Western military access to Svalbard. The Soviets have not deployed their own forces or military devices on the archipelago, as far as can be ascertained. In practice, the very size of their non-military presence helps them satisfy their verification requirements.[42]

The Soviets seem to have learned to live with the present verification arrangements in view of the relatively tolerant Norwegian attitude towards Soviet activities and the small number of foreigners on Svalbard. However, a resurgence of foreign interest in the archipelago's resources, coupled with the steady intensification of Norwegian regulatory activities that affect Soviet freedom of movement, may revive earlier Soviet designs for some form of condominium arrangement with Norway in both military and economic matters.

Jursidiction

Initial Soviet resistance to the expansion of Norwegian regulatory activity in several functional areas on Svalbard has gradually given way to a grudging acceptance of Norway's jurisdiction outside the Soviet mining communities and, to a more limited extent, within them.[43] The Soviet press seems to have abandoned even oblique assertions that Norway's jurisdiction does not extend to Soviet citizens on the archipelago or that Svalbard is not a sovereign part of the Norwegian kingdom. Soviet citizens on Svalbard have failed to comply with laws that require the registration of land vehicles, permission for use of radio frequencies by expeditions, and registration of power-stations and helicopters. Yet the Soviets have accepted and complied with other regulations, such as those concerning provision of data for taxes, dues and duties, and have helped the local Norwegian governor to enforce fines against Soviet personnel behaving in an unruly manner or hunting illegally.[44]

The Soviets base their objections to various Norwegian regulatory acts on a restrictive interpretation of Article 1 of the Svalbard Treaty, which accords sovereignty to Norway. They also rely on an expansive treatment of Articles 2 and 3, which grant all signatories an equal right to fish and hunt and conduct maritime, industrial, mining and commercial activities in the lands and territorial waters of the archipelago, according to local laws and regulations. These rights seem to be viewed as absolute material rights, rather than merely rights of equal treatment with respect to Norwegian and other nationals. Economic activities are held to be subject solely to the Mining Code, which should not be affected by any other constraining legislation. Parties are entitled to conduct any activities necessary to modern operations, unaffected by Norwegian national legislation: i.e., no authorization is required or must be given if requested. Thus, the Soviets objected to the 1971 Safety and the 1973 Conservation regulations as Norwegian attempts to restrict Soviet economic activities and as excuses to reinforce Oslo's sovereignty and jurisdiction. They regard Norwegian national legislation that affects operations under Articles 2 and 3 as amending the mining regulations, and consequently they think it should be submitted for approval by other Treaty signatories. Since the Treaty, under Article 8, required Norway to submit the original Mining Code for approval by other parties (which it did), they consider it carries an implicit obligation for Norway to consult with its Treaty partners on subsequent changes in any regulations.[45]

The USSR does not register scientific expeditions to Svalbard.

Although there is as yet no regulation requiring this, other states do register scientific expeditions, whereas forthcoming Soviet visits to the islands tend to be announced in the press. In commenting on the ESRO affair the Soviets argued rather suspectly that, in the absence of international conventions on scientific research provided for by Treaty Article 5, international cooperation on Svalbard could only be conducted through a special agreement among Treaty members or after prior consultations between them.[46] The ESRO incident prompted Moscow to suggest Soviet–Norwegian cooperation in scientific research on Svalbard, despite its implications for Norwegian jurisdiction over such research. Moscow may now come to assert that Norwegian hopes for increased Western scientific research to counterbalance the Soviet presence on Svalbard constitute the kind of 'unequal treatment' proscribed by the Treaty.[47]

In the future the USSR could be persuaded that effective control of the Western presence on Svalbard necessitates Soviet acquiescence in the application of the Treaty principle of equal treatment to the Soviet mining communities themselves. However, Moscow might alternatively become more resistant to unilateral Norwegian constraints on the exercise of its Treaty rights, and apply renewed pressure on Oslo to accept restrictions, partly shaped by the USSR, on the foreign presence on Svalbard.

The Svalbard shelf and zone

When Norway in 1970 issued a declaration that its Barents Sea continental shelf extended beyond Svalbard and that the archipelago had no shelf of its own, the Soviet Union alone explicitly rejected it, stating that Svalbard had a shelf, to which the Treaty regime should apply. This was consistent with Moscow's restrictive interpretation of Norwegian sovereignty under the Treaty, and reflected a concern not to acquiesce in the Norwegian position on Svalbard or the Barents Sea.

The Soviet Union questioned the legal basis of Norway's introduction of a 200-mile fisheries protection zone around the archipelago in June 1977 with the same motives as for its earlier objection. In this case, the USSR was joined by Spain, which had growing fishing interests in the Barents. The Soviets have, however, largely complied with the regulations, conforming with required net sizes, observing off-limits areas and allowing net inspections by Norwegian fisheries protection vessels.[48]

Although Soviet catches find their way into ICES statistics, reporting catch sizes directly to Norway was doubtless seen as implicit legal recognition of the Norwegian right to establish the zone and as a precedent. Soviet compliance nonetheless marks the common interest in conserving the vulnerable fish stocks around Svalbard, which are of some importance to Soviet fisheries.[49] That the zone is non-discriminatory could be interpreted by the USSR as confirmation of the applicability of the equal access and treatment provisions in the Treaty beyond Svalbard's territorial waters. Furthermore, Norway consulted Moscow and the EEC before introducing the detailed regulations in 1978.

Soviet opposition to Norway's assertion of sovereignty beyond Svalbard's 4-mile territorial sea cannot be seen solely as a tactical ploy with a view to wresting concessions on the shelf boundary in the Barents in return for Moscow's submission to the Norwegian position. The Soviets probably expect economic considerations and the archipelago's remoteness to discourage major Western interest in the seabed resources around Svalbard, which would have serious implications for Soviet security in the Barents Sea. Moscow evidently hopes that if it maintains its insistence on equal and unfettered access to the shelf and zone, a *de facto* regime based on Soviet consent will gradually emerge.[50] This would improve the prospects for a similar arrangement in the disputed area of the Barents Sea. Furthermore, the difficulties Norway would face in verifying the military provisions of the Treaty offshore would, while leaving the Soviet military relatively unaffected, afford Moscow a further opportunity to rationalize its own presence there as necessary to ensure other states' respect for Svalbard's 'demilitarized' status.

If the major Western powers were to accept Norway's position, the USSR would probably follow suit, arguing instead for a 12-mile territorial sea in which the Treaty would apply. Norway would almost certainly take Soviet security interests into account in regulating the activities of NATO members in the economic zone, yet Soviet naval patrols and surveillance would nonetheless intensify in order to measure Norwegian restraint.

As things stand in the mid-1980s, Soviet interests in the Barents Sea and wider Northern Waters are best suited by the absence of both Soviet and Western agreement with Norway on the status of Svalbard's shelf and waters. Non-resolution of the issues has so far served to restrain Norwegian activity on the continental shelf and helped to discourage a major West European or US presence in the Barents. The Soviet Union can also make common cause with Spain — and conceivably in future with the European Commission — over fisheries jurisdiction around Svalbard. Soviet hopes of access to Greenlandic waters could be encouraged not only by the present dispute over Jan Mayen's fisheries zone, but also by the prospect of similar complications surrounding the future delimitation of the Svalbard and Greenlandic continental shelves.

Notes

1. *Jane's Defence Weekly*, 14 July 1984, pp. 3-4.
2. 'Soviet Naval Activities 1977-84', *NATO Review*, No. 1 (1985), pp. 17-20.
3. See Press and Information Department, Royal Ministry of Defence, Fact Sheet No. 0383, 'Foreign Submarines in Norwegian Waters' (Oslo, May 1983). On probable sightings of Soviet submarines close to the west coast of Greenland, see *Politiken*, 9-16 December 1983, p. 16.
4. See Chs. 5 and 9 in this volume.
5. Tacitly acknowledged in V. Afanasyev, 'Canadian Naval Forces', *Zarubezhnoye voyennoye obozreniye (ZVO)*, No. 5 (1985), p. 61.
6. See *Aviation Week and Space Technology*, 10 December 1984, pp. 16-17, and 3 June 1985, p. 387.
7. W. Harriet Critchley, 'Polar Deployment of Soviet Submarines', *International Journal*, Vol. 39 (1984), No. 4, pp. 859-60.
8. Barry Posen, 'The Military Build-Up in the High North: The US Military Response to Soviet Naval Developments', paper presented at the Harvard Nordic Conference, April 1985, p. 16.
9. See G.M. Sturua, '"Strategic ASW": US Views and Policy', *S.Sh.A. Ekonomika, Politika, Ideologia (S.Sh.A.)*, No. 2 (1985), p. 38.
10. Soviet commentaries occasionally claim that the Western SOSUS system extends from North Cape beyond Bear Island to Spitsbergen itself; see G. Lukyanov, 'NATO and the Atlantic', *Morskoi Sbornik*, No. 3 (1981), p. 78.
11. See V.F. Petrenko, 'The US and North European Security, *S.Sh.A.*, No. 2 (1982), pp. 18-30.
12. See Ch. 12.
13. (a) S.V. Molodtsov, 'Delimitation of Maritime Zones in International Law', in Institute of State and Law, *Mezhdunarodnaya bezopasnost i mirovoi okean* (International Security and the Oceans) (Moscow: 'Nauka', 1982), Ch. 3, p. 59. (b) S.V. Molodtsov, *Pravovoi rezhim morskikh vod* (Legal Regime of the Seas) (Moscow: 'Mezhdunarodnye otnoshenia', 1982), p. 217.
14. Moscow has made little reference to the unusual configuration of the coastline from which Norway projected its median line in the Barents Sea. See Kim Traavik and Willy Østreng, 'Security and Ocean Law: Norway and the Soviet Union in the Barents Sea', *Ocean Development and International Law Journal*, Vol. 4 (1977), No. 4, p. 357.
15. Molodtsov merely notes that Norway 'made its observations on this important point'; see S.V. Molodtsov, as Note 13 (a), pp. 59-60.
16. Boleslaw A. Boczek, 'The Soviet Union and the Antarctic Regime',

American Journal of International Law, Vol. 87 (1984), No. 4, p. 842. For a striking recent example of the Soviet double standard regarding 'red seas' and 'blue seas' high seas freedoms and the effort not to address the contrast between Soviet practice in the Arctic and Moscow's position on freedom of navigation, etc., elsewhere, see M.L. Lopatin, *Mezhdunarodnye prolivy i kanaly*, (International Straits and Canals) (Moscow: 'Mezhdunarodnye otnoshenia', 1985), esp. p. 16.

17. For a pessimistic Norwegian assessment of the implications of Oslo's recognition of special circumstances in its dispute with Iceland, see Finn Sollie, 'Jan Mayen sonen — Forhandlingene med Island', *Internasjonal Politikk*, No. 3 (1981), pp. 383-406. For a well-argued dismissal of the Jan Mayen solution as a legal precedent relevant to the Barents Sea, see Robin Churchill, 'Marine Delimitation in the Jan Mayen Area', *Marine Policy*, Vol. 9 (1985), No. 1, pp. 16-38. Soviet awareness of Norwegian anxiety was expressed in O.V. Cherstvova, *Islandia. Problemy vneshnei politiki* (Iceland. Foreign Policy Issues) (Moscow: 'Mezhdunarodnye otnoshenia', 1983), pp. 91-2. Moscow withdrew its original objection to Norway's declaration of a Jan Mayen fisheries zone, in June 1981. Norway allowed the USSR to catch 280,000 tons of blue whiting around the island in 1981, and allocated to the USSR 485,000 and 385,000 tons off the Norwegian coast and Jan Mayen in 1983 and 1984 respectively. Moscow agreed to Norwegian fisheries inspection in the whole Jan Mayen zone, including that portion disputed with Greenland/Denmark.

18. Interview with S.I. Yudin, Director of Glavmorneftegazprom, in *Izvestia*, 15 April 1984.

19. Finn Sollie, 'Borepunkter på midtlinjen — Hvor kritisk er det?', *Nyhetsbrev*, No. 2 (Oslo: Fridtjof Nansen Institute, 1983), pp. 17-20; *Lloyds List*, 13 June 1983.

20. Traavik and Østreng, as Note 14, p. 344.

21. *Guardian*, 30 July 1985. Geco is a marine surveying company based in Norway.

22. Falk Bomsdorff, 'Norway's Nordpolitik and the Soviet Union', *Aussenpolitik*, Vol. 30 (1979), No. 3, pp. 258-73.

23. Molodtsov, as Note 13 (a), p. 60.

24. Peter Colins, 'Swedish Concern About Soviet Boarding of Fishing Vessels in Disputed Baltic Waters', *Radio Liberty Research*, RL 132/85, 20 April 1985.

25. Article by A. Monin, Director of the Institute of Oceanology, *Pravda*, 3 October 1983. The Institute has campaigned, so far without success, for a northwestern division to be set up in Murmansk.

26. *Noroil*, August 1984, p. 31; *Petroleum Economist*, November 1984, p. 427. Those hints preceded the resumption of shelf negotiations agreed for December by just a few weeks, and their timing may have been more than a coincidence.

27. *Oil and Gas Journal*, 4 February 1985; *Petroleum Economist*, July 1985, pp. 254-5. The Soviets purchased saturation diving systems for use on this latest *Shelf* semi-sub series abroad, with Seaforth Maritime of Aberdeen providing the system for installation on this first rig for Arctic use.

28. *Petroleum Economist*, April 1984, p. 145.

29. Soviet oil production failed to grow for the first time in 1984, and the first quarter of 1985 saw a 4 per cent output drop compared with the same period for 1984.

30. *The Financial Times*, 12 August 1982; 'Interview with Soviet Geology Minister', *Soviet News* (London), 15 May 1985; *Izvestia*, 15 April 1984.

31. See, for example, M.P. Krasnov, 'Exploitation of the Canadian Shelf', *S.Sh.A.*, No. 2 (1981), pp. 87-94; O. Kazakova, 'The Scandinavian Concept of an "Industrial Niche"', *Mirovaya ekonomika i mezhdunarodnye otnoshenia*

(MEMO), No. 6 (1984), pp. 53-65; Yu Denisov, 'The International Significance of Soviet–Finnish Cooperation', *MEMO*, No. 2 (1985), pp. 21-31.

32. *Norinform*, 30 August 1983; *Noroil*, November 1984, p. 38, and May 1985, pp. 19, 26.

33. Credit terms proved to be one of the more intractable issues that delayed agreement on the movement to production in the Chaivo field in cooperation with the Japanese consortium Sodeco: *Petroleum Economist*, October 1984, p. 387.

34. Finn Sollie, 'Oil and Foreign Policy', *Nyhetsbrev* No. 4 (Oslo: Fridtjof Nansen Institute, 1984), p. 20.

35. Growing Soviet sensitivity to environmental degradation in Karelia and Western Siberia was reflected in a new decree on environmental protection in the Far North and on the coastline of the northern seaboard. See *Izvestia*, 6 March 1985. On pollution of the Ob Gulf and Kara Sea, see Zeev Wolfson, *The Environmental Risk of the Developing Oil and Gas Industry in Western Siberia*, Research Paper No. 52 (Jerusalem: Hebrew University of Jerusalem, Soviet and East European Research Centre, October 1983), p. 14.

36. Soviet acceptance of Norwegian sovereignty was also indicated by the coordinates of the 1926 Sector Decree, which laid claim to polar territories not belonging to another power.

37. R.V. Dekanozov, 'The Demilitarization and Neutralization of Spitsbergen', in *Sovetskii ezhegodnik mezhdunarodnovo prava 1966-67* (Soviet Yearbook of International Law — *SYIL*) (Moscow: 'Nauka', 1968), p. 188. The thrust of the Resolution actually lay in the reassertion of sole Norwegian responsibility for Svalbard's defence and the rejection of Soviet military bases there, while allowing for talks with Moscow in view of Soviet economic interests, provided that other signatories of the Treaty were not excluded from the process.

38. Philippe Bretton, 'L'Union soviétique et la clause de non-militarisation du Spitsberg', *Annuaire Français de Droit International*, 1965, p. 138.

39. Willy Østreng, *Politics in High Latitudes: The Svalbard Archipelago* (London: C. Hurst & Co., 1977), pp. 55-8.

40. G.M. Melkov, 'The Legal Meaning of "Exclusively for Peaceful Purposes"', in *SYIL 1971* (Moscow: 'Nauka', 1973), pp. 153-61; B.M. Klimenko, 'The Neutralization of Territories in Contemporary International Law', in *SYIL 1961* (Moscow: 'Nauka', 1962), pp. 213-9.

41. See Dekanozov, as Note 37.

42. Aeroflot's presence at Longyearbyen airport exceeds that strictly needed to deal with the volume of air traffic from the USSR. Soviet helicopters based nearby at Kap Heer sometimes visit and often overfly the camps of foreign scientific expeditions.

43. Soviet wariness of Norwegian inspections of their mining communities may stem partly from a record of defections by Soviet and East European citizens to the local authorities on Svalbard. Activities on Svalbard are legally regulated by three principal instruments: the 1920 Treaty; the 1925 Mining Code; and the Norwegian Svalbard Act of 1925, which laid the framework for the exercise of Norwegian jurisdiction.

44. Helicopter facilities at Kap Heer were built without seeking Norwegian permission, and the aircraft initially operated unregistered and failed to report their flights to the Norwegian control tower at Longyearbyen. Flights are now notified, yet occasional crashes are not reported, being discovered by the Norwegian authorities themselves. In 1981 a group of Soviet geologists paid fines imposed after they had damaged airport warning lights while intoxicated.

45. The mining regulations are considered to form part of Norwegian legislation, except by the USSR. For a detailed exposition of the Norwegian argument regarding precedence of Article 1 over other Treaty articles and an

indirect exposure of the dissenting Soviet legal position, see Carl August Fleischer, 'Le Régime d'exploitation du Spitsberg', *Annuaire Français de Droit International*, Vol. 24 (1978), pp. 275-300, and *Problemer om folkerett og sikkerhet i nordområdene. Jus, milliarder og storpolitik*, Atlanterhavskomitéens Serier No. 8 (Oslo: Norwegian Atlantic Committee, 1984).

46. As Note 37, p. 190. Notably Dekanozov omitted to include consultations with *all* the treaty parties. Moscow officially protested at the unilateral decision by Norway to permit the ESRO station, which was taken 'without the agreement of the treaty parties and, furthermore, without the agreement of the Soviet Union, whose interests ... are substantially affected', *Pravda*, 20 February 1965, quoted in Bretton, as Note 38, p. 143. The Treaty text does not specifically require such agreements to include parties to the Treaty.

47. On the political dimension of scientific research in Svalbard, see Arild Moe, *Forskning og politik på Svalbard, EP-5* (Oslo: Fridtjof Nansen Institute, 1983).

48. Norway faced enforcement difficulties mainly with Spanish rather than Eastern bloc fishing vessels.

49. In 1981 and 1982 the USSR took approximately 21% and 28% of the total nominal catch in the Spitsbergen/Bear Island fishing area, with Norway taking 76% and 65% respectively. In 1982 Denmark took 2%, the Faroes 1.9%, Spain 1.6% and the GDR 0.3%. The USSR took 20% of the capelin, 96% of the redfish, 88% of the Greenland halibut and 52% of the cod (in order of catch size). See *Bulletin Statistique Des Pêches Maritimes*, Vol. 67 for 1982 (Copenhagen: ICES, 1985).

50. The Soviet formula for fisheries management around Svalbard was hinted at in P. Krymov, 'The Soviet Union and the North European Countries', *International Affairs* (Moscow), No. 9 (1979), pp. 15-16.

INDEX

air forces 70-1, 72-7
  Canada 147-8
  Greenland 175, 183, 184
  Iceland 204
  NATO 71, 81-2, 225
  new technology and 94
  USSR 71, 75, 80, 209
air passage, right of 14
Alaska 19, 50
  resources 43, 45, 49, 109;
    exploited 51, 67, 110, 112-14
Alpha Ridge 139
amphibious assault 81-2
animals 131-3, 136
  see also conservation; polar bears;
    seals; whales
anti-submarine warfare 78, 92, 94,
  102, 117-19, 122, 211
Archer, C. 1
Arctic Islands 19, 110, 114, 125-7,
  138
Arctic Ocean
  boundaries, lack of 12
  definition 1, 11, 30
  see also individual seas
Arctic Pilot Project 8, 66, 127, 136
armed forces *see* air forces; ground
  forces; navies
arms control 17, 100, 104-5, 106
Armstrong, T. 55
army *see* ground forces
Asgeirsson, A. 198

Baffin Bay 30
  passage through 1, 60, 128, 136
Baffin Island 56, 58, 125, 130-1
Baltic Sea 26, 60, 71
Barents Sea 22, 155
  continental shelf 20, 32, 38
  disputes over 3, 7, 8, 111, 158,
    163-71, 211-22
  fisheries 26, 57-8, 101, 216-18
  passage through 1, 49
  resources 47-8, 52, 64, 101,
    218-22
  strategic importance 4, 5, 70, 74,
    79, 92, 100, 117-18
baselines 13, 20-3

bays 13, 20-3
Bear Island 225
Beaufort Sea 19, 128, 137
  disputes over 111, 138-9, 141
  resources 45, 51, 53, 66, 125, 131,
    134
Bering Sea 19, 50, 113
  resources 45, 49, 112, 113, 131
Bering Straits 49, 109, 113
Bethge, A. 73
Birnie, P. 11

Canada 1, 13
  EC and 134-5
  fisheries 26, 27, 36, 58, 131,
    134-6, 137
  Greenland/Denmark and 3, 7, 8,
    36, 135-6, 139-40, 179, 180,
    188
  LOSC and 19, 23, 26-7, 31-2, 36
  NATO and 146, 148, 151, 153-4
  Norway and 36
  resources 2, 9, 49, 51-2, 109,
    125-45; international
    uncertainties 138-41; national
    uncertainties 136-8;
    non-renewable 126-31; oil and
    gas 125-30; renewable 131-6
  shipping 8, 56, 58, 61-2, 64, 67
  strategy 82, 146-54; air forces
    147-8; conflict control 98, 100,
    104; domestic intra-regional
    dimension 152-3; East-West
    dimension 146-8; ground
    forces 148; USA and 149-52
  USA and 110, 112, 114, 138-9,
    141, 146-52
  USSR and 141, 209-10
Carney, P. 137
chromium 181
Chryssostomidis, C. 98
Chukchi Sea 21, 45, 49, 99, 131
Churchill, R. 35
Clark, J. 138
coal 55, 181
Cod War *see under* Iceland
communication, sea lines of, defended
  80-1

communications satellites 86, 89-90
Conant, M. 109
conflict, control of 97-108
    concepts 97-8
    potential for 98-104
    tools of control 104-6
    see also strategy
conservation 8, 131, 134, 135, 136,
    137-8
    conventions on 12, 13-14, 29, 31-2
contiguous zones 13
continental shelf
    conventions on 12, 14, 19, 22, 25,
        27-8, 32-4, 163-4, 211
    disputes *see under* Barents Sea; Jan
        Mayen
    resources 43-6, 49
conventions *see* Law of the Sea
Crombie, D. 137

Davis Strait 3
    resources 46, 52, 130, 135
    shipping through 1, 8, 50, 60, 128
de Lee, N. 190
defence *see* strategy
Dekanozov, R.V. 226
demilitarized zones 224-6
Denmark *see* Greenland/Denmark
Denmark Strait 20, 50
deterrence *see* nuclear weapons
'development issue area' 98, 104
DEW Line (Distant Early Warning)
    111, 147, 149, 151, 176
disarmament *see* arms control;
    demilitarized zones
Dyer, I. 98

East Siberian Sea 21, 30, 48, 50, 99
EC (European Community) 7, 18
    Canada and 134-5
    fisheries 3, 14-15, 26-7, 35, 36,
        135, 187-8, 201, 229
    Greenland/Denmark/Faroes and
        178-9, 184, 187
    *see also individual member
        countries*
economic zones disputes *see* Barents
    Sea; Exclusive Economic Zones
ecosystems, rare and fragile 31-2
    see also animals; conservation
EEZ *see* Exclusive Economic Zones
electronic navigational aids 60
Ellesmere Island 23
environment

'issue areas' 98, 102-3
    nations 98; *see also individual
        countries*
    protection of *see* conservation
Escamilla Case 23
Europe *see* EC *and individual
    countries*
Evensen, J. 161
Exclusive Economic Zones (EEZs)
    18-19
    agreements 36, 106
    problems and conflicts 34, 35, 100,
        103, 217
    resource rights in 25-33 *passim*
Exclusive Fisheries Zones *see* fisheries,
    zones
exploration
    council 28, 29, 37, 218, 229
    see also research

Faroes 1, 7, 99, 152
    defence 4, 105, 118-19
    EC and 187
    fisheries 15, 26, 36, 58, 135, 179,
        187-8
    resources 46
    shipping 55-6
    see also Greenland/Denmark
Finland
    shipping 61-3
    strategy 81, 98
fisheries 2-3, 57
    conventions on 12, 13, 14-15,
        35-6, 264
    EC and 3, 14-15, 26-7, 35, 36,
        135, 187-8, 201, 229
    NATO and 27, 158, 201
    organizations 26, 27, 135
    size of catch 58
    zones 26-7, 166-8, 200, 217
    see also under individual countries
fleets *see* navies; resources,
    transportation
forces *see* armed forces; strategy
forecasting
    ice 64
    weather 86, 91, 176
Franz Josef Land 48, 49, 215
freight *see* resources, transportation

Galbraith, J.K. 155, 160
gas *see* oil and gas
geology 44-5
Germany

Democratic Republic 188
Federal Republic 18, 98
in World Wars 115-16, 146
Gestsson, S. 195
GIUK gap (Greenland/Iceland/UK)
    4, 5, 92-3, 121, 189, 203
Global Positioning System 90
Golovko, A.G. 163
Gorshkov, S.G. 69, 70, 72, 77, 79
Greenland Sea 5, 20, 30, 209-10
Greenland/Denmark 1, 13, 152,
    174-86
    Canada and 3, 7, 8, 36, 135-6,
        139-40, 179, 180, 188
    climate 180
    EC and 178-9, 184
    fisheries 13, 15, 26, 58, 103,
        179-81
    historical perspective 174-5
    Iceland and 3, 22, 36, 103, 179,
        188, 191, 198, 200-1
    LOSC and 18, 19, 22, 23, 26, 32,
        34-6, 180
    NATO and 176, 184, 189
    Norway and 3, 8, 34-5, 36, 179,
        188
    politics 176-8, 185-6
    resources 2, 7, 9, 46, 64-5, 181;
        exploitation 49, 52, 53, 182
    shipping 50, 55-6, 58
    social and economic conditions
        177
    strategy 74, 175-6, 182-4; air
        forces 175, 183, 184; conflict
        control 98, 99, 100, 103-4, 105
    UK and 186-7, 188
    USA and 176, 184, 188
    USSR and 179
    see also Faroes; GIUK gap
'Grey Zone' Agreement 3, 36, 164,
    213, 214, 216-18, 222
ground forces
    Canada 148
    Greenland 183-4
    NATO 71, 81, 82, 117
    new technology and 94

Hans Island 36, 126, 139
Hayward, T.B. 76
Hedtoft, H. 176
high seas, convention on 12, 14, 15,
    25
'historic bays' 13
Hobbs, D. 85

'horizontal escalation' 121-2
Hudson Bay 56, 60, 130

ice
    changes in conditions 67
    forecasting 64
    LOSC and 31
    navigation hazard 57-60, 136
    shelves, floes and islands 22-3
icebreakers 21, 60-1, 65, 139
    list of 62-3
Iceland 1, 18, 152, 200
    fisheries 26, 36, 57-8, 103, 200-2;
        dispute with UK (Cod War)
        2-3, 7, 9, 102, 194, 198, 199
    Greenland/Denmark and 3, 22,
        36, 103, 179, 188, 191, 198,
        200-1
    NATO and 158, 162, 190-9, 201,
        203-4
    Norway and 3, 8, 34-5, 155-8,
        160-2, 198, 200
    resources 9, 46, 199-205
    shipping 55-6
    strategy 74, 190-207; conflict
        control 98-9, 105; political
        background 191-7; threat
        perception 197-9
    UK and 22, 201; see under
        fisheries above
    USA and 190-1, 195, 198-200,
        202, 204, 205
    USSR and 194, 195, 196-9
    whaling 15
    see also GIUK gap
ice-strengthened freighters 61
indigenous people 179, 214
    'issue area' 98, 103-4
    rights 137, 152-3
intelligence-gathering satellites 86-9
interest nations 98
    see also individual countries
International Maritime Organization
    (IMO) 15, 16, 17, 29, 31
Ireland 22, 99, 135
iron ore 130-1
islands 22
    see also individual islands
'issue areas' 98-104

Jan Mayen Island 1, 22, 27, 32, 46,
    155
    disputes and agreements 3, 8,
        34-5, 156-62, 167-9, 215

Japan 15, 98, 219
Johannesson, D. 194
Johnston, D. 67
jurisdictional 'issue areas' 32, 33,
    98-9, 138-41, 200

Kara Sea 21, 30, 48, 50, 52, 99, 102
Kola Peninsula and Seas 1
    shipping route 20, 49, 91
    strategic importance 214; air force
        in 71, 75, 80, 209; amphibious
        units in 82; attacks on, possible
        94, 121; missiles explosion
        208; Northern Fleet in 4, 5, 74,
        78, 91, 116, 158, 210; numbers
        in 88

Labrador Sea 45
land claims 137
land forces *see* ground forces
Laptev Sea 21, 30, 48, 50, 99
Law of the Sea Convention (LOSC)
    11-37, 155, 160, 169, 180, 200
    applicable law after UNCLOS
        12-17
    delimitation problems 34-6
    relevant provisions 19-25
    resources rights 25-34
    see also under United Nations
lead 125, 130
'lead time' in resource development
    42, 52-3
Lehman, J. 74-5, 120-1
Lie, T. 69
Lippmann, W. 116
Little Cornwallis Island 57, 125
LNG (liquefied natural gas) 57,
    112-13
    see also oil and gas
Lofoten Islands 46
LOSC *see* Law of the Sea Convention
Lynge, F. 185

Mackenzie Delta 128, 137
    resources 45, 51, 52, 125, 127, 131
MacKenzie King, W.L. 149, 150
merchant shipping *see* resources,
    transportation
meteorology satellites 86, 91, 176
military activities *see* strategy
Miller, S. 115
minerals 2, 7, 181-2
    Canada 125, 130-1
    'issue areas' 98, 101

Norway 222
    seabed 20
    USSR 222
    see also oil and gas; resources
        under individual countries
missiles 2, 4-5, 70, 76, 78-9, 146-8,
    176, 184, 209
    control 105
    new technology and 92-4
    warfare against 117-18, 122
    see also nuclear weapons;
        submarines
Molodtsov, S.V. 214
Molotov, V.M. 69, 70, 224
Motzfeldt, J. 184
Mulroney, B. 137

NATO 72, 79
    air forces 71, 81-2, 225
    Canada and 146, 148, 151, 153-4
    conflict control 100-2, 105
    fisheries problems 27, 158, 201
    Greenland/Denmark and 176,
        184, 189
    ground forces 71, 81, 82, 117
    Iceland and 158, 162, 190-9, 201,
        203-4
    Norway and 71, 158-9, 163, 225,
        229
    nuclear deterrence and new
        technology 78-9, 85, 92-5, 146
    resources problems 3, 7, 111
    sea forces 71-5, 77-8, 81-2, 92-5,
        116-22, 148, 209-10
    surveillance and anti-submarine
        warfare *see* GIUK gap
    territorial seas disputes 99
    UK and 158, 201
    USA and 116-22, 148, 151, 184
Navarin Basin 51, 112, 113
navies
    new technology and 91-5
    see also under NATO; strategy
        under individual countries
navigation
    electronic aids 60
    freedom of 14
    ice hazard 57-60, 136
    'issue area' 98, 101-2
    problems in resource
        transportation 57-60
    satellites 60, 86, 90-1
    see also shipping
Netherlands 82

Nordic Nuclear-Free Zone 105, 199, 203, 211
North Atlantic, strategic importance of 115-22 *passim*
    see also NATO
Northeast Passage 20, 21-2
Northern Fleet *see* USSR, sea forces *and under* Kola
Northwest Passage 20, 56, 128
    ice problems 60, 136
    legal status unclear 138, 141, 149-50
    mining and 130
    oil transport through 66-7, 149-50
    short-cut to Japan 125
Norway 13, 152
    Canada and 36
    fisheries 57-8; agreements 26-7, 135, 155-7, 161; disputes 20, 103, 163-4, 166, 211, 215-18, 228
    Greenland/Denmark and 3, 8, 34-5, 36, 179, 188
    Iceland and 3, 8, 34-5, 155-8, 160-2, 198, 200
    Jan Mayen and 34-5, 158-62, 167-9
    LOSC and 18, 19-20, 22, 23, 26-7, 32, 34-6, 169
    NATO and 71, 158-9, 163, 225, 229
    resources 7, 9, 46-7, 65; exploitation 50-1, 52; oil and gas 155, 157-8, 161, 163
    shipping 35-6, 58
    Spitsbergen and 35
    strategy 7, 71-3, 80, 81-2, 116-18, 158, 163
    conflict control 98-9, 100-1
    reassurance and deterrence 159-61
    UK and 20, 36
    USA and 159, 211
    USSR and *see under* USSR
Norwegian Sea 30, 155
    fisheries 57-8
    passage through 1, 20, 49
    resources 47, 50
    strategic importance 5, 73, 79, 80, 116-17, 118, 122, 210
nuclear
    energy, 16, 29
    shipping, passage of 17, 19, 24; *see also* SSBNs; submarines
    waste dumping 16-17

weapons 77-80; control 17, 100, 104-5, 106; new technology and 78-9, 85, 92-5, 146
    see also missiles

Ob delta 43, 51
ocean nations 98
    see also individual countries
offshore oil and gas 49-53, 219, 220
    see also oil and gas
oil and gas 7
    Canada 125-30
    exploitation 43-6, 49-53, 218-19, 220-1
    'issue areas' 98, 101
    Norway 155, 157-8, 161, 163
    resources 43-9, 53, 155, 157-8, 161, 163, 181, 216, 218-19, 221
    USA 109-14; *see also* Alaska
    USSR 216, 218-19, 220-1
    see also minerals; resources
Okhotsk Sea 21, 79
Østreng, W. 155

passage, rights of 13, 23-5
passages, major 20
    see also Northeast; Northwest
petroleum *see* oil and gas
Poland 98, 222
polar bears, agreement on 12, 31-2, 134, 136
pollution 103, 110
    conventions on 15-17, 19, 28-30, 36
Pope, M. 149, 151
protection of environment *see* conservation; pollution
Prudhoe Bay 51, 67

radioactivity *see* nuclear
Reagan. R. 101, 120-2, 150
reconnaissance *see* spy satellites
research 180-1
    'issue areas' 98, 102
    rights and LOSC 27-8
    USSR 208, 218-21, 227
    see also exploration
resources 2-4, 7
    endowment 42-9
    exploitation 49-53
    'issue areas' 98, 101, 102-3
    rights and LOSC 25-34
    security and 6-8

transportation 6-7, 8, 55-68,
128-9; future possibilities 64-7;
ice-going equipment 60-3;
navigational problems 57-60;
present pattern 55-7
see also fisheries; minerals; oil and
gas *and under individual
countries*
rights of passage 13, 23-5
Rink, H.J. 177
Rockall 22, 32, 46, 99, 188, 201
rocks 22
Russett, B. 6

safety at sea, conventions on 15-16
'sanctuaries' 105-6
satellites 60, 86-91, 176, 225
Scanlan, T. 42
Scrivener, D. 208
seabed minerals 20
sea-control, struggle for 72-7
see also navies; submarines
Seal Island 51
seals 36, 131, 133, 134, 136
security *see* strategy
semi-enclosed seas 30
Severnaya Zemlya 23, 48, 49
Shetlands 1, 4, 7, 9
shipping 1, 2
see also navies; resources,
transportation
silver 130
SLOCs (Sea Lines of Communication)
1, 4, 7, 92, 93, 95, 115-16, 204,
209, 210
Sollie, F. 42
Soviet Union *see* USSR
space 147
see also satellites
Spain 102-3, 228
special areas 30-1
Spitsbergen (Svalbard) 20, 22, 35-6
spy satellites 86-9, 225
SSBNs (nuclear submarines) 119, 122,
203
numbers of 70, 91
strategic reserve 4, 77-80, 91-2,
117, 159, 204, 209-10
under ice 4, 92, 106
see also submarines
'Star Wars' 147
strategy 4-6, 69-84
amphibious assault 81-2
conflict control 9

importance of area 69-72
'issue areas' 98, 99-101
nuclear deterrence 77-80; *see also*
missiles; nuclear weapons
resources and 6-8
sea-control, struggle for 72-7
sea-lines of communication
defended 80-1
see also under individual countries;
technologies
submarine cables and pipelines 14
submarines 70, 148, 210
anti-submarine warfare 78, 92, 94,
102, 117-19, 122, 211
freighters 63
new technology and 92-5
passage of 12, 19, 25
under ice 4, 79-80, 92, 106, 209
see also missiles; SSBNs
surveillance *see* spy
Svalbard 1, 23, 49
demilitarization 224-6
disputes and treaties 8, 99, 104,
106, 111, 163, 165-8, 211,
222-30
fisheries 8, 36, 58
jurisdiction 226-8
resources 2, 46, 52, 53, 64-5
sovereignty 224
see also Spitsbergen
Sverdrup Islands 45, 49, 51
Sweden
fisheries 26, 135
shipping 61
strategy 81, 98, 99, 105

Taagholt, J. 174
technologies, new military 9, 70,
85-96, 209
naval 91-5
space-based 85-91
see also satellites
territorial seas, convention on 12-13,
24
Till, G. 69
Tracy, N. 146
Train, H.D. 79
trained manpower for freighters 64
transport 'issue areas' 98, 101-2
see also under resources
Trudeau, P. 137, 150-1
Tuktoyaktuk peninsula 52

UNCLOS *see* United Nations

United Kingdom 1, 13
  fisheries 13, 20, 26; dispute *see*
    under Iceland
  Greenland/Denmark and 186-7,
    188
  Iceland and 22, 201; *see also under*
    Iceland
  LOSC and 18, 20, 22, 23, 26, 28,
    36
  NATO and 158, 201
  Norway and 20, 36
  resources 7, 9, 46-7
  strategy 2, 7, 74, 82; conflict control
    98-9, 100, 101, 102, 103
  see also GIUK gap
United Nations 16, 29
  Law of the Sea Convention 3, 8,
    11, 19, 20-1, 30-1, 160, 206,
    211, 215; applicable law after
    12-17
  see also Law of the Sea
United States
  Canada and 110, 112, 114, 138-9,
    141, 146-52
  fisheries 13, 26, 135
  Greenland/Denmark and 176,
    184, 188
  Iceland and 190-1, 195, 198-200,
    202, 204, 205
  LOSC and 18, 19, 21, 23-6, 28,
    31-2
  NATO and 116-22, 148, 151, 184
  Norway and 159, 211
  resources 2, 43, 45, 49;
    exploitation 51, 53; oil and gas
    109-14; *see also* Alaska
  shipping 61-2, 63, 64, 66, 115-17
  strategic interests 70, 74-6, 79,
    115-24; anti-submarine
    warfare 117-18; Canada and
    149-52; changed situation
    118-20; control of conflict
    98-102, 104-6; new military
    technology 86-93 *passim*;
    Reagan's defence policy 120-2;
    safeguarding sea-lanes 115-17
  USSR and 21, 210; *see also*
    strategy
uranium 7, 181
USSR 13
  Canada and 141, 209-10

  fisheries 26, 57, 211, 214-18
    passim, 228-9
  Greenland/Denmark and 179
  Iceland and 194, 195, 196-9
  LOSC and 15, 18, 19, 21-5, 30,
    32, 36
  Northeast Passage and 21-2, 25
  Norway and 3-4, 8, 22, 36, 111,
    155, 188, 209; and Barents Sea
    211-21; and Svalbard 222-30
  resources 2, 7, 45, 47-9, 64, 216,
    218-22; exploitation 51, 52,
    218-19, 220-1; oil and gas
    216-21
  shipping 8, 50, 55-7, 60-7, 101,
    103, 113; *see also under*
    strategy *below*
  strategy 4-6, 7, 69-82, 116,
    147-15, 208-11; air forces 71,
    75, 80, 209; amphibious assault
    81-2; conflict control 98-9,
    101-2, 104-6; new military
    technology 85, 87-8, 90-5,
    209; nuclear deterrence 77-80,
    105, 209, *see also* missiles; sea
    forces 4-5, 24, 72-7, 116-20,
    122, 163, 208-11, *see also*
    Kola; SSBNs; submarines
  Svalbard and 222-30
  USA and 21, 210; *see also* strategy

VanderZwaag, D. 125
Vil'kitsky Strait 21

Wadhams, P. 58
Warsaw Pact countries, disputes with
  NATO 3, 122
weapons *see under* nuclear
weather *see* meteorology
Weinberger, C. 121
Weinland, R. 75
West, F. 121
whales 131, 133, 134, 136
  convention on 5, 29
White Sea 60, 70
Wrangel Island 48-9, 50

Young, E. 97

zinc 125, 130

AUG 1 3 1987